The Hills and the Vale

RICHARD JEFFERIES

The
Hills AND THE *Vale*

With an introduction by
Edward Thomas

DESORMAIS

Oxford New York Toronto Melbourne

OXFORD UNIVERSITY PRESS

1980

Oxford University Press, Walton Street, Oxford OX2 6DP

OXFORD LONDON GLASGOW
NEW YORK TORONTO MELBOURNE WELLINGTON
KUALA LUMPUR SINGAPORE JAKARTA HONG KONG TOKYO
DELHI BOMBAY CALCUTTA MADRAS KARACHI
NAIROBI DAR ES SALAAM CAPE TOWN

The Hills and the Vale was first published in 1909
This edition first published as an
Oxford University Press paperback 1980

British Library Cataloguing in Publication Data
Jefferies, Richard
The hills and the vale
1. England – Social life and custom – 19th century
2. Country life – England
I. Title
942'.00973'4   DA533   79-41413
ISBN 0-19-281294-7

Printed in Great Britain by
Cox & Wyman Ltd, Reading

CONTENTS

INTRODUCTION

THIS book consists of three unpublished essays and of fifteen reprinted from *Longman's Magazine*, *Fraser's Magazine*, the *New Quarterly*, *Knowledge*, *Chambers's Magazine*, the *Graphic*, and the *Standard*, where they have probably been little noticed since the time of their appearance. Several more volumes of this size might have been made by collecting all the articles which were not reprinted in Jefferies' lifetime, or in 'Field and Hedgerow' and 'Toilers of the Field,' shortly after his death. But the work in such volumes could only have attracted those very few of the omnivorous lovers of Jefferies who have not already found it out. After the letters on the Wiltshire labourer, addressed to the *Times* in 1872, he wrote nothing that was not perhaps at the time his best, but, being a journalist, he had often to deal immediately, and in a transitory manner, with passing events, or to empty a page or two of his note-books in response to an impulse assuredly no higher than habit or necessity. Many of these he passed over or rejected in making up volumes of essays for publication ; some he certainly included. Of those he passed over, some are equal to the best, or all but the best, of those which he admitted, and I think these will be found in 'The Hills and the Vale.' There are others which need more excuse. The two early papers on 'Marlborough Forest' and 'Village Churches,' which were quoted in Besant's 'Eulogy,' are interesting on account of their earliness (1875), and charming enough to please those who read all Jefferies' books. 'The Story of Swindon,' 'Unequal Agriculture,' and 'Village Organization,' will be valued for their matter, and because they are examples of his writing, and of his interests and opinions, before he was thirty. That they are partly out of date is true, but they are worth remembering by the student of Jefferies and of his times ; they do credit to his insight and even to his foresight ; and there is still upon them, here and there, some ungathered fruit. The later agricultural articles, 'The Idle Earth,' 'After the County Franchise,' and 'The Wiltshire Labourer,' are the work of his ripe years. There were also several papers published not only after his death, but after the posthumous collections. I have included all of these, for none of them needs defence, while 'Nature and Eternity' ranks with his finest work. The three papers now for the first time printed might have been, but are not, admitted on that ground alone. 'On Choosing a Gun' and 'Skating' belong to the period of 'The Amateur Poacher,' and are still alive, and too good to destroy. 'The Dawn' is beautiful.

Among these eighteen papers are examples from nearly every kind and period of Jefferies' work,

though his earliest writing is still decently interred
where it was born, in Wiltshire and Gloucestershire
papers (chiefly the *North Wilts Herald*), except such
as was disinterred by the late Miss Toplis for
' Jefferies Land,' 'T. T. T.,' and 'The Early Fiction
of Richard Jefferies.' From his early youth Jefferies
was a reporter in the north of Wiltshire and south of
Gloucestershire, at political and agricultural meetings,
elections, police-courts, markets, and Boards of Guardians. He inquired privately or officially into the
history of the Great Western Railway works at New
Swindon, of the local churches and families, of ancient
monuments, and he announced the facts with such
reflections as came to him, or might be expected from
him, in newspaper articles, papers read before the Wiltshire Archæological Society, and in a booklet on ' The
Goddards of North Wilts.' As reporter, archæologist,
and sportsman, he was continually walking to and
fro across the vale and over the downs ; or writing
down what he saw, for the most part in a manner
dictated by the writing of other men engaged in the
same way ; or reading everything that came in his
way, but especially natural history, chronicles, and
Greek philosophy in English translations. He was
bred entirely on English, and in a very late paper he
could be so hazy about the meaning of ' illiterate ' as to
say that the labourers ' never were illiterate mentally ;
they are now no more illiterate in the partial sense of
book-knowledge.' He tried his hand at topical
humour, and again and again at short sensational
tales. But until he was twenty-four he wrote nothing

which could have suggested that he was much above the cleverer young men of the same calling. There was nothing fine or strong in his writing. His researches were industrious, but not illuminated. If his range of reading was uncommon, it gave him only some quotations of no exceptional felicity. His point of view could have given no cause for admiration or alarm. And yet he was not considered an ordinary young man, being apparently idle, ambitious, discontented, and morose, and certainly unsociable and negligently dressed. He walked about night and day, chiefly alone and with a noticeable long stride. But if he was ambitious, it was only that he desired success—the success of a writer, and probably a novelist, in the public eye. His possessions were the fruits of his wandering, his self-chosen books and a sensitive, solitary temperament. He might have been described as a clever young man, well-informed, a little independent, not first-rate at short-hand, and yet possibly too good for his place ; and the description would have been all that was possible to anyone not intimate with him, and there was no one intimate with him but himself. He had as yet neither a manner nor a matter of his own. It is not clear from anything remaining that he had discovered that writing could be something more than a means of making party views plausible or information picturesque. In 1867, at the age of nineteen, he opened a description of Swindon as follows :

'Whenever a man imbued with republican politics and progressionist views ascends the platform and delivers an oration, it is a safe wager that he makes some allusion at least to Chicago, the famous mushroom city of the United States, which sprang up in a night, and thirty years ago consisted of a dozen miserable fishermen's huts, and now counts over two hundred thousand inhabitants. Chicago! Chicago! look at Chicago! and see in its development the vigour which invariably follows republican institutions. . . . Men need not go so far from their own doors to see another instance of rapid expansion and development which has taken place under a monarchical government. The Swindon of to-day is almost ridiculously disproportioned to the Swindon of forty years ago. . . .'

Eight years later Jefferies rewrote 'The Story of Swindon' as it is given in this book, and the allusion to Chicago was reduced to this:

'The workmen required food; tradesmen came and supplied that food, and Swindon rose as Chicago rose, as if by magic.'

Yet it is certain that in 1867 Jefferies was already carrying about with him an experience and a power which were to ripen very slowly into something unique. He was observing; he was developing a sense of the beauty in Nature, in humanity, in thought, and the arts; and he was 'not more than eighteen when an inner and esoteric meaning began to come to him from all the visible universe, and undefinable aspirations filled him.'

In 1872 he discovered part of his power almost in its perfection. He wrote several letters to the *Times*

about the Wiltshire labourer, and they were lucid,
simple, moderate, founded on his own observation,
and arranged in a telling, harmonious manner. What
he said and thought about the labourers then is of
no great importance now, and even in 1872 it was
only a journalist's grain in the scale against the
labourer's agitation. But it was admirably done.
It was clear, easy writing, and a clear, easy writer he
was thenceforth to the end.

These letters procured for him admission to
Fraser's and other magazines, and he now began for
them a long series of articles, mainly connected with
the land and those who work on the land. He had
now freedom and space to put on paper something
of what he had seen and thought. The people,
their homes, and their fields, he described and
criticized with moderation and some spirit. He
showed that he saw more things than most writing
men, but it was in an ordinary light, in the same
way as most of the readers whom he addressed. His
gravity, tenderness and courage were discernible, but
the articles were not more than a clever presentation
of a set of facts and an intelligent, lucid point
of view, which were good grist to the mills of that
decade. They had neither the sagacity nor the
passion which could have helped that calm style to
make literature.

'The Story of Swindon' (*Fraser's*, May, 1875)
is one of three or four articles which Jefferies wrote
at that time on a subject not purely his own. As a
journalist he had had to do a hundred things for which

he had no strong natural taste. This article is a good example of his adaptable gifts. He was probably equal to grappling with any set of facts and ideas at the word of command. In 'coming to this very abode of the Cyclops' the *North Wilts Herald* reporter survives, and nothing could be more like everybody else than the phrasing and the atmosphere of the greater part, as in 'the ten minutes for refreshment, now in the case of certain trains reduced to five, have made thousands of travellers familiar with the name of the spot.' This is probably due to lack not so much of skill as of developed personality. When he describes and states facts, he is lucid and forcible ; when he reflects or decorates, he is often showy or ill at ease, or both, though the thought on p. 130 is valid enough. Through the cold, colourless light between him and the object, he saw and remembered clearly ; short of creativeness, he was a master—or one of those skilled servants who appear masters—of words. The power is, at this distance, more worthy of attention than the achievement. The power of retaining and handling facts was one which he never lost, but it was absorbed and even concealed among powers of later development, when reality was a richer thing to him than is to be surmised from anything in 'The Story of Swindon.'

'Unequal Agriculture' (*Fraser's*, May, 1877) and 'Village Organization' (*New Quarterly*, October, 1875) belong to the same period. They describe and debate matters which are now not so

new, though often as debatable. The description
is sometimes felicitous, as in the 'steady jerk' of the
sower's arm, but is not destined for immortality ;
and the picture of a steam-plough at work he himself surpassed in a later paper. But it is sufficiently
vivid to survive for another generation. Since
Cobbett no keener agriculturist's eye or better pen
had surveyed North Wiltshire. The most advanced
and the most antiquated style of farming remain the
same in our own day. Whether these articles were
commissioned or not, their form and direction was
probably dictated as much by the expressed or
supposed needs of the magazine as by Jefferies himself. His own line was not yet clear and strong,
and he consciously or unconsciously adopted one
which was a compromise between his own and that
of his contemporaries. In fact, it is hard in places
to tell whether he is expressing his own opinion or
those of the farmers whom he has consulted ; and he
still writes as one of an agricultural community who
is to remain in it. But many of the suggestions in
' Village Organization ' may still be found stimulating,
and the inactivity of men in country parishes is not yet
in need of further description ; while the fact that ' the
great centres of population have almost entirely occupied the attention of our legislators of late years ' is
still only fitfully perceived. It should be noticed, also,
that he is true to himself and his later self, if not in
his valiant asseveration of the farmer's sturdy independence, yet in the wish that there should be an
authority to ' cause a parish to be supplied with

good drinking water,' or that there should be a tank, 'the public property of the village.'

To 'Unequal Agriculture' the editor of *Fraser's Magazine* appended a note, saying that if England were to be brought to such a pitch of perfection under scientific cultivation as Jefferies desired, 'a few of us would then prefer to go away and live elsewhere.' And there is no doubt that he was carried away by his subject into an indiscriminate optimism, for he turned upon it sadly and with equal firmness in later life. But the writing is beyond that of the letters to the *Times*, and in the sentences—

'The plough is drawn by dull, patient oxen, plodding onwards now just as they were depicted upon the tombs and temples, the graves and worshipping-places, of races who had their being three thousand years ago. Think of the suns that have shone since then ; of the summers and the bronzed grain waving in the wind ; of the human teeth that have ground that grain, and are now hidden in the abyss of earth ; yet still the oxen plod on, like slow Time itself, here this day in our land of steam and telegraph '

—in these sentences, though they are commonplace enough, there is proof that the writer already had that curious consciousness of the past which was to give so deep a tone to many of his pages later on. But in these papers, again, what is most noticeable is the practical knowledge and the power of handling practical things. Though he himself, brought up on his father's farm, had no taste for farming, and seldom did any practical work except splitting timber, he yet confines himself severely to things as they are, or as they may quickly be made to become by a patching-up. These are 'practical politics for practical men.' Consequently the clear and forcible writing is only better in degree than other writing of the moment with an element of controversy, and represents not the whole truth, but an aspect of selected portions of the truth. When it is turned to other purposes it shows a poor grace, as in ' a widespread ocean of wheat, an English gold-field, a veritable Yellow Sea, bowing in waves before the southern breeze—a sight full of peaceful poetry ;' and the sluggish, customary euphemism of phrases like ' a few calves find their way to the butcher ' is tedious enough.

'The Idle Earth ' (*Longman's*, December, 1894), ' After the County Franchise' (*Longman's*, February, 1884), and 'The Wiltshire Labourer' (*Longman's*, 1887), belong to Jefferies' later years. 'The Idle Earth ' was published only after his death, but, like the other two, was written, probably, between 1884 and 1887. He was no longer writing as a practical man, but as a critical outsider with an inside know-ledge. 'The Idle Earth' is an astonishing curiosity —an extreme example of Jefferies' discontent with things as they are. 'Why is it,' he asks, 'that this cry arises that agriculture will not pay ? ... The answer is simple enough. It is because the earth is idle one-third of the year.' He looks round a January field and sees 'not an animal in sight, not a single machine for making money, not a penny being turned.' He wishes to know, 'What would a manufacturer think of a business in which he was compelled to let his engines rest for a third of the year?' Then he falls upon the miserable Down-land because that is still more idle and still less productive. 'With all its progress,' he cries, 'how little real advance has agriculture made! All because of the stubborn, idle earth.' It is a genuine cry, to be paralleled by 'Life is short, art long,' and by his own wonder that 'in twelve thousand written years the world has not yet built itself a House, unfilled a Granary, nor organized itself for its own comfort,' by his contempt for 'this little petty life of seventy years,' and for the short sleep permitted to men.

The editor of *Longman's* had to explain that, in publishing 'After the County Franchise,' he was not really 'overstepping the limit which he laid down in undertaking to keep *Longman's Magazine* free from the strife of party politics, because it might be profitable to consider what changes this Bill will make, when it becomes law, in the lives and the social relations of our rural population.' It was true that Jefferies was no longer a party politician. He was by that time above and before either party. He is so still, and the reappearance of these no longer novel ideas is excusable simply because Jefferies' name is likely to gain for them still more of the consideration and support which they deserve, for it may be hoped that our day is ready to receive the seed of trouble and advance contained in the modest suggestion which he believed to be compatible with 'the acquisition of public and the preservation of private liberty.'

[' We now govern our village ourselves ;] why should we not possess our village? Why should we not live in our own houses? Why should we not have a little share in the land, as much, at least, as we can pay for? . . . Can an owner of this kind of property be permitted to refuse to sell? Must he be compelled to sell?'

Twenty-five years ago Jefferies, knowing that neither land nor cottages were to be had, that there was no security of tenure for the labourer, hoped for the day when 'some, at least, of our people may be able to set up homes for themselves in their own country.' He believed that 'the greater his freedom, the greater his attachment to home, the more settled the labourer,' the firmer would become the position of labourer, farmer, and landowner. Yet an advanced reformer of our own day—Mr. Montague Fordham in ' Mother Earth'—has still to cry the same thing in the wilderness ; and it is still true that 'you cannot have a fixed population unless it has a home, and the labouring population is practically homeless.' On the other hand, it should be remembered that Jefferies also says : ' Parks and woods are becoming of priceless value ; we should have to preserve a few landowners, if only to have parks and woods.'

These later articles are far more persuasive than their predecessors, for here there is no doubt, not merely that they are sincere, but that they are the unprejudiced opinion of the man as well as of the agriculturist. He has ceased to be concerned only with things as they are, or as they may be made to-morrow. He allows himself to think as much of justice as of expediency, of what is fitting as well as of what is at once possible. The phrases, 'Sentiment is more stubborn than fact,' 'Service is no inheritance,' 'I do not want any paupers,' 'I should not like men under my thumb,' 'Men demanding to be paid in full for full work, but refusing favours and petty assistance to be recouped hereafter ; . . . men with the franchise, voting under the protection of the ballot, and voting first and foremost for the demolition of the infernal Poor Law and workhouse system'—these simple phrases fall with peculiar and even pathetic force, in their context, from the mystic optimist whom pain was ripening fast in those last years. Even here he uses phrases like 'the serious work which brings in money' and commends 'push and enter-prise' as a substitute for 'the slow plodding manner of the labourer.' But these are exceptional. As to the writing itself, of which this is an example,

'By home life I mean that which gathers about a house, however small, standing in its own grounds. Something comes into existence about such a house, an influence, a pervading feeling, like some warm colour softening the whole, tinting the lichen on the wall, even the very smoke-marks on the chimney. It is home, and the men and women born there will never lose the tone it has given them. Such homes are the strength of a land '

—it remains simple; but by the use of far fewer words, and of fewer orator's phrases, its unadorned directness has almost a positive spiritual quality.

But these agricultural essays, good as they were, and absorbing as they did all of Jefferies' social thoughts to the end of his life, became less and less frequent as he grew less inclined and less able to adapt his mind and style to the affairs of the moment.

In the same year as 'The Story of Swindon' he published 'Village Churches' and 'Marlborough Forest' (*Graphic*, December 4 and October 23, 1875). These and his unsuccessful novels remain to show the direction of his more intimate thoughts in the third decade of his life. They are as imperfect in their class as 'The Story of Swindon' is perfect in its own. They are the earliest of their kind from Jefferies' pen which have survived. He is dealing already with another and a more individual kind of reality, and he is not yet at home with it in words. He approaches it with ceremony—with the ceremony of phrases like 'the great painter Autumn,' 'a very tiger to the rabbit,' 'the titles and pomp of belted earl and knight.' But here for the first time he is so bent upon himself and his object that he casts only an occasional glance upon his audience, whereas in his practical papers he has it continually in view, or even ready to jog his elbow if he dreams. The full English hedges, which he condemns as an agriculturist, he would now save from the modern Goths; he can even be sorry for the death of beautiful jays.   Here, for the first time, it might occur to a student of the man that he is more than his words express.   He does not see Nature as he sees the factory, and when he and Nature touch there is an emotional discharge which blurs the sight, though presently it is to enrich it.   As yet we cannot be sure whether he is perfectly genuine or is striving for an effect based upon a recollection of someone else—probably it is both—when he writes :

'The heart has a yearning for the unknown, a longing to penetrate the deep shadow and the winding glade, where, as it seems, no human foot has been ';

when he speaks of the '*visible* silence' of the old church, or exclaims:

'To us, each hour is of consequence, especially in this modern day, which has invented the detestable creed that time is money.   But time is not money to Nature.   She never hastens. . . .'

But already he is expressing a thought, which he was often to repeat in his maturity and in his best work, when he says of the church-bell that 'In the day when this bell was made, men put their souls into their works.   Their one great object was not to turn out 100,000 all alike.'

It was in the next year, 1876, that he began to think of using his observation and feeling in a 'chatty style,' of setting down 'some of the glamour—the magic of sunshine, and green things, and clear waters.'   But it was not until 1878 that he succeeded in doing so. In 'The Amateur Poacher' and its companions, there was not between Jefferies and Nature the colourless, clear light of the factory or the journalist's workshop, but the tender English atmosphere or, if you like, that of the happy and thoughtful mind which had grown up in that atmosphere.

'Choosing a Gun' and 'Skating' belong to the period, if not the year, of 'The Amateur Poacher.' In fact, the passage about the pleasure of having the freedom of the woods with a wheel-lock, is either a first draft of one of the best in that book, or it is an unconscious repetition. Here again is a characteristic complaint that 'the leading idea of the gunmaker nowadays is to turn out a hundred thousand guns of one particular pattern.' The suggestion that some clever workman should go and set himself up in some village is one that has been followed in other trades, and is not yet exhausted. The writing is now excellent of its kind, but for the word 'Metropolis' and the phrase 'no great distance from' Pall Mall. The negligent—but slowly acquired—conversational simplicity captures the open air as calmly and pleasantly as the humour of the city dialogue.

'Skating' is slight enough, but ends with grace and an unsought solemnity which comes more and more into his later writing, so that in 'The Spring of the Year' (*Longman's*, June, 1894), after many notes about wood-pigeons, there comes such a genuine landscape as this ·

'The bare, slender tips of the birches on which they perched exposed them against the sky. Once six alighted on a long birch-branch, bending it down with their weight, not unlike a heavy load of fruit. As the stormy sunset flamed up, tinting the fields with momentary red, their hollow voices sounded among the trees.'

These notes for April and May, 1881, were continued in 'The Coming of Summer,' which forms part of 'Toilers of the Field.' This informal chit-chat, addressed chiefly to the amateur naturalist, became an easy habit with Jefferies. The talk is of the plainest and pleasantest here, and full of himself. With his 'I like sparrows,' he was an older and tenderer man than in 'The Gamekeeper' period. The paper gives some idea of his habits and haunts round about Surbiton before the fatal chain of illnesses began at the end of this year. Personally, I like to know that it was finished on May 10, 1881, at midnight, with 'Antares visible, the summer star,' very low in the south-east above Banstead Downs, and Lyra and Arcturus high above in the south, if Jefferies was writing at Tolworth, as presumably he was. This paper is to be preferred to 'Birds of Spring'—likeable mainly for the pages on the chiff-chaff and sedge-warbler—which does much the same thing, in a more formal manner, for the instruction of readers of *Chambers's* (March, 1884), who wished to know about our 'feathered visitors.'

'Vignettes from Nature' were posthumously published in *Longman's* (July, 1895). They abound in touches from the depth and tenderness of his nature, and when they were written Jefferies had passed into the most distinct period of his life—the period which gave birth to his mature ideas, and, in particular, to 'The Story of My Heart.' The light which he had carried about with him since his youth —a light so faint that we cannot be sure he was aware of it in retrospect—now leaped up with a mystic significance. Professor William James, in 'Varieties of Religious Experience,' describes four marks by which states of mind may be recognized as mystical. The subject says that they defy expression. They are 'states of insight into depths of truth unplumbed by the discursive intellect . . . and, as a rule, they carry with them a curious sense of authority for after-time,' because the mystic believes that 'we both become one with the Absolute, and we become aware of our oneness.' They 'cannot be sustained for long . . . except in rare instances half an hour, or at most an hour or two, seems to be the limit beyond which they fade into the light of common day.' And when the mystic consciousness has set in, 'the mystic feels as if his own will were in abeyance, and, indeed, sometimes as if he were grasped and held by a superior power.' Most of the striking cases in Professor James's collection occurred out of doors. These marks may all be recognized in Jefferies' record of his own experience—'The Story of My Heart.' Yet it was, in the opinion of a very high authority—Dr. Maurice Bucke, in 'Cosmic Consciousness'—an imperfect experience, and his

state is described as 'the twilight of cosmic consciousness.' Dr. Bucke gives as the marks of the cosmic
sense—a subjective light on its appearance ; moral
elevation ; intellectual illumination ; the sense of immortality ; loss of the fear of death and of the sense
of sin ; the suddenness of the awakening which
takes place usually at a little past the thirtieth year,
and comes only to noble characters (*e.g.*, Pascal,
Blake, Balzac, and Whitman) ; a charm added to
the personality ; a transfiguration of the subject in
the eyes of others when the cosmic sense is actually
present. Jefferies appears to have lacked the subjective light and the full sense of immortality. 'If,'
says Dr. Bucke, ' he had attained to cosmic consciousness, he would have entered into eternal life, and
there would be no " seems " about it ;' while he finds
positive evidence against Jefferies' possession of the
perfect cosmic sense in his ' contempt for the assertion
that all things occur for the best.' The sense varied
in intensity with Jefferies, and in its everyday force
was not much more than Kingsley's ' innate feeling
that everything I see has a meaning, if I could but
understand it,' which ' feeling of being surrounded
with truths which I cannot grasp amounts to indescribable awe sometimes.'

Cosmic consciousness, the half-grasped power
which gave its significance to his autobiography, to
'The Dawn,' ' The Sun and the Brook ' (*Knowledge*,
October 13, 1882), 'On the Downs' (*Standard*,
March 23, 1883), ' Nature and Eternity ' (*Longman's*,
May, 1895), and many other papers, may have been

the faculty for which Jefferies prayed in ' The Story of My Heart,' and to which he desired that mankind should advance. In Dr. Bucke's view, an imperfectly supported one, men with this faculty are becoming more and more common, and he thinks that ' our descendants will sooner or later reach, as a race, the condition of cosmic consciousness, just as long ago our ancestors passed from simple to self consciousness.'

In Jefferies the development of this sense was gradual. Phrases suggesting that it is in progress may be found in earlier books—in the novels, in ' Wood Magic ' and ' Bevis '—but ' The Story of My Heart ' is the first that is inspired by it; and after that, all his best work is affected either by the same fervour and solemnity, or by its accompanying ideas, or by both. It is to be detected in many sentences in ' Vignettes,' and in the concluding prayer, ' Let the heart come out from the shadow of roofs to the open glow of the sky . . .'—even in the plea to the mechanics in ' A King of Acres ' (*Chambers's*, January, 1884) not to ' pin their faith to any theory born and sprung up among the crushed and pale-faced life of modern time, but to look for themselves at the sky above the highest branches . . . that they might gather to themselves some of the leaves— mental and spiritual leaves—of the ancient forest, feeling nearer to the truth and soul, as it were, that lives on in it.' It is in the aspiration and hope—in the sense of ' hovering on the verge of a great truth,' of ' a meaning waiting in the grass and water,' of a ' wider existence yet to be enjoyed on the earth '—in the 'increased consciousness of our own life,' gained from sun and sky and sea—it is everywhere in 'Sun and Brook' and 'On the Downs.' It suffuses the sensuous delicacy and exuberance and the spiritual joy of 'Nature and Eternity.' That paper belongs to, and in a measure corrects, 'The Story of My Heart.' There is less eloquence than in the autobiography, and a greater proportion of that beautiful simplicity that is so spiritual when combined with the characteristic cadence of Jefferies at his best. The mystic has a view of things by which all knowledge becomes real—or disappears—and all things are seen related to the whole in a manner which gives a wonderful value to the least of them. The combination of sensuousness and spiritual aspiration in this and other essays produces a beauty perhaps peculiar to Jefferies—often a vague beauty imperfectly adumbrated, as was the meaning of the universe itself in his mood of 'thoughts without words, mobile like the stream, nothing compact that can be grasped and stayed : dreams that slip silently as water slips through the fingers.' In 'Nature and Eternity' this is all the more impressive because Coate Farm and its fields, Jefferies' birthplace and early home, is the scene of it. That beauty haunts the last four essays of this book as it haunts 'The Story of My Heart,' like a theme of music, always a repetition, and yet never exactly the same. 'The Dawn' is one of the most beautiful things which Jefferies wrote after his awakening. The cadences are his best—gentle, wistful, not quite certain cadences, where the effect of the mere sound cannot be detached from the effect of the thought hovering behind the sound. How they kindle such a passage as this, where Jefferies again brings before us his sense of past time !—

' But though so familiar, that spectral light in the silence has never lost its meaning, the violets are sweet year by year though never so many summers pass away ; indeed, its meaning grows wider and more difficult as the time goes on. For think, this spectre of light—light's double-ganger—has stood by the couch of every human being for thousands and thousands of years. Sleeping or waking, happily dreaming, or wrenched with pain, whether they have noticed it or not, the finger of this light has pointed towards them. When they were building the pyramids, five thousand years ago, straight the arrow of light shot from the sun, lit their dusky forms, and glowed on the endless sand. . . .'

The whole essay is delicately perfect—as free from the spiritual eloquence of the autobiography and from the rhetoric of the agricultural papers as from the everyday atmosphere of earlier work and the decoration of the first outdoor essays. It is pure spirit. Take any passage, and it will be seen that in thought and style Jefferies' evolution is now complete. He has mounted from being a member of a class, at first undistinguishable from it, then clearly more enlightened, but still of it, and seeing things in the same way, up to the position of a poet with an outlook that is purely individual, and, though deeply human, yet of a spirituality now close as the grass, and now as the stars. The date of ' The Dawn ' is uncertain. It may have been 1883, the year of ' The Story of My Heart,' or it may have been as late as 1885. This book, therefore, contains, like no other single volume, the record of Jefferies' progress during about ten of his most important years. It was not for nothing that Jefferies, man and boy, had gone through the phases of sportsman, naturalist, and artist, and always worshipper, upon the hills, ' that he lived in a perpetual commerce with external Nature, and nourished himself upon the spirit of its forms.' Air and sun so cleaned and sweetened his work that in the end the cleanness and sweetness of Nature herself become inseparable from it in our minds.

CHOOSING A GUN

The first thought of the amateur sportsman naturally refers to his gun, and the questions arise : What sort of a gun do I want ? Where can I get it ? What price shall I pay ? In appearance there can be no great difficulty in settling these matters, but in practice it is really by no means easy. Some time since, being on a visit to the Metropolis, I was requested by a friend to get him a gun, and accepted the commission, as M. Emile Ollivier went to war, with a light heart, little dreaming of the troubles that would start up in the attempt to conscientiously carry it out. He wanted a good gun, and was not very scrupulous as to maker or price, provided that the latter was not absolutely extravagant. With such *carte blanche* as this it seemed plain-sailing, and, indeed, I never gave a second thought to the business till I opened the door of the first respectable gunmaker's shop I came across, which happened to be no great distance from Pall Mall. A very polite gentleman immediately came forward, rubbing his hands as if he were washing them (which is an odd habit with many), and asked if there was anything he could do for me. Well, yes, I wanted a gun. Just so—they had one of the largest stocks in London, and would be most happy to show me specimens of all kinds. But was there any special sort of gun required, as then they could suit me in an instant.

'Hum! Ah! Well, I — I ' — feeling rather vague—' perhaps you would let me see your catalogue——'

' Certainly.' And a handsomely got-up pamphlet, illustrated with woodcuts, was placed in my hands, and I began to study the pages. But this did not suit him ; doubtless, with the practice of his profession, he saw at once the uncertain manner of the customer who was feeling his way, and thought to bring it to a point.

' You want a good, useful gun, sir, I presume ?'

' That is just it '—shutting the catalogue ; quite a relief to have the thing put into shape for one !

' Then you can't do better than take our new patent double-action so-and-so. Here it is '—handing me a decent-looking weapon in thorough polish, which I begin to weigh in my hands, poise it to ascertain the balance, and to try how it comes to the present, and whether I can catch the rib quick enough, when he goes on : ' We can let you have that gun, sir, for ten guineas.'

' Oh, indeed! But that's very cheap, isn't it ?' I thoughtlessly observe, putting the gun down.

My friend D. had mentioned a much higher amount as his ultimatum. The next instant I saw in what light my remark would be taken. It would be interpreted in this way : Here we have either a rich amateur, who doesn't care what he gives, or else a fool who knows nothing about it.

'Well, sir, of course it's our very plainest gun'—the weapon is tossed carelessly into the background—'in fact, we sometimes call it our gamekeeper gun. Now, here is a really fine thing—neatly finished, engraved plates, first choice stock, the very best walnut, price——' He names a sum very close to D.'s outside.

I handle the weapon in the same manner, and for the life of me cannot meet his eye, for I know that he is reading me, or thinks he is, like a book. With the exception that the gun is a trifle more elaborately got up, I cannot see or feel the slightest difference, and begin secretly to suspect that the price of guns is regulated according to the inexperience of the purchaser—a sort of sliding scale, gauged to ignorance, and rising or falling with its density! He expatiates on the gun and points out all its beauties.

'Shooting carefully registered, sir. Can see it tried, or try it yourself, sir. Our range is barely three-quarters of an hour's ride. If the stock doesn't quite fit your shoulder, you can have another—the same price. You won't find a better gun in all London.'

I can see that it really is a very fair article, but do not detect the extraordinary excellencies so glibly described. I recollect an old proverb about the fool and the money he is said to part with hastily. I resolve to see more variety before making the final plunge ; and what the eloquent shopkeeper thinks is my growing admiration for the gun which I continue to handle is really my embarrassment, for as yet I am not hardened, and dislike the idea of leaving the shop without making a purchase after actually touching the goods.   But D.'s money—I must lay it out to the best advantage.   Desperately I fling the gun into his hands, snatch up the catalogue, mutter incoherently, ' Will look it through—like the look of the thing—call again,' and find myself walking aimlessly along the pavement outside.

An unpleasant sense of having played a rather small part lingered for some time, and ultimately resolved itself into a determination to make up my mind as to exactly what D. wanted, and on entering the next shop, to ask to see that, and that only.   So, turning to the address of another gunmaker, I walked towards it slowly, revolving in my mind the sort of shooting D. usually enjoyed.   Visions of green fields, woods just beginning to turn colour, puffs of smoke hanging over the ground, rose up, and blotted out the bustling London scene.   The shops glittering with their brightest goods placed in front, the throng of vehicles, the crowds of people, faded away, the pace increased and the stride lengthened as if stepping over the elastic turf, and the roar of the traffic sounded low, like a distant waterfall.   From this reverie the rude apostrophes of a hansom-cabman awoke me—I had walked right into the stream of the street, and instead of the awning boughs of the wood found a whip upheld, threatening chastisement for getting in the way. This brought me up from imagination to logic with a jerk, and I began to check off the uses D. could put his gun to on the fingers. (1) I knew he had a friend in Yorkshire, and shot over his moor every August. His gun, then, must be suited to grouse-shooting, and must be light, because of the heat which often prevails at that time, and renders dragging a heavy gun many miles over the heather—before they pack—a serious drawback to the pleasure of the sport. (2) He had some partridge-shooting of his own, and was peculiarly fond of it. (3) He was always invited to at least two battues. (4) A part of his own shooting was on the hills, where the hares were very wild, where there was no cover, and they had to be knocked over at long distances, and took a hard blow. That would require (*a*) a choke-bore, which was not suitable either, because in covers the pheasants at short ranges would not unlikely get 'blown,' which would annoy the host; or (*b*) a heavy, strong gun, which would take a stiff charge without too much recoil. But that, again, clashed with the light gun for shooting in August. (5) He had latterly taken a fancy to wild-fowl shooting by the coast, for which a very hard-hitting, long-range gun was needed. It would never do if D. could not bring down a duck. (6) He was notorious as a dead shot on snipe—this told rather in favour of a light gun, old system of boring; for where would a snipe or a woodcock be if it chanced to get 200 pellets into it at twenty yards? You might find the claws and fragments of the bill if you looked with a microscope. (7) No delicate piece of workmanship would do, because he was careless of his gun, knocked it about anyhow, and occasionally dropped it in a brook. And here was the shop-door ; imagine the state of confusion my mind was in when I entered !

This was a very ' big ' place : the gentleman who approached had a way of waving his hand—very white and jewelled—and a grand, lofty idea of what a gun should cost. ' Twenty, thirty, forty pounds —some of the £30 were second-hand, of course—we have a few, a very few, second-hand guns '—such was the sweeping answer to my first mild inquiry about prices. Then, seeing at once my vacillating manner, he, too, took me in hand, only in a terribly earnest, ponderous way from which there was no escape. ' You wanted a good general gun—yes ; a thoroughly good, well-finished, *plain* gun (great emphasis on the ' plain '). Of course, you can't get anything new for *that* money, finished in style. Still, the plain gun will shoot just as well (as if the shooting part was scarcely worth consideration). We make the very best plain-finished article for five-and-twenty guineas in London. By-the-by, where is your shooting, sir ?' Thrust home like this, not over-gratified by a manner which seemed to say, ' Listen to an authority,' and desiring to keep an incog., I mutter something about ' abroad.' ' Ah— well, then, this article is precisely the thing, because it will carry ball, an immense advantage in any country where you may come across large game.'

'How far will it throw a ball?' I ask, rather curious on that subject, for I was under the impression that a smooth-bore of the usual build is not much to be relied on in that way—far less, indeed, than the matchlocks made by semi-civilized nations. But it seems I was mistaken.

'Why—a hundred yards point-blank, and ten times better to shoot with than a rifle.'

'Indeed!'

'Of course, I mean in cover, as you're pretty sure to be. Say a wild boar is suddenly started : well, you pull out your No. 4 shot-cartridge, and push in a ball; you shoot as well again—snap-shooting with a smooth-bore in jungle or bush. There's not a better gun turned out in town than that. It's not the slightest use your looking for anything cheaper— rebounding locks, best stocks, steel damascene barrels ; fit for anything from snipe to deer, from dust to buck-shot——'

'But I think——' Another torrent overwhelms me.

'Here's an order for twenty of these guns for Texas, to shoot from horseback at buffalo—ride in among them, you know.'

I look at my watch, find it's much later than I imagine, remark that it is really a difficult thing to pick out a gun, and seize the door-handle.

'When gentlemen don't exactly know what they're looking for it *is* a hard job to choose a gun '—he smiles sarcastically, and shuts me out politely.

The observation seems hard, after thinking over guns so intently ; yet it must be aggravating to attempt to serve a man who does not know what he wants—yet (one's mood changes quickly) it was his own fault for trying to force, to positively force, that twenty-five-guinea thing on me instead of giving me a chance to choose. I had seen rows on rows of guns stacked round the shop, rank upon rank ; in the background a door partly open permitted a glimpse of a second room, also perfectly coated with guns, if such an expression is permissible. Now, I look on ranges of guns like this much the same as on a library. Is there anything so delicious as the first exploration of a great library—alone—unwatched ? You shut the heavy door behind you slowly, reverently, lest a noise should jar on the sleepers of the shelves. For as the Seven Sleepers of Ephesus were dead and yet alive, so are the souls of the authors in the care of their ancient leathern binding. You walk gently round the walls, pausing here to read a title, there to draw out a tome and support it for a passing glance—half in your arms, half against the shelf. The passing glance lengthens till the weight becomes too great, and with a sigh you replace it, and move again, peering up at those titles which are foreshortened from the elevation of the shelf, and so roam from folio to octavo, from octavo to quarto, till at last, finding a little work whose value, were it in the mart, would be more than its weight in gold, you bear it to the low leather-covered arm-chair and enjoy it at your ease. But to sip the full pleasure of a library you must be alone, and you must take the books yourself from the shelves. A man to read must read

alone. He may make extracts, he may *work* at books
in company ; but to read, to absorb, he must be
solitary. Something in the same way—except in the
necessity for solitude, which does not exist in this
case—I like to go through a battery of guns, picking
up this one, or that, glancing up one, trying the locks
of another, examining the thickness of the breech.
Why did not the fellow say, ' There are our guns;
walk round, take down what you please, do as you
like, and don't hurry. I will go on with some work
while you examine them. Call me if you want any
explanation. Spend the day there if you like, and
come again to-morrow.' It would have been a hundred
chances to one that I had found a gun to suit D.,
for the shop was a famous one, the guns really good,
the workmanship unimpeachable, and the stock to
select from immense. But let a thing be never so
good, one does not care to have it positively thrust
on one.

By this time my temper was up, and I determined
to go through with the business, and get the precise
article likely to please D., if I went to every maker
in the Metropolis. I went to very nearly every
prominent man—I spent several days at it. I called
at shops whose names are household words wherever
an English sportsman can be found. Some of them,
though bright to look at from the pavement, within
were mean, and even lacked cleanliness. The attendants were often incapable of comprehending that
a customer *may* be as good a judge of what he wants
as themselves; they have got into a narrow routine

of offering the same thing to everybody. No two
shops were of the same opinion: at one you were
told that the choke was the greatest success in the
world; at another, that they only shot well for one
season, quickly wearing out; at a third, that such and
such a 'grip' or breech-action was perfect; at a
fourth, that there never was such a mistake; at a
fifth, that hammerless guns were the guns of the
future, and elsewhere, that people detested hammerless guns because it seemed like learning to shoot
over again. Finally, I visited several of the second-
hand shops. They had some remarkably good
guns—for the leading second-hand shops do not
care to buy a gun unless by a crack maker—but the
cheapness was a delusion. A new gun might be got
for the same money, or very little more. Their
system was like this. Suppose they had a really good
gun, but, for aught you could tell, twenty or thirty
years old (the breech-action might have been altered),
for this they would ask, say £25. The original
price of the gun may have been £50, and if viewed
only with regard to the original price, of course that
would be a great reduction. But for the £25 a new
gun could be got from a maker whose goods, if not so
famous, were thoroughly reliable, and who guaranteed
the shooting. In the one case you bought a gun
about whose previous history you knew absolutely
nothing beyond the mere fact of the barrels having
come at first-hand from a leading maker. But they
may have been battered about—rebored; they may
be scored inside by someone loading with flints;

twenty things that are quite unascertainable may have combined to injure its original perfection. The cheapness will not stand the test of a moment's thought—that is, if you are in search of excellence. You buy a name and trust to chance. After several days of such work as this, becoming less and less satisfied at every fresh attempt, and physically more fatigued than if I had walked a hundred miles, I gave it up for awhile, and wrote to D. for more precise instructions.

When I came to quietly reflect on these experiences, I found that the effect of carefully studying the subject had been to plunge me into utter confusion. It seemed as difficult to choose a gun as to choose a horse, which is saying a good deal. Most of us take our shooting as we take other things—from our fathers—very likely use their guns, get into their style of shooting; or if we buy guns, buy them because a friend wants to sell, and so get hold of the gun that suits us by a kind of happy chance. But to begin *de novo*, to select a gun from the thousand and one exhibited in London, to go conscientiously into the merits and demerits of the endless varieties of locks and breeches, and to come to an impartial decision, is a task the magnitude of which is not easily described. How many others who have been placed in somewhat similar positions must have felt the same ultimate confusion of mind, and perhaps at last, in sheer despair, plunged, and bought the first that came to hand, regretting for years afterwards that they had not bought this or that weapon, which had taken their fancy, but which some gunsmith interested in a patent had declared obsolete !

D. settled the question, so far as he was concerned, by ordering two guns : one bored in the old style for ordinary shooting, and a choked gun of larger bore for the ducks. But all this trouble and investigation gave rise to several not altogether satisfactory reflections. For one thing, there seems a too great desire on the part of gunmakers to achieve a colossal reputation by means of some new patent, which is thrust on the notice of the sportsman and of the public generally at every step and turn. The patent very likely is an admirable thing, and quite fulfils the promise so far as the actual object in view is concerned. But it is immediately declared to supersede everything—no gun is of any use without it : you are compelled to purchase it whether or no, or you are given to understand that you are quite behind the age. The leading idea of the gunmaker nowadays is to turn out a hundred thousand guns of one particular pattern, like so many bales of cloth ; everybody is to shoot with this, their speciality, and everything that has been previously done is totally ignored. The workman in the true sense of the word—the artist in guns—is either extinct, or hidden in an obscure corner. There is no individuality about modern guns. One is exactly like another. That is very well, and necessary for military arms, because an army must be supplied with a single pattern cartridge in order to simplify the difficulty of providing ammunition. They fail even in the matter of ornament. The design—if it can be called design —on one lock-plate is repeated on a thousand others, so with the hammers. There is no originality about a modern gun ; as you handle it you are conscious that it is well put together, that the mechanism is perfect, the barrels true, but somehow it feels *hard ;* it conveys the impression of being machine-made. You cannot feel the *hand* of the maker anywhere, and the failure, the flatness, the formality of the supposed ornament, is depressing. The ancient harquebuss makers far surpassed the very best manufacturers of the present day. Their guns are really artistic—works of true art. The stocks of some of the German wheel-lock guns of the sixteenth and seventeeth centuries are really beautiful specimens or carving and design. Their powder-horns are gems of workmanship—hunting-scenes cut out in ivory, the minutest detail rendered with life-like accuracy. They graved their stags and boars from Nature, not from conventional designs ; the result is that we admire them now because Nature is constant, and her fashions endure. The conventional 'designs' on our lock-plates, etc., will in a few years be despised ; they have no intrinsic beauty. The Arab of the desert, wild, untrammelled, ornaments his matchlock with turquoise. Our machine - made guns, double-barrel, breech-loading, double-grip, rebounding locks, first-choice stocks, laminated steel, or damascus barrels, choke-bore, and so forth, will, it is true, mow down the pheasants at the battue as the scythe cuts down the grass. There is slaughter

in every line of them.   But is slaughter everything?
In my idea it is not, but very far from it.   Were I
offered the choice of participation in the bloodiest
battue ever arranged—such as are reserved for
princes—the very best position, and the best-finished
and swiftest breech-loader invented, or the freedom
of an English forest, to go forth at any time and
shoot whatever I chose, untrammelled by any attendants, on condition that I only carried a wheel-lock,
I should unhesitatingly select the second alternative.
There would be an abiding pleasure in the very fact
of using so beautiful a weapon—just in the very
handling of it, to pass the fingers over the intricate
and exquisite carving.   There would be pleasure in
winding up the lock with the spanner ; in adjusting
the pyrites to strike fire from the notches of the
wheel ; in priming from a delicate flask graven with
stag and hounds.   There would be delight in steal-
ing from tree to tree, in creeping from bush to
bush, through the bracken, keeping the wind carefully, noiselessly gliding forward—so silently that
the woodpecker should not cease tapping in the
beech, or the pigeon her hoarse call in the oak,
till at last within range of the buck.   And then!
First, if the ball did not hit the vital spot, if
it did not pass through the neck, or break the
shoulder, inevitably he would be lost, for the round
bullet would not break up like a shell, and smash
the creature's flesh and bones into a ghastly jelly, as
do the missiles from our nineteenth century express
rifles.   Secondly, if the wheel did not knock a spark

out quickly, if the priming had not been kept dry, and did not ignite instantly, the aim might waver, and all the previous labour be lost. Something like skill would be necessary here. There would be art in the weapon itself, skill in the very loading, skill in the approach, nerve in holding the gun steady while the slow powder caught from the priming and expelled the ball. That would be sport. An imperfect weapon—well, yes ; but the imperfect weapon would somehow harmonize with the forest, with the huge old hollow oaks, the beeches full of knot-holes, the mysterious thickets, the tall fern, the silence and solitude. It would make the forest seem a forest— such as existed hundreds of years ago ; it would make the chase a real chase, not a foregone conclusion. It would equalize the chances, and give the buck 'law.' In short, it would be real shooting. Or with smaller game—I fancy I could hit a pheasant with a wheel-lock if I went alone, and *flushed the bird myself*. In that lies all the difference. If your birds are flushed by beaters, you may be on the watch, but that very watching unnerves by straining the nerves, and then the sudden rush and noise flusters you, and even with the best gun of modern construction you often miss. If you spring the bird yourself the noise may startle you, and yet somehow you settle down to your aim and drop him. With a wheel-lock, if I could get a tolerably clear view, I think I could bring him down. If only a brace rewarded a day's roaming under oak and beech, through fern and past thicket, I should be amply satisfied. With the antique weapon the spirit of the wood would enter into one. The chances of failure add zest to the pursuit. For slaughter, however, our modern guns are unsurpassed.

Another point which occurs to one after such an overhauling of guns as I went through is the price charged for them. There does seem something very arbitrary in the charges demanded, and one cannot help a feeling that they bear no proportion to the real value or cost of production. It may, of course, be said that the wages of workmen are very high— although workmen as a mass have long been complaining that such is not really the case. The rent of premises in fashionable localities is also high, no doubt. For my part, I would quite as soon buy a gun in a village as in a crowded thoroughfare of the Metropolis ; indeed rather sooner, since there would probably be a range attached where it could be tried. To be offered a range, as is often the case in London, half an hour out—which, with getting to the station and from the station at the other end, to the place and back, may practically mean half a day—is of little use. If you could pick up the gun in the shop, stroll outside and try it at once, it would be ten times more pleasant and satisfactory. A good gun is like the good wine of the proverb—if it were made in a village, to that village men would go or send for it. The materials for gunmaking are, surely, not very expensive—processes for cheapening steel and metal generally are now carried to such an extent, and the market for metals has fallen to an extraordinary extent. Machinery and steam-power to drive it is, no doubt, a very heavy item ; but are we so anxious for machinery and machine-made guns? Are you and I anxious that ten thousand other persons should shoot with guns exactly, precisely like ours in every single particular? That is the meaning of machinery. It destroys the individuality of sport. We are all like so many soldiers in an army corps firing Government Martini-Henries. In the sporting ranks one does not want to be a private. I wonder some clever workman does not go and set himself up in some village where rent and premises are low, and where a range could be got close to his door, and deliberately set down to make a name for really first-rate guns, at a moderate price, and with some pretensions to individuality and beauty. There is water-power, which is cheaper than steam, running to waste all over the country now. The old grist-mills, which may be found three or four in a single parish sometimes, are half of them falling into decay, because we eat American wheat now, which is ground in the city steam-mills, and a good deal imported ready ground as flour. Here and there one would think sufficient water-power might be obtained in this way. But even if we admit that great manufactories are extremely expensive to maintain, wages high, rent dear, premises in fashionable streets fabulously costly, yet even then there is something in the price of guns not quite the thing. You buy a gun and pay a long price for it : but if you attempt to sell it again you find it is the same as with jewellery, you can get hardly a third of its original cost. The intrinsic value of the gun then is less than half its advertised first cost-price. The second-hand gun offered to you for £20 has probably cost the dealer about £6, or £10 at the most. So that, manage it ' how you will,' you pay a sum quite out of proportion to the intrinsic value. It is all very well to talk about the market, custom of trade, supply and demand, and so forth, though some of the cries of the political economist (notably the Free Trade cry) are now beginning to be questioned. The value of a thing is what it will fetch, no doubt, and yet that is a doctrine which metes out half-justice only. It is justice to the seller, but, argue as sophistically as you like, it is *not* justice to the purchaser.

I should recommend any gentleman who is going to equip himself as a sportsman to ask himself before he starts the question that occurred to me too late in D.'s case: What kind of shooting am I likely to enjoy? Then, if not wishing to go to more expense than absolutely necessary, let him purchase a gun precisely suited to the game he will meet. As briefly observed before, if the sportsman takes his sport early in the year, and practically in the summer— August is certainly a summer month—he will like a light gun ; and as the grouse at that time have not packed, and are not difficult of access, a light gun will answer quite as well as a heavy arm, whose powerful charges are not required, and which simply adds to the fatigue. Much lighter guns are used now than formerly ; they do not last so long, but few of us now look forward forty years. A gun of $6\frac{1}{2}$ pounds' weight will be better than anything else for summer work. All sportsmen say it is a toy and so it is, but a very deadly one. The same weapon will equally well do for the first of September (unless the weather has been very bad), and for a few weeks of partridge-shooting. But if the sport comes later in the autumn, a heavier gun with a stronger charge (alluding to guns of the old style of boring) will be found useful. For shooting when the leaves are off a heavier gun has, perhaps, some advantages.

Battue-shooting puts a great strain upon a gun, from the rapid and continuous firing, and a pheasant often requires a hard knock to grass him successfully. You never know, either, at what range you are likely to meet with him. It may be ten yards, it may be sixty ; so that a strong charge, a long range, and considerable power of penetration are desirable, if it is wished to make a good performance. I recommend a powerful gun for pheasant-shooting, because probably in no other sport is a miss so annoying. The bird is large and in popular estimation, therefore ought not to get away. There is generally a party at the house at the time, and shots are sure to be talked about, good or bad, but especially the latter, which some men have a knack of noticing, though they may be apparently out of sight, and bring up against you in the pleasantest way possible : 'I say, you were rather in a fluster, weren't you, this morning? Nerves out of order—eh?' Now, is there anything so aggravating as to be asked about your nerves? It is, perhaps, from the operation of competition that pheasants, as a rule, get very little law allowed them. If you want to shine at this kind of sport, knock the bird over, no matter when you see him—if his tail brushes the muzzle of your gun: every head counts. The fact is, if a pheasant is allowed law, and really treated as game, he is not by any means so easy a bird to kill as may be supposed.

If money is no particular object, of course the sportsman can allow himself a gun for every different kind of sport, although luxury in that respect is apt to bring with it its punishment, by making him but an indifferent shot with either of his weapons. But if anyone wishes to be a really good shot, to be equipped for almost every contingency, and yet not to go to great expense, the very best course to follow is to buy two good guns, one of the old style of boring, and the other nearly or quite choked. The first should be neither heavy nor light—a moderately weighted weapon, upon which thorough reliance may be placed up to fifty yards, and that under favourable circumstances may kill much farther. Choose it with care, pay a fair price for it, and adhere to it. This gun, with a little variation in the charge, will suit almost every kind of shooting, from snipe to pheasant. The choke-bore is the reserve gun, in case of specially long range and great penetration being required. It should, perhaps, be a size larger in the bore than the other. Twelve-bore for the ordinary gun, and ten for the second, will cover most contingencies. With a ten-bore choke, hares running wild on hills without cover, partridge coveys getting up at fifty or sixty yards in the same kind of country, grouse wild as hawks, ducks, plovers, and wild-fowl generally, are pretty well accessible. If not likely to meet with duck, a twelve-bore choke will do equally well. Thus armed, if opportunity offers, you may shoot anywhere in Europe. The cylinder-bore will carry an occasional ball for a boar, a wolf, or fallow-deer, though large shot out of the choke will, perhaps, be more effective—so far, at least, as small deer are concerned. If you can afford it, a spare gun (old-style boring) is a great comfort, in case of an accident to the mechanism.

SKATING

THE rime of the early morning on the rail nearest the bank is easily brushed off by sliding the walking-stick along it, and then forms a convenient seat while the skates are fastened. An old hand selects his gimlet with the greatest care, for if too large the screw speedily works loose, if too small the thread, as it is frantically forced in or out by main strength, cuts and tears the leather. A bad gimlet has spoilt many a day's skating. Nor should the straps be drawn too tight at first, for if hauled up to the last hole at starting the blood cannot circulate, and the muscles of the foot become cramped. What miseries have not ladies heroically endured in this way at the hands of incompetent assistants! In half an hour's time the straps will have worked to the boot, and will bear pulling another hole or even more without pain. On skates thus fastened anything may be accomplished.

Always put your own skates on, and put them on deliberately; for if you really mean skating in earnest, limbs, and even life, may depend on their running true, and not failing at a critical moment. The slope of the bank must be descended sideways—

avoid the stones concealed by snow, for they will destroy the edge of the skate. When within a foot or so, leap on, and the impetus will carry you some yards out upon the lake, clear of the shadow of the bank and the willows above, out to where the ice gleams under the sunshine. A glance round shows that it is a solitude; the marks of skates that went past yesterday are visible, but no one has yet arrived: it is the time for an exploring expedition. Following the shore, note how every stone or stick that has been thrown on by thoughtless persons has sunk into and become firmly fixed in the ice. The slight heat of midday has radiated from the surface of the stone, causing the ice to melt around it, when it has sunk a little, and at night been frozen hard in that position, forming an immovable obstacle, extremely awkward to come into contact with. A few minutes and the marks of skates become less frequent, and in a short time almost cease, for the gregarious nature of man exhibits itself even on ice. One spot is crowded with people, and beyond that extends a broad expanse scarcely visited. Here a sand-bank rises almost to the surface, and the yellow sand beneath causes the ice to assume a lighter tint; beyond it, over the deep water, it is dark.

Then a fir-copse bordering the shore shuts out the faintest breath of the north wind, and the surface in the bay thus sheltered is sleek to a degree. This is the place for figure-shating; the ice is perfect, and the wind cannot interfere with the balance. Here you may turn and revolve and twist and go through those endless evolutions and endless repetitions of curves which exercise so singular a fascination. Look at a common figure of 8 that a man has cut out! How many hundreds of times has he gone round and round those two narrow crossing loops or circles! No variation, no change; the art of it is to keep almost to the same groove, and not to make the figure broad and splay. Yet by the wearing away of the ice it is evident that a length of time has been spent thus for ever wheeling round. And when the skater visits the ice again, back he will come and resume the wheeling at intervals. On past a low waterfall where a brook runs in—the water has frozen right up to the cascade. A long stretch of marshy shore succeeds—now frozen hard enough, at other times not to be passed without sinking over the ankles in mud. The ice is rough with the aquatic weeds frozen in it, so that it is necessary to leave the shore some thirty yards. The lake widens, and yonder in the centre—scarcely within range of a deer-rifle—stand four or five disconsolate wild-duck watching every motion. They are quite unapproachable, but sometimes an unfortunate dabchick that has been discovered in a tuft of grass is hunted and struck down by sticks. A rabbit on ice can also be easily overtaken by a skater. If one should venture out from the furze there, and make for the copse opposite, put on the pace, and you will be speedily alongside. As he doubles quickly, however, it is not so easy to catch him when overtaken: still, it can be done. Rabbits previously netted are occasionally turned out on purpose for a course, and afford considerable sport, with a very fair chance—if dogs be eschewed—of gaining their liberty. But they must have 'law,' and the presence of a crowd spoils all; the poor animal is simply surrounded, and knows not where to run. Tracks of wild rabbits crossing the ice are frequent. Now, having gained the farthest extremity of the lake, pause a minute and take breath for a burst down the centre. The regular sound of the axe comes from the wood hard by, and every now and then the crash as some tall ash-pole falls to the ground, no more to bear the wood-pigeon's nest in spring, no more to impede the startled pheasant in autumn as he rises like a rocket till clear of the boughs.

Now for it: the wind, hardly felt before under shelter of the banks and trees, strikes the chest like the blow of a strong man as you rush against it. The chest responds with a long-drawn heave, the pliable ribs bend outwards, and the cavity within enlarges, filled with the elastic air. The stride grows longer and longer—the momentum increases—the shadow slips over the surface; the fierce joy of reckless speed seizes on the mind. In the glow, and the speed, and the savage north wind, the old Norse spirit rises, and one feels a giant. Oh that such a sense of vigour—of the fulness of life—could but last!

By now others have found their way to the shore; a crowd has already assembled at that spot which a gregarious instinct has marked out for the ice-fair, and approaching it speed must be slackened. Sounds of merry laughter, and the 'knock, knock' of the hockey-sticks arise. Ladies are gracefully gliding hither and thither. Dancing-parties are formed, and thus among friends the short winter's day passes too soon, and sunset is at hand. But how beautiful that sunset! Under the level beams of the sun the ice assumes a delicate rosy hue; yonder the white snow-covered hills to the eastward are rosy too. Above them the misty vapour thickening in the sky turns to the dull red the shepherd knows to mean another frost and another fine day. Westwards where the disc has just gone down, the white ridges of the hills stand out for the moment sharp against the sky, as if cut by the graver's tool. Then the vapours thicken; then, too, behind them, and slowly, the night falls.

Come back again in a few hours' time. The laugh is still, the noise has fled, and the first sound of the skate on the black ice seems almost a desecration. Shadows stretch out and cover the once gleaming surface. But through the bare boughs of the great oak yonder the moon—almost full—looks athwart the lake, and will soon be high in the sky.

MARLBOROUGH FOREST

THE great painter, Autumn, has just touched with the tip of his brush a branch of the beech-tree, here and there leaving an orange spot, and the green acorns are tinged with a faint yellow. The hedges, perfect mines of beauty, look almost red from a distance, so innumerable are the peggles.* Let not the modern Goths destroy our hedges, so typical of an English landscape, so full of all that can delight the eye and please the mind. Spare them, if only for the sake of the 'days when we went gipsying— a long time ago'; spare them for the children to gather the flowers of May and the blackberries of September.

When the orange spot glows upon the beech, then the nuts are ripe, and the hawthorn-bushes are hung with festoons of the buff-coloured, heart-shaped leaves of a once-green creeper. That 'deepe and enclosed country of Northe Wiltes,' which old Clarendon, in his famous 'Civill Warre,' says the troops of King Charles had so much difficulty to hurry through, is pleasant to those who can linger by the wayside and the copse, and do not fear to hear the ordnance make

* A Wiltshire name for hawthorn-berries.

the 'woods ring again,' though to this day a rusty old cannon-ball may sometimes be found under the dead brown leaves of Aldbourne Chase, where the skirmish took place before 'Newbury Battle.'

Perhaps it is because no such outbursts of human passions have swept along beneath its trees that the 'Forest' is unsung by the poet and unvisited by the artist. Yet its very name is poetical—Savernake— *i.e.*, savernes-acres—like the God's-acres of Long-fellow. Saverne—a peculiar species of sweet fern ; acre—land.' So we may call it 'Fern-land Forest,' and with truth, for but one step beneath those beeches away from the path plunges us to our shoulders in an ocean of bracken.

The yellow stalks, stout and strong as wood, make walking through the brake difficult, and the route pursued devious, till, from the constant turning and twisting, the way is lost. For this is no narrow copse, but a veritable forest in which it is easy to lose one-self ; and the stranger who attempts to pass it away from the beaten track must possess some of the Indian instinct which sees signs and directions in the sun and wind, in the trees and humble plants of the ground.

And this is its great charm. The heart has a yearning for the unknown, a longing to penetrate the deep shadow and the winding glade, where, as it seems, no human foot has been.

High overhead in the beech-tree the squirrel peeps down from behind a bough, his long bushy tail curled up over his back, and his bright eyes full of mischievous cunning. Listen, and you will hear the tap, tap of the woodpecker, and see! away he goes in undulating flight with a wild, unearthly chuckle, his green and gold plumage glancing in the sun, like the parrots of far-distant lands. He will alight in some open space upon an ant-hill, and lick up the red insects with his tongue. In the fir-tree there, what a chattering and fluttering of gaily-painted wings!—three or four jays are quarrelling noisily. These beautiful birds are slain by scores because of their hawk-like capacities for destruction of game, and because of the delicate colours of their feathers, which are used in fly-fishing.

There darts across the glade a scared rabbit, straining each little limb for speed, almost rushing against us, a greater terror overcoming the less. In a moment there darts forth from the dried grass a fierce red-furred hunter, a very tiger to the rabbit tribe, with back slightly arched, bounding along, and sniffing the scent; another, and another, still a fourth — a whole pack of stoats (elder brothers of the smaller weasels). In vain will the rabbit trust to his speed, these untiring wolves will overtake him. In vain will he turn and double: their unerring noses will find him out. In vain the tunnels of the 'bury,' they will as surely come under ground as above. At last, wearied, panting, frightened almost to death, the timid creature will hide in a cul-de-sac, a hole that has no outlet, burying its head in the sand. Then the tiny bloodhounds will steal with swift, noiseless rush, and fasten upon the veins of the neck. What a rattling the wings of the pigeons make as they rise out of the trees in hot haste and alarm! As we pass a fir-copse we stoop down and look along the ground under the foliage. The sharp 'needles' or leaves which fall will not decay, and they kill all vegetation, so that there is no underwood or herbage to obstruct the view. It is like looking into a vast cellar supported upon innumerable slender columns. The pheasants run swiftly away underneath.

High up the cones are ripening—those mysterious emblems sculptured in the hands of the gods at Nineveh, perhaps typifying the secret of life. More bracken. What a strong, tall fern! it is like a miniature tree. So thick is the cover, a thousand archers might be hid in it easily. In this wild solitude, utterly separated from civilization, the whistle of an arrow would not surprise us—the shout of a savage before he hurled his spear would seem natural, and in keeping. What are those strange, clattering noises, like the sound of men fighting with wooden 'backswords'? Now it is near—now afar off—a spreading battle seems to be raging all round, but the combatants are out of sight. But, gently—step lightly, and avoid placing the foot on dead sticks, which break with a loud crack—softly peep round the trunk of this noble oak, whose hard furrowed bark defends it like armour.

The red-deer! Two splendid stags are fighting —fighting for their lady-love, the timid doe. They rush at each other with head down and horns extended ; the horns meet and rattle ; they fence with them skilfully. This was the cause of the noise. It is the tilting season—these tournaments between the knights of the forest are going on all around. There is just a trifle of danger in approaching these combatants, but not much, just enough to make the forest still more enticing ; none whatever to those who use common caution. At the noise of our footsteps away go the stags, their 'branching antlers' seen high above the tall fern, bounding over the ground in a series of jumps, all four feet leaving the earth at once. There are immense oaks that we come to now, each with an open space beneath it, where Titania and the fairies may dance their rings at night. These enormous trunks—what *time* they represent! To us, each hour is of consequence, especially in this modern day, which has invented the detestable creed that time is money. But time is not money to Nature. She never hastens. Slowly from the tiny acorn grew up this gigantic trunk, and spread abroad those limbs which in themselves are trees. And from the trunk itself to the smallest leaf, every infinitesimal atom of which it is composed was perfected slowly, gradually—there was no hurry, no attempt to discount effect. A little farther and the ground declines ; through the tall fern we come upon a valley. But the soft warm sunshine, the stillness, the solitude, have induced an irresistible idleness. Let us lie down upon the fern, on the edge of the green vale, and gaze up at the slow clouds as they drift across the blue vault.

The subtle influence of Nature penetrates every limb and every vein, fills the soul with a perfect contentment, an absence of all wish except to lie there, half in sunshine, half in shade, for ever in a Nirvana of indifference to all but the exquisite delight of simply *living*. The wind in the tree-tops overhead sighs in soft music, and ever and anon a leaf falls with a slight rustle to mark time.

The clouds go by in rhythmic motion, the ferns whisper verses in the ear, the beams of the wondrous sun in endless song, for he, also,

> In his motion like an angel sings,
> Still quiring to the young-eyed cherubim,
> Such harmony is in immortal souls !

Time is to us now no more than it was to the oak ; we have no consciousness of it. Only we feel the broad earth beneath us, and as to the ancient giant, so there passes through us a strength renewing itself, of vital energy flowing into the frame. It may be an hour, it may be two hours, when, without the aid of sound or sight, we become aware by an indescribable, supersensuous perception that living creatures are approaching. Sit up without noise and look : there is a herd of deer feeding down the narrow valley close at hand, within a stone's-throw. And these are deer indeed—no puny creatures, but the ' tall deer' that William the Conqueror loved ' as if he were their father.' Fawns are darting here and there, frisking round the does. How many may there be in this herd ? Fifty, perhaps more. Nor is this a single isolated instance, but dozens more of such herds may be found in this true old English forest, all running free and unconstrained.

But the sun gets low. Following this broad green drive, it leads us past vistas of endless glades, going no man knows where, into shadow and gloom; past grand old oaks; past places where the edge of a veritable wilderness comes up to the trees—a wilderness of gnarled hawthorn trunks of unknown ages, of holly with shining metallic-green leaves, and hazel-bushes. Past tall trees bearing the edible chestnut in prickly clusters; past maples which in a little while will be painted in crimson and gold, with the deer peeping out of the fern everywhere, and once, perhaps, catching a glimpse of a shy, beautiful, milk-white doe. Past a huge hollow trunk in the midst of a green-sward, where merry picnic parties under the 'King Oak' tread the social quadrille, or whirl waltzes to the harp and flute. For there are certain spots even in this grand solitude consecrated to Cytherea and Bacchus, as he is now worshipped in champagne. And where can graceful forms look finer, happy eyes more bright, than in this natural ballroom, under its incomparable roof of blue, supported upon living columns of stately trees? Still onward, into a gravel carriage-road now, returning by degrees to civilization, and here, with happy judgment, the hand of man has aided Nature. Far as the eye can see extends an avenue of beech, passing right through the forest. The tall, smooth trunks rise up to a great height, and then branch overhead, looking like the roof of a Gothic cathedral. The growth is so regular and so perfect that the comparison springs unbidden to the lip, and here, if anywhere, that order

of architecture might have taken its inspiration.
There is a continuous Gothic arch of green for miles,
beneath which one may drive or walk, as in the aisles
of a forest abbey.   But it is impossible to even mention all the beauties of this place within so short a
space.   It must suffice to say that the visitor may
walk for whole days in this great wood, and never
pass the same spot twice.   No gates or jealous walls
will bar his progress.   As the fancy seizes him, so
he may wander.   If he has a taste for archæological
studies, especially the prehistoric, the edge of the
forest melts away upon downs that bear grander
specimens than can be seen elsewhere.   Stonehenge
and Avebury are near.   The trout-fisher can approach very close to it.   The rail gives easy communication, but has not spoilt the seclusion.

Monsieur Lesseps, of Suez Canal fame, is reported
to have said that Marlborough Forest was the finest
he had seen in Europe.   Certainly no one who had
not seen it would believe that a forest still existed in
the very heart of Southern England so completely
recalling those woods and ' chases ' upon which the
ancient feudal monarchs set such store.

VILLAGE CHURCHES

THE black rooks are busy in the old oak-trees, carrying away the brown acorns one by one in their strong beaks to some open place where, undisturbed, they can feast upon the fruit. The nuts have fallen from the boughs, and the mice garner them out of the ditches ; but the blue-black sloes cling tight to the thorn-branch still. The first frost has withered up the weak sap left in the leaves, and they whirl away in yellow clouds before the gusts of wind. It is the season, the hour of half-sorrowful, half-mystic thought, when the past becomes a reality and the present a dream, and unbidden memories of sunny days and sunny faces, seen when life was all spring, float around :

> Dim dream-like forms ! your shadowy train
> Around me gathers once again ;
> The same as in life's morning hour,
> Before my troubled gaze you passed.
>
> * * * * *
>
> Forms known in happy days you bring,
> And much-loved shades amid you spring,
> Like a tradition, half expired,
> Worn out with many a passing year.

35

In so busy a land as ours there is no place where the mind can, as it were, turn in upon itself so fully as in the silence and solitude of a village church.

There is no ponderous vastness, no oppressive weight of gloomy roof, no weird cavernous crypts, as in the cathedral ; only a *visible* silence, which at once isolates the soul, separates it from external present influences, and compels it, in falling back upon itself, to recognize its own depth and powers. In daily life we sit as in a vast library filled with tomes, hurriedly writing frivolous letters upon ' vexatious nothings,' snatching our food and slumber, for ever rushing forward with beating pulse, never able to turn our gaze away from the goal to examine the great storehouse, the library around us. Upon the infinitely delicate organization of the brain innumerable pictures are hourly painted ; these, too, we hurry by, ignoring them, pushing them back into oblivion. But here, in silence, they pass again before the gaze. Let no man know for what real purpose we come here ; tell the aged clerk our business is with brasses and inscriptions, press half a crown into his hand, and let him pass to his potato-digging. There is one advantage at least in the closing of the church on week-days, so much complained of—to those who do visit it there is a certainty that their thoughts will not be disturbed. And the sense of man's presence has departed from the walls and oaken seats ; the dust here is not the dust of the highway, of the quick footstep ; it is the dust of the past. The ancient heavy key creaks in the cumbrous lock, and the iron latch-ring has worn a deep groove in the solid stone. The narrow nail-studded door of black oak yields slowly to the push—it is not easy to enter, not easy to quit the present—but once close it, and the living world is gone. The very style of ornament upon the door, the broad-headed nails, has come down from the remotest antiquity. After the battle, says the rude bard in the Saxon chronicle,

> The Northmen departed
> In their nailed barks,

and, earlier still, the treacherous troop that seized the sleeping magician in iron, Wayland the Smith, were clad in 'nailed armour,' in both instances meaning ornamented with nails. Incidentally, it may be noted that, until very recently, at least one village church in England had part of the skin of a Dane nailed to the door—a stern reminder of the days when 'the Pagans' harried the land. This narrow window, deep in the thick wall, has no painted magnificence to boast of ; but as you sit beside it in the square, high-sided pew, it possesses a human interest which even art cannot supply.

The tall grass growing rank on the graves without rustles as it waves to and fro in the wind against the small diamond panes, yellow and green with age— rustles with a melancholy sound ; for we know that this window was once far above the ground, but the earth has risen till nearly on a level—risen from the accumulation of human remains. Yet, but a day or two before, on the Sunday morning, in this pew, bright, restless children smiled at each other, exchanged guilty pushes, while the sunbeams from the arrow-slit above shone upon their golden hair.

Let us not think of this further, but dimly through the window, 'as through a glass darkly,' see the green yew with its red berries, and afar the elms and beeches, brown and yellow. The steep down rises over them, and the moving grey patch upon it is a flock of sleep. The white wall is cold and damp, and the beams of the roof overhead, though the varnish is gone from them, are dark with slow decay.

In the recess lies the figure of a knight in armour, rudely carved, beside his lady, still more rudely rendered in her stiff robes, and of him an ill-spelt inscription proudly records that he 'builded ye greate howse at'—no matter where; but history records that cruel war wrapped it in flames before half a generation was gone, so that the boast of his building great houses reads as a bitter mockery. There stands opposite a grander monument to a mighty earl, and over it hangs a breastplate and gauntlets of steel.

The villagers will tell that in yonder deep shady 'combe' or valley, in the thick hazel-bushes, when the 'beetle with his drowsy hum' rises through the night air, there comes the wicked old earl, wearing this very breastplate, these iron gloves, to expiate one evil deed of yore. And if we sit in this pew long enough, till the mind is magnetized with the spirit of the past, till the early evening sends its shadowy troops to fill the distant corners of the silent church, then, perhaps, there may come to us forms gliding noiselessly over the stone pavement of the aisles—forms not repelling or ghastly, but filling us with an eager curiosity. Then through the slit made for that very purpose centuries since, when the pew was in a family chapel—through the slit in the pillar, we may see cowled monks assemble at the altar, muttering as magicians might over vessels of gold. The clank of scabbards upon the stones is stilled, the rustle of gowns is silent; if there is a sound, it is of subdued sobs, as the aged monk blesses the troop on the eve of their march. Not even yet has the stern idol of war ceased to demand its victims; even yet brave hearts and noble minds must perish, and leave sterile the hopes of the elders and the love of woman. There is still light enough left to read the few simple lines on the plain marble slab, telling how ' Lieutenant ——,' at Inkerman, at Lucknow, or, later still, at Coomassie, fell doing his duty. And these plain slabs are dearer to us far than all the sculptured grandeur, and the titles and pomp of belted earl and knight; their simple words go straighter to our hearts than all the quaint curt Latin of the olden time.

The belfry door is ajar—those winding stairs are not easy of access. The edges are worn away, and the steps strewn with small sticks of wood; sticks once used by the jackdaws in building their nests in the tower. It is needful to take much care, lest the foot should stumble in the semi-darkness. Listen !

there is now a slight sound : it is the dull ticking of
the old, old clock above. It is the only thing with
motion here ; all else is still, and even its motion is
not life. A strange old clock, a study in itself ;
all the works open and visible, simple, but ingenious.
For a hundred years it has carried round the one
hour-hand upon the square-faced dial without, marking every second of time for a century with its pen-
dulum. Here, too, are the bells, and one, the chief
bell, is a noble tenor, a mighty maker of sound. Its
curves are full and beautiful, its colour clear ; its
tone, if you do but tap it, sonorous, yet not harsh.
It is an artistic bell. Round the rim runs a rhyme
in the monkish tongue, which has a chime in the
words, recording the donor, and breathing a prayer
for his soul. In the day when this bell was made
men put their souls into their works. Their one
great object was not to turn out 100,000 all alike,
it was rarely they made two alike. Their one
great object was to construct a work which should
carry their very spirit in it, which should excel all
similar works, and cause men in after-times to inquire
with wonder for the maker's name, whether it was
such a common thing as a knife-handle, or a bell, or
a ship. Longfellow has caught the spirit well in the
saga of the ' Long Serpent,' where the builder of the
vessel listens to axe and hammer :

> All this tumult heard the master,
>   It was music to his ear ;
> Fancy whispered all the faster,
> ' Men shall hear of Thorberg Skafting
>   For a hundred year !'

Would that there were more of this spirit in the
workshops of our day ! They did not, when such a
work was finished, hasten to blaze it abroad with
trumpet and shouting ; it was not carried to the
topmost pinnacle of the mountain in sight of all
the kingdoms of the earth. They were contented
with the result of their labour, and cared little where
it was placed or who saw it ; and so it is that some
of the finest-toned bells in the world are at this
moment to be found in village churches; and for so
local a fame the maker worked as truly, and in as
careful a manner, as if he had known his bell was to
be hung in St. Peter's, at Rome. This was the true
spirit of art. Yet it is not altogether pleasant to
contemplate this bell ; the mind cannot but reflect
upon the length of time it has survived those to
whose joys or sorrows it has lent a passing utter-
ance, and who are dust in the yard beneath.

> For full five hundred years I've swung
> In my old grey turret high,
> And many a changing theme I've sung
> As the time went stealing by.

Even the ' old grey turret ' shows more signs of
age and of decay than the bell, for it is strengthened
with iron clamps and rods to bind its feeble walls
together. Of the pavements, whose flagstones are
monuments, the dates and names worn by footsteps ;
of the vaults beneath, with their grim and ghastly
traditions of coffins moved out of place, as was supposed, by supernatural agency, but, as explained, by
water ; of the thick walls, in which, in at least one

village church, the trembling victim of priestly cruelty was immured alive—of these and a thousand other matters that suggest themselves there is no time to speak.

But just a word must be spared to notice one lovely spot where two village churches stand not a hundred yards apart, separated by a stream, both in the hands of one Vicar, whose 'cure' is, nevertheless, so scant of souls that service in the morning in one and in the evening in the other church is amply sufficient. And where is there a place where spring-time possesses such a tender yet melancholy interest to the heart as in a village churchyard, where the budding leaves and flowers in the grass may naturally be taken as symbolical of a still more beautiful spring-time yet in store for the soul?

BIRDS OF SPRING

THE birds of spring come as imperceptibly as the leaves. One by one the buds open on hawthorn and willow, till all at once the hedges appear green, and so the birds steal quietly into the bushes and trees, till by-and-by a chorus fills the wood, and each warm shower is welcomed with varied song. To many, the majority of spring-birds are really unknown; the cuckoo, the nightingale, and the swallow, are all with which they are acquainted, and these three make the summer. The loud cuckoo cannot be overlooked by anyone passing even a short time in the fields; the nightingale is so familiar in verse that everyone tries to hear it; and the swallows enter the towns and twitter at the chimney-top. But these are really only the principal representatives of the crowd of birds that flock to our hedges in the early summer; and perhaps it would be accurate to say that no other area of equal extent, either in Europe or elsewhere, receives so many feathered visitors. The English climate is the established subject of abuse, yet it is the climate most preferred and sought by the birds, who have the choice of immense continents.

Nothing that I have ever read of, or seen, or that I expect to see, equals the beauty and the delight of

a summer spent in our woods and meadows. Green
leaves and grass, and sunshine, blue skies, and sweet
brooks—there is nothing to approach it ; it is no
wonder the birds are tempted to us. The food they
find is so abundant, that after all their efforts, little
apparent diminution can be noticed ; to this fertile
and lovely country, therefore, they hasten every year.
It might be said that the spring-birds begin to come
to us in the autumn, as early as October, when
hedge-sparrows and golden-crested wrens, larks,
blackbirds, and thrushes, and many others, float over
on the gales from the coasts of Norway. Their
numbers, especially of the smaller birds, such as larks,
are immense, and their line of flight so extended that
it strikes our shores for a distance of two hundred
miles. The vastness of these numbers, indeed, makes
me question whether they all come from Scandinavia.
That is their route ; Norway seems to be the last
land they see before crossing ; but I think it possible
that their original homes may have been farther still.
Though many go back in the spring, many individuals remain here, and rejoice in the plenty of the
hedgerows. As all roads of old time led to Rome,
so do bird-routes lead to these islands. Some of
these birds appear to pair in November, and so have
settled their courtship long before the crocuses of
St. Valentine. Much difference is apparent in the
dates recorded of the arrivals in spring ; they vary
year by year, and now one and now another bird
presents itself first, so that I shall not in these notes
attempt to arrange them in strict order.

One of the first noticeable in southern fields is the common wagtail. When his shrill note is heard echoing against the walls of the outhouses as he rises from the ground, the carters and ploughmen know that there will not be much more frost. If icicles hang from the thatched eaves, they will not long hang, but melt before the softer wind. The bitter part of winter is over. The wagtail is a house-bird, making the houses or cattle-pens its centre, and remaining about them for months. There is not a farmhouse in the South of England without its summer pair of wagtails—not more than one pair, as a rule, for they are not gregarious till winter; but considering that every farmhouse has its pair, their numbers must be really large.

Where wheatears frequent, their return is very marked; they appear suddenly in the gardens and open places, and cannot be overlooked. Swallows return one by one at first, and we get used to them by degrees. The wheatears seem to drop out of the night, and to be showered down on the ground in the morning. A white bar on the tail renders them conspicuous, for at that time much of the surface of the earth is bare and dark. Naturally birds of the wildest and most open country, they yet show no dread, but approach the houses closely. They are local in their habits, or perhaps follow a broad but well-defined route of migration; so that while common in one place, they are rare in others. In two localities with which I am familiar, and know every path, I never saw a wheatear. I heard of them occasionally as passing over, but they were not birds of the district. In Sussex, on the contrary, the wheatear is as regularly seen as the blackbird; and in the spring and summer you cannot go for a walk without finding them. They change their ground three times : first, on arrival, they feed in the gardens and arable fields ; next, they go up on the hills ; lastly, they return to the coast, and frequent the extreme edge of the cliffs and the land by the shore. Every bird has its different manner ; I do not know how else to express it. Now, the wheatears move in numbers, and yet not in concert ; in spring, perhaps twenty may be counted in sight at once on the ground, feeding together and yet quite separate ; just opposite in manner to starlings, who feed side by side and rise and fly as one. Every wheatear feeds by himself, a space between him and his neighbour, dotted about, and yet they obviously have a certain amount of mutual understanding : they recognize that they belong to the same family, but maintain their individuality. On the hills in their breeding season they act in the same way: each pair has a wide piece of turf, sometimes many acres. But if you see one pair, it is certain that other pairs are in the neighbourhood. In their breeding-grounds they will not permit a man to approach so near as when they arrive, or as when the nesting is over. At the time of their arrival, anyone can walk up within a short distance ; so, again, in autumn. During the nesting-time the wheatear perches on a molehill, or a large flint, or any slight elevation above the open surface of the downs, and allows no one to come closer than fifty yards.

The hedge-sparrows, that creep about the bushes of the hedgerow as mice creep about the banks, are early in spring joined by the whitethroats, almost the first hedge-birds to return. The thicker the undergrowth of nettles and wild parsley, rushes and rough grasses, the more the whitethroat likes the spot. Amongst this tangled mass he lives and feeds, slipping about under the brambles and ferns as rapidly as if the way was clear. Loudest of all, the chiff-chaff sings in the ash woods, bare and leafless, while yet the sharp winds rush between the poles, rattling them together, and bringing down the dead twigs to the earth. The violets are difficult to find, few, and scattered; but his clear note rings in the hushes of the eastern breeze, encouraging the flowers. It is very pleasant indeed to hear him. One's hands are dry, and the skin rough with the east wind; the trunks of the trees look dry, and the lichens have shrivelled on the bark; the brook looks dark; grey dust rises and drifts, and the grey clouds hurry over; but the chiff-chaff sings, and it is certainly spring. The first green leaves which the elder put forth in January have been burned up by frost, and the woodbine, which looked as if it would soon be entirely green then, has been checked, and remains a promise only. The chiff-chaff tells the buds of the coming April rains and the sweet soft intervals of warm sun. He is a sure forerunner. He defies the bitter wind; his little heart is as true as steel. He is one of the birds in which I feel a personal interest, as if I could converse with him. The willow-wren, his friend, comes later, and has a gentler, plaintive song.

Meadow-pipits are not migrants in the sense that the swallows are; but they move about and so change their localities that when they come back they have much of the interest of a spring-bird. They rise from the ground and sing in the air like larks, but not at such a height, nor is the song so beautiful. These, too, are early birds   They often frequent very exposed places, as the side of a hill where the air is keen, and where one would not expect to meet with so lively a little creature. The pond has not yet any of the growths that will presently render its margin green; the willow-herbs are still low, the aquatic grasses have not become strong, and the osiers are without leaf. If examined closely, evidences of growth would be found everywhere around it; but as yet the surface is open, and it looks cold. Along the brook the shoals are visible, as the flags have not risen from the stems which were cut down in the autumn. In the sedges, however, the first young shoots are thrusting up, and the reeds have started slender green stalks tipped with the first leaves. At the verge of the water, a thick green plant of marsh-marigold has one or two great golden flowers open. This is the appearance of his home when the sedge-reedling returns to it. Sometimes he may be seen flitting across the pond, or perched for a moment on an exposed branch; but he quickly returns to the dry sedges or the bushes, or climbs in and out the willow-stoles. It is too bare and open for him at the pond, or even by the brook-side. So much does he love concealment, that although to be near the water is his habit, for a while he prefers to keep back among the bushes. As the reeds and reed canary-grass come up and form a cover—as the sedges grow green and advance to the edge of the water—as the sword-flags lift up and expand, opening from a centre, the sedge-reedling issues from the bushes and enters these vigorous growths, on which he perches, and about which he climbs as if they were trees. In the pleasant morn-ings, when the sun grows warm about eleven o'clock, he calls and sings with scarcely a cessation, and is answered by his companions up and down the stream. He does but just interrupt his search for food to sing; he stays a moment, calls, and im-mediately resumes his prying into every crevice of the branches and stoles. The thrush often sits on a bough and sings for a length of time, apart from his food, and without thinking of it, absorbed in his song, and full of the sweetness of the day. These restless sedge-reedlings cannot pause; their little feet are for ever at work, climbing about the willow-stoles where the wands spring from the trunk; they never reflect; they are always engaged. This restlessness is to them a great pleasure; they are filled with the life which the sun gives, and express it in every motion; they are so joyful, they cannot be still. Step into the osier-bed amongst them gently; they will chirp—a note like a sparrow's—just in front, and only recede a yard at a time as you push through the tall grass, flags, and underwood. Stand where you can see the brook, not too near, but so as to see it through a fringe of sedges and willows. The pink lychnis or ragged robin grows among the grasses; the iris flowers higher on the shore. The water-vole comes swimming past, on his way to nibble the green weeds in the stream round about the great branch which fell two winters since, and remains in the water. Aquatic plants take root in its shelter. There, too, a moorhen goes, sometimes diving under the bough. A blackbird flies up to drink or bathe, never at the grassy edge, but always choosing a spot where he can get at the stream free from obstruction. The sound of many birds singing comes from the hedge across the meadow; it mingles with the rush of the water through a drawn hatch—finches and linnets, thrush and chiff-chaff, wren and whitethroat, and others farther away, whose louder notes only reach. The singing is so mixed and interwoven, and is made of so many notes, it seems as if it were the leaves singing—the countless leaves—as if they had voices.

A brightly-coloured bird, the redstart, appears suddenly in spring, like a flower that has bloomed before the bud was noticed. Red is his chief colour, and as he rushes out from his perch to take an insect on the wing, he looks like a red streak. These birds sometimes nest near farm-houses in the rickyards, sometimes by copses, and sometimes in the deepest and most secluded combes or glens, the farthest places from habitation ; so that they cannot be said to have any preference, as so many birds have, for a particular kind of locality ; but they return year by year to the places they have chosen. The return of the corncrake or landrail is quickly recognized by the noise he makes in the grass; he is the noisiest of all the spring-birds. The return of the goat-sucker is hardly noticed at first. This is not at all a rare, but rather a local bird, well known in many places, but in others unnoticed, except by those who feel a special interest. A bird must be common and plentiful before people generally observe it, so that there are many of the labouring class who have never seen the goat-sucker, or would say so, if you asked them.

Few observe the migration of the turtle-doves, perhaps confusing them with the wood-pigeons, which stay in the fields all the winter. By the time the sap is well up in the oaks all the birds have arrived, and the tremulous cooing of the turtle-dove is heard by those engaged in barking the felled trees. The sap rises slowly in the oaks, moving gradually through the minute interstices or capillary tubes of this close-grained wood ; the softer timber-trees are full of it long before the oak ; and when the oak is putting forth its leaves it is high spring. Doves stay so much at this time in the great hawthorns of the hedgerows and at the edge of the copses that they are seldom noticed, though comparatively large birds. They are easily seen by any who wish ; the 'coo-coo' tells where they are; and in walking gently to find them, many other lesser birds will be observed. A wryneck may be caught sight of on a bough over-head; a black-headed bunting, in the hedge where there is a wet ditch and rushes; a blackcap, in the birches; and the 'zee-zee-zee' of the tree-pipit by the oaks just through the narrow copse.

This is the most pleasant and the best way to observe—to have an object, when so many things will be seen that would have been passed unnoticed. To steal softly along the hedgerow, keeping out of sight as much as possible, pausing now and then to listen as the 'coo-coo' is approached; and then, when near enough to see the doves, to remain quiet behind a tree, is the surest way to see everything else. The thrush will not move from her nest if passed so quietly; the chaffinch's lichen-made nest will be caught sight of against the elm-trunk—it would escape notice otherwise; the whitethroat may be watched in the nettles almost underneath; a rabbit will sit on his haunches and look at you from among the bare green stalks of brake rising; mice will rustle under the ground-ivy's purple flowers; a mole perhaps may be seen, for at this time they often leave their burrows and run along the surface; and, indeed, so numerous are the sights and sounds and interesting things, that you will soon be conscious of the fact that, while you watch one, two or three more are escaping you. It would be the same with any other search as well as the dove; I choose the dove because by then all the other creatures are come and are busy, and because it is a fairly large bird with a distinctive note, and consequently a good guide.

But these are not all the spring-birds : there are the whinchats, fly-catchers, sandpipers, ring-ousels, and others that are occasional or rare. There is not a corner of the fields, woods, streams, or hills, which does not receive a new inhabitant: the sandpiper comes to the open sandy margins of the pool; the fly-catcher, to the old post by the garden ; the whin-chat, to the furze ; the tree-pipit, to the oaks, where their boughs overhang meadow or cornfield ; the sedge-reedling, to the osiers; the dove, to the thick hedgerows ; the wheatear, to the hills ; and I see I have overlooked the butcher-bird or shrike, as, indeed, in writing of these things one is certain to overlook something, so wide is the subject. Many of the spring-birds do not sing on their first arrival, but stay a little while; by that time others are here. Grass-blade comes up by grass-blade till the meadows are freshly green ; leaf comes forth by leaf till the trees are covered ; and, like the leaves, the birds gently take their places, till the hedges are imper-ceptibly filled.

THE SPRING OF THE YEAR

'There's the cuckoo!' Everyone looked up and listened as the notes came indoors from the copse by the garden. He had returned to the same spot for the fourth time. The tallest birch-tree—it is as tall as an elm—stands close to the hedge, about three parts of the way up it, and it is just round there that the cuckoo generally sings. From the garden gate it is only a hundred yards to this tree, walking beside the hedge which extends all the way, so that the very first time the cuckoo calls upon his arrival he is certain to be heard. His voice travels that little distance with ease, and can be heard in every room. This year (1881) he came back to the copse on April 27, just ten days after I first heard one in the fields by Worcester Park. The difference in time is usual ; the bird which frequents this copse does not arrive there till a week or so after others in the neighbourhood may be heard calling. So marked is the interval that once or twice I began to think the copse would be deserted—there were cuckoos crying all round in the fields, but none came near. He has, however, always returned, and this difference in time makes his notes all the more remarked. I have, therefore, always two dates for the cuckoo : one, when I first hear the note, no matter where, and the second, when the copse bird sings. When he once comes he continues so long as he stays in this country, visiting the spot every day, sometimes singing for a few minutes, sometimes for an hour, and one season he seemed to call every morning and all the morning long. In the copse the ring of the two notes is a little toned down and lost by passing through the boughs, which hold and check the vibration of the sound. One year a detached ash in Cooper's Field, not fifty yards from the houses, was a favourite resort, and while perched there the notes echoed along the buildings, one following the other as waves roll on the summer sands. Flying from the ash to the copse, or along the copse hedge, the cuckoo that year was as often seen as the sparrows, and as little notice was taken of him. Several times cuckoos have flown over this house, but just clearing the roof, and descending directly they were over to the copse. He has not called so much this year yet, but on the evening of May 8 he was crying in the copse at half-past eight while the moon was shining.

On the morning of May 2, standing in the garden, or at the window of any of the rooms facing south, you could hear five birds calling together. The cuckoo was calling not far from the tallest birch ; there was a turtle-dove cooing in the copse much closer ; and a wood-pigeon overpowered the dove's soft voice every two or three minutes—the pigeon was not fifty yards distant ; a wryneck was perched up in an oak at the end of the garden, and uttered his peculiar note from time to time, and a nightingale was singing on Tolworth Common, just opposite the house, though on the other side. These were all audible, sometimes together, sometimes alternately ; and if you went to the northern windows or the front door, looking towards the common, then you might also hear the chatter of a brook-sparrow. The dove has a way of gurgling his coo in the throat. The wryneck's 'kie-kie-kie,' the last syllable plaintively prolonged, is not like the call or songs of other birds ; it reminds one of the peacock's strange scream, not in its actual sound, but its singularity. When it is suddenly heard from the midst of the thick green hedges of a summer's day, the bird itself unseen, it has a weird sound, which does not accord, like the blackbird's whistle, with our trees ; it seems as if some tropical bird had wandered hither. I have heard the wryneck calling in the oak at the end of the garden every morning this season before rising, and suspect, from his constant presence, that a nest will be built close by. Last year the wryneck was a scarce bird in this neighbourhood ; in all my walks I heard but two or three, and at long intervals. This year there are plenty ; I hear them in almost every walk I take. There is one in the orchard beside the Red Lion Inn ; another frequents the hedges and trees behind St. Matthew's Church ; up Claygate Lane there is another—the third or fourth gateway on the left side is the place to listen. One year a pair built, I am sure, close to the cottage which stands by itself near the road on Tolworth Common. I saw them daily perched on the trees in front, and heard them every time I passed. There were not many, or we did not notice them, at home, and therefore I have observed them with interest. Now there is one every morning at the end of the garden. This nightingale, too, that sings on Tolworth Common just opposite, returns there every year, and, like the cuckoo to the copse, he is late in his arrival—at least a week later than other nightingales whose haunts are not far off. His cover is in some young birch-trees, which form a leafy thicket among the furze. On the contrary, the brook-sparrow, or sedge-reedling, that sings there is the first, I think, of all his species to return in this place. He comes so soon that, remembering the usual date in other districts, I have more than once tried to persuade myself that I was mistaken, and that it was not the sedge-bird, but some other. But he has a note that it is not possible to confuse, and as it has happened several seasons running, this early appearance, there can be no doubt it is a fixed period with him. These two, the sedge-bird and the nightingale, have their homes so near together that the one often sings in the branches above, while the other chatters in the underwood beneath.

Besides these, before I get up I hear now a wren regularly. Little as he is, his notes rise in a crescendo above all; he sings on a small twig growing from the trunk of an oak—a bare twig which gives him a view all round. There is a bold ring in some

of the notes of the wren which might give an idea to
a composer desirous of producing a merry tune.
The chirp of sparrows, of course, underlies all. I
like sparrows. The chirp has a tang in it, a sound
within a sound, just as a piece of metal rings ; there
is not only the noise of the blow as you strike it, but
a sound of the metal itself. Just now the cock birds
are much together ; a month or two since the little
bevies of sparrows were all hens, six or seven together, as if there were a partial separation of the
sexes at times. I like sparrows, and am always glad
to hear their chirp ; the house seems still and quiet
after this nesting-time, when they leave us for the
wheatfields, where they stay the rest of the summer.
What happy days they have among the ripening corn !

But this year the thrushes do not sing : I have
listened for them morning after morning, but have
not heard them. They used to sing so continuously
in the copse that their silence is very marked : I see
them, but they are silent—they want rain. Nor
have our old missel-thrushes sung here this spring.
One season there seem more of one kind of bird, and
another of another species. None are more constant
than the turtle-dove : he always comes to the same
place in the copse, about forty yards from the garden
gate.

The wood-pigeons are the most prominent birds
in the copse this year. In previous seasons there
were hardly any—one or two, perhaps ; sometimes
the note was not heard for weeks. There might
have been a nest ; I do not think so ; the pigeons

that come seemed merely to rest *en route* elsewhere—occasional visitors only. But last autumn (1880) a small flock of seven or eight took up their residence here, and returned to roost every evening. They remained the winter through, and even in the January frosts, if the sun shone a little, called now and then. Their hollow cooing came from the copse at midday on January 1, and it was heard again on the 2nd. During the deep snows they were silent, but I constantly saw them flying to and fro, and immediately it became milder they recommenced to call. So that the wood-pigeon's notes have been heard in the garden—and the house—with only short intervals ever since last October, and it is now May. In the early spring, while walking up the Long Ditton road towards sunset, the place from whence you can get the most extended view of the copse, they were always flying about the tops of the trees preparatory to roosting. The bare slender tips of the birches on which they perched exposed them against the sky. Once six alighted on a long birch-branch, bending it down with their weight, not unlike a heavy load of fruit. As the stormy sunset flamed up, tinting the fields with momentary red, their hollow voices sounded among the trees.

Now, in May, they are busy; they have paired, and each couple has a part of the copse to themselves. Just level with the gardens the wood is almost bare of undergrowth; there is little to obstruct the sight but the dead hanging branches, and one couple are always up and down here. They are near enough for us to see the dark marking at the end of the tail as it is spread open to assist the upward flight from the ground to the tree. Outside the garden gate, about twenty yards distant, there stand three or four young spruce-firs ; they are in the field, but so close as to touch the copse hedge. To the largest of these one of the pigeons comes now and then ; he is half inclined to choose it for his nest, and yet hesitates. The noise of their wings, as they rise and thresh their strong feathers together over the tops of the trees, may often be heard in the garden ; or you may see one come from a distance, swift as the wind, suddenly half close two wings, and, shooting forward, alight among the branches. They seem with us like the sparrows, as much as if the house stood in the midst of the woods at home. The coo itself is not tuneful in any sense ; it is hoarse and hollow, yet it has a pleasant sound to me—a sound of the woods and the forest. I can almost feel the gun in my hand again. They are pre-eminently the birds of the woods. Other birds frequent them at times, and then quit the trees : but the ring-dove is the woodbird, always there some part of the day. So that the sound soothes by its associations.

Coming down the Long Ditton road on May 1, at the corner of the copse, where there are some hornbeams, I heard some low sweet notes that came from the trees, and, after a little difficulty, discovered a blackcap perched on a branch, humped up. Another answered within ten yards, and then they sang one against the other. The foliage of the hornbeam was

still pale, and the blackcaps' colours being so pale
also (with the exception of the poll), it was not easy
to see them. The song is sweet and cultured, but
does not last many seconds. In its beginning it
something resembles that of the hedge-sparrow—not
the pipe, but the song which the hedge-sparrows are
now delivering from the top sprays of the hawthorn
hedges. It is sweet indeed and cultured, and it is a
pleasure to welcome another arrival, but I do not feel
enraptured with the blackcap's notes. One came
into the garden, visiting some ivy on the wall, but
they are not plentiful just now. By these hornbeam
trees a little streamlet flows out from the copse and
under the road by a culvert. At the hedge it is
crossed by a pole (to prevent cattle straying in), and
this pole is the robin's especial perch. He is always
there, or near; he was there all through the winter,
and is there now. Beneath, where there are a few
inches of sand beside the water, a wagtail comes now
and then ; but the robin does not like the intrusion,
and drives him away.

The same oak at the end of the garden, where the
wryneck calls, is also the favourite tree of a cock
chaffinch, and every morning he sings there for at
least two hours at a stretch. I hear him first between waking and sleeping, and listen to his song
before my eyes are open. No starlings whistle on
the house-tops this year ; I am disappointed that
they have not returned ; last year, and the year
before that—indeed, since we have been here—a pair
built under the eaves just above the window of the

room I then used.   Last spring, indeed, they filled
the gutter with the materials of their nest, and long
after they had left a storm descended, and the rain,
unable to escape, flooded the corner.   It cost eight
shillings to repair the damage; but it did not matter,
they had been happy.   It is a disappointment not to
hear their whistle again this spring, and the flutter
of their wings as they vibrate them superbly while
hovering a moment before entering their cavern.
A pair of house-martins built under the eaves near
by one season; they, too, have disappointed me by
not returning, though their nest was not disturbed.
Some fate has probably overtaken late starlings and
house-martins.

Then in the sunny mornings, too, there is the
twittering of the swallows.   They were very late
this spring at Surbiton.   The first of the species was
a bank-martin flying over the Wandle by Wimbledon
on April 25 ; the first swallow appeared at Surbiton
on April 30.   As the bank-martins skim the surface
of the Thames—there are plenty everywhere near
the osier-beds and eyots, as just below Kingston
Bridge—their brown colour, and the black mark
behind the eye, and the thickness of the body near
the head, cause them to bear a resemblance to moths.
A fortnight before the first swallow the large bats
were hawking up and down the road in the evenings.
They seem to prefer to follow the course of the
road, flying straight up it from the copse to the
pond, half-way to Red Lion Lane, then back again,
and so to and fro, sometimes wheeling over the

Common, but usually resuming their voyaging above
the highway. Passing on a level with the windows
in the dusk, their wings seem to expand nine or ten
inches. Bats are sensitive to heat and cold. When
the north or east wind blows they do not come out;
they like a warm evening.

A shrike flew down from a hedge on May 9, just
in front of me, and alighted on a dandelion, bending
the flower to the ground and clasping the stalk in
his claws. There must have been an insect on the
flower: the bright yellow disk was dashed to the
ground in an instant by the ferocious bird, who came
with such force as almost to lose his balance. Though
small, the butcher-bird's decision is marked in every
action, in his very outline. His eagle-like head
sweeps the grass, and in a second he is on his victim.
Perhaps it was a humble-bee. The humble-bees are
now searching about for the crevices in which they
make their nests, and go down into every hole or
opening, exploring the depressions left by the hoofs
of horses on the sward when it was wet, and peering
under stones and flints beside the way. Wasps, too, are
about with the same purpose, and wild bees hover in
the sunshine. The shrikes are numerous here, and
all have their special haunts, to which they annually
return. The bird that darted on the dandelion flew
from the hedge by the footpath, through the meadow
where the stag is generally uncarted, beside the
Hogsmill brook. A pair frequent the bushes beside
the Long Ditton road, not far from the milestone;
another pair come to the railway arch at the foot of

Cockrow Hill.   In Claygate Lane there are several
places, and in June and July, when they are feeding
their young, the ' chuck-chucking ' is incessant.

Beside the copse on the sward by the Long
Ditton road is a favourite resort of peacock butterflies.   On sunny days now one may often be seen
there floating over the grass.   White butterflies go
flutter - flutter, continually fanning ; the peacock
spreads his wide wings and floats above the bennets.
Yellow or sulphur butterflies are almost rare—things
common enough in other places.   I seldom see one
here, and, unless it is fancy, fewer the last two
seasons than previously.

In the ploughed field by Southborough Park,
towards the Long Ditton road, partridges sometimes
call now as the sun goes down.   The corn is yet so
short and thin that the necks of partridges stand up
above it.   One stole out the other evening from the
hedge of a field beside the Ewell road into the
corn ; his head was high over the green blades.
The meadow close by, the second past the turn, is a
favourite with partridges, though so close to the
road and to Tolworth Farm.   Beside Claygate Lane,
where the signpost points to Hook, there is a withy-
bed which is a favourite cover for hares.   There is
a gateway (on the left of the lane) just past the signpost, from which you can see all one side of the
osiers ; the best time is when the clover begins to
close its leaves for the evening.   On May 3, looking
over the gate there, I watched two hares enjoying
themselves in the corn ; they towered high above it

—it was not more than four or five inches—and fed with great unconcern, though I was not concealed. A nightingale sang in the bushes within a few yards, and two cuckoos chased each other, calling as they flew across the lane; once one passed just overhead. The cuckoo has a note like ' chuck, chuck,' besides the well-known cry, which is uttered apparently when the bird is much exerted. These two were quite restless; they were to and fro from the fields on one side of the lane to those on the other, now up the hedge, now in a tree, and continually scolding each other with these ' chuck - chucking ' sounds. Chaffinches were calling from the tops of the trees ; the chaffinches now have a note much like one used by the yellow-hammer, different from their song and from their common ' fink tink.' I was walking by the same place, on April 24, when there was suddenly a tremendous screaming and threatening, and, glancing over the fields bordering on the Waffrons, there were six jays fighting. They screamed at and followed each other in a fury, real or apparent, up and down the hedge, and then across the fields out of sight. There were three jays together in a field by the Ewell road on May 1.

Just past the bridge over the Hogsmill brook at Tolworth Court there begins, on the left-hand side of the road, a broad mound, almost a cover in itself. At this time, before the underwood is up, much that goes on in the mound can be seen. There are several nightingales here, and they sometimes run or dart along under the trailing ivy, as if a mouse had rushed through it. The rufous colour of the back increases the impression; the hedgerows look red in the sunshine. Whitethroats are in full song everywhere: they have a twitter sometimes like swallows. A magpie flew up from the short green corn to a branch low down an elm, his back towards me, and as he rose his tail seemed to project from a white circle. The white tips of his wings met—or apparently so—as he fluttered, both above and beneath his body, so that he appeared encircled with a white ring.

The swifts have not come, up to the 10th, but there are young thrushes about able to fly. There was one at the top of the garden the other day almost as large as his parent. Nesting is in the fullest progress. I chanced on a hedge-sparrow's lately, the whole groundwork of which was composed of the dry vines of the wild white convolvulus. All the birds are come, I think, except the swift, the chat, and the redstart: very likely the last two are in the neighbourhood, though I have not seen them. In the furze on Tolworth Common—a resort of chats—the land-lizards are busy every sunny day. They run over the bunches of dead, dry grass— quite white and blanched—grasping it in their claws, like a monkey with hands and prehensile feet. They are much swifter than would be supposed. There was one on the sward by the Ewell road the other morning, quite without a tail; the creature was as quick as possible, but the grass too short to hide under till it reached some nettles.

The roan and white cattle happily grazing in the meadows by the Hogsmill brook look as if they had never been absent, as if they belonged to the place, like the trees, and had never been shut up in the yards through so terrible a winter. The water of the Hogsmill has a way of escaping like that of larger channels, and has made for itself a course for its overflow across a corner of the meadow by the road. A thin place in the rather raised bank lets it through in flood-time (like a bursting loose of the Mississippi), and down it rushes towards the moat. Beside the furrows thus soaked now and then, there are bunches of marsh-marigold in flower, and though the field is bright with dandelions and buttercups, the marigolds are numerous enough to be visible on the other side of it, 300 yards or more distant, and are easily distinguished by their different yellow. White cuckoo-flowers (*Cardamine*) are so thick in many fields that the green tint of the grass is lost under their silvery hue. Bluebells are in full bloom. There are some on the mound between Claygate and the Ewell road ; the footpath to Chessington from Roxby Farm passes a copse on the left which shimmers in the azure ; on the mound on the right of the lane to Horton they are plentiful this year—the hedge has been cut, and consequently more have shot up. Cowslips innumerable. The pond by the Ewell road, between this and Red Lion Lane, is dotted with white water-crowfoot. The first that flowered were in the pond in the centre of Tolworth Common. The understalks are long and slender,

and with a filament rather than leaves—like seaweed
—but when the flower appears these larger leaves
float on the surface. Quantities of this ranunculus
come floating down the Hogsmill brook, at times
catching against the bridge. A little pond by the
lane near Bone's Gate was white with this flower
lately, quite covered from bank to bank, not a
spare inch without its silver cup. Vetches are in
flower; there are always some up the Long
Ditton road on the bank by Swaynes-Thorp. Shepherd's purse stands up in flower in the waste places,
and on the side of the ditches thick branches of
hedge-mustard lift their white petals. The delicate
wind anemones flowered thickly in Claygate Lane
this year. On April 24 the mound on the right-
hand side was dotted with them. They had pushed
up through the dead dry oak-leaves of last autumn.
The foliage of the wind anemone is finely cut and
divided, so that it casts a lovely shadow on any
chance leaf that lies under it : it might suggest a
design. The anemones have not flowered there like
this since I have known the lane before. They were
thicker than I have ever seen them there. Dog-
violets, barren strawberry, and the yellowish-green
spurge are in flower there now.

The pine in front of my north window began to
put forth its catkins some time since ; those up the
Long Ditton road are now covered thick with the
sulphur farina or dust. I fancy three different sets of
fruit may sometimes be seen on pines : this year's
small and green, last year's ripe and mature, and

that of the year before dry and withered. The trees
are all in leaf now, except the Turkey oaks—there
are some fine young Turkey oaks by Oak Hill Path
—and the black poplars. Oaks have been in leaf
some time, except those that flower and are now
garlanded with green. Ash, too, is now in leaf, and
beech. The bees have been humming in the syca-
mores ; the limes are in leaf, but their flower does
not come yet. There were round, rosy oak-apples
on the oak by the garden in the copse on the 9th.
This tree is singular for bearing a crop of these
apples every year. Its top was snapped by the snow
that fell last October while yet the leaf was on. I
think the apples appear on this oak earlier than on
any about here. As for the orchards, now they are
beautiful with bloom; walking along the hedges,
too, you light once now and then on a crab or a
wild apple, with its broad rosy petals showing
behind the hawthorn. On the 7th I heard a corncrake in the meadow over Thames, opposite the
Promenade, a hundred yards below Messenger's
Eyot. It is a favourite spot with the corncrake
—almost the only place where you are nearly sure
to hear him. Crake! crake! So it is now high
May, and now midnight. Antares is visible—the
summer star.

VIGNETTES FROM NATURE

I.—SPRING

The soft sound of water moving among thousands of grass-blades is to the hearing as the sweetness of spring air to the scent. It is so faint and so diffused that the exact spot whence it issues cannot be discerned, yet it is distinct, and my footsteps are slower as I listen. Yonder, in the corners of the mead, the atmosphere is full of some ethereal vapour. The sunshine stays in the air there as if the green hedges held the wind from brushing it away. Low and plaintive comes the notes of a lapwing; the same notes, but tender with love.

On this side by the hedge the ground is a little higher and dry, hung over with the lengthy boughs of an oak which give some shade. I always feel a sense of regret when I see a seedling oak in the grass. The two green leaves—the little stem so upright and confident, and though but a few inches high, already so completely a tree—are in themselves beautiful. Power, endurance, grandeur are there; you can grasp all with your hand and take a ship between the finger and thumb. Time, that sweeps away everything, is for a while repelled : the oak

will grow when the time we know is forgotten, and
when felled will be mainstay and safety of a generation in a future century. That the plant should
start among the grass to be severed by the scythe, or
crushed by cattle, is very pitiful; I cannot help wishing that it could be transplanted and protected. O
the countless acorns that drop in autumn not one in
a million is permitted to become a tree : a vast waste
of strength and beauty. From the bushes by the
stile on the left hand (which I have just passed)
follows the long whistle of a nightingale. His nest
is near; he sings night and day. Had I waited on the
stile, in a few minutes, becoming used to my presence,
he would have made the hawthorn vibrate, so powerful is his voice when heard close at hand. There
is not another nightingale along this path for at least
a mile, though it crosses meadows and runs by hedges
to all appearance equally suitable. But nightingales
will not pass their limits ; they seem to have a
marked-out range as strictly defined as the line of
a geological map. They will not go over to the
next hedge, hardly into the field on one side of a
favourite spot, nor a yard farther along the mound.
Opposite the oak is a low fence of serrated green.
Just projecting above the edges of a brook, fast-
growing flags have thrust up their bayonet-tips.
Beneath, these stalks are so thick in the shallow
places that a pike can scarcely push a way
between them. Over the brook stand some high
maple-trees : to their thick foliage wood-pigeons
come. The entrance to a combe—the widening

mouth of a valley—is beyond, with copses on the slopes.

Again the plover's notes, this time in the field immediately behind ; repeated, too, in the field on the right hand. One comes over, and as he flies he jerks a wing upwards and partly turns on his side in the air, rolling like a vessel in a swell. He seems to beat the air sideways, as if against a wall, not downwards. This habit makes his course appear so uncertain : he may go there, or yonder, or in a third direction, more undecided than a startled snipe. Is there a little vanity in that wanton flight ? Is there a little consciousness of the spring-freshened colours of his plumage and pride in the dainty touch of his wings on the sweet wind ? His love is watching his wayward course. He prolongs it. He has but a few yards to fly to reach the well-known feeding-ground by the brook where the grass is short ; perhaps it has been eaten off by sheep. It is a straight and easy line—as a starling would fly. The plover thinks nothing of a straight line : he winds first with the curve of the hedge, then rises, uttering his cry, aslant, wheels, and returns ; now this way, direct at me, as if his object was to display his snowy breast ; suddenly rising aslant again, he wheels once more, and goes right away from his object over above the field whence he came. Another moment and he returns, and so to and fro, and round and round, till, with a sidelong, unexpected sweep, he alights by the brook. He stands a minute, then utters his cry, and runs a yard or so forward. In a little while a second plover arrives from the field behind; he, too, dances a maze in the air before he settles. Soon a third joins them. They are visible at that spot because the grass is short; elsewhere they would be hidden. If one of these rises and flies to and fro, almost instantly another follows, and then it is indeed a dance before they alight. The wheeling, maze-tracing, devious windings continue till the eye wearies and rests with pleasure on a passing butterfly. These birds have nests in the meadows adjoining; they meet here as a common feeding-ground. Presently they will disperse, each returning to his mate at the nest. Half an hour afterwards they will meet once more, either here or on the wing.

In this manner they spend their time from dawn, through the flower-growing day, till dusk. When the sun arises over the hill into the sky, already blue, the plovers have been up a long while. All the busy morning they go to and fro: the busy morning when the wood-pigeons cannot rest in the copses on the combe side, but continually fly in and out; when the blackbirds whistle in the oaks; when the bluebells gleam with purplish lustre. At noontide in the dry heat it is pleasant to listen to the sound of water moving among the thousand thousand grass-blades of the mead. The flower-growing day lengthens out beyond the sunset, and till the hedges are dim the lapwings do not cease.

Leaving now the shade of the oak, I follow the path into the meadow on the right, stepping by the way over a streamlet which diffuses its rapid current broadcast over the sward till it collects again and pours into the brook. This next meadow is somewhat more raised, and not watered; the grass is high, and full of buttercups. Before I have gone twenty yards a lapwing rises out in the field, rushes towards me through the air, and circles round my head, making as if to dash at me, and uttering shrill cries. Immediately another comes from the mead behind the oak; then a third from over the hedge, and all those that have been feeding by the bank, till I am encircled with them. They wheel round, dive, rise aslant, cry, and wheel again, always close over me, till I have walked some distance, when one by one they fall off, and, still uttering threats, retire. There is a nest in this meadow, and, although it is, no doubt, a long way from the path, my presence even in the field, large as it is, is resented. The couple who imagine themselves threatened are quickly joined by their friends, and there is no rest till I have left their treasures far behind.

*   *   *   *   *

II.—THE GREEN CORN

Pure colour almost always gives the idea of fire, or, rather, it is perhaps as if a light shone through as well as the colour itself. The fresh green blade of corn is like this—so pellucid, so clear and pure in its green as to seem to shine with colour. It is not brilliant—not a surface gleam nor an enamel—it is stained through. Beside the moist clods the slender flags arise, filled with the sweetness of the earth. Out of the darkness under—that darkness which knows no day save when the ploughshare opens its chinks—they have come to the light. To the light they have brought a colour which will attract the sunbeams from now till harvest. They fall more pleasantly on the corn, toned, as if they mingled with it. Seldom do we realize that the world is practically no thicker to us than the print of our footsteps on the path. Upon that surface we walk and act our comedy of life, and what is beneath is nothing to us. But it is out from that underworld, from the dead and the unknown, from the cold, moist ground, that these green blades have sprung. Yonder a steam-plough pants up the hill, groaning with its own strength, yet all that strength and might of wheels, and piston, and chains cannot drag from the earth one single blade like these. Force cannot make it ; it must grow—an easy word to speak or write, in fact full of potency.

It is this mystery—of growth and life, of beauty and sweetness and colour, and sun-loved ways starting forth from the clods—that gives the corn its power over me. Somehow I identify myself with it ; I live again as I see it. Year by year it is the same, and when I see it I feel that I have once more entered on a new life. And to my fancy, the spring, with its green corn, its violets, and hawthorn leaves, and increasing song, grows yearly dearer and more dear to this our ancient earth. So many centuries have flown. Now it is the manner with all natural things to gather as it were by smallest particles. The merest grain of sand drifts unseen into a crevice, and by-and-by another; after a while there is a heap; a century and it is a mound, and then everyone observes and comments on it. Time itself has gone on like this; the years have accumulated, first in drifts, then in heaps, and now a vast mound, to which the mountains are knolls, rises up and over-shadows us. Time lies heavy on the world. The old, old earth is glad to turn from the cark and care of driftless centuries to the first sweet blades of green.

There is sunshine to-day, after rain, and every lark is singing. Across the vale a broad cloud-shadow descends the hillside, is lost in the hollow, and pre-sently, without warning, slips over the edge, crossing swiftly along the green tips. The sunshine follows —the warmer for its momentary absence. Far, far down in a grassy combe stands a solitary corn-rick, conical-roofed, casting a lonely shadow—marked because so solitary—and beyond it, on the rising slope, is a brown copse. The leafless branches take a brown tint in the sunlight; on the summit above there is furze; then more hill-lines drawn against the sky. In the tops of the dark pines at the corner of the copse, could the glance sustain itself to see them, there are finches warming themselves in the sunbeams. The thick needles shelter them from the current of air, and the sky is bluer above the pines. Their hearts are full already of the happy days to come, when the moss yonder by the beech, and the lichen on the fir-trunk, and the loose fibres caught in the fork of an unbending bough, shall furnish forth a sufficient mansion for their young. Another broad cloud-shadow, and another warm embrace of sunlight. All the serried ranks of the green corn bow at the word of command as the wind rushes over them.

There is largeness and freedom here. Broad as the down and free as the wind, the thought can roam high over the narrow roofs in the vale. Nature has affixed no bounds to thought. All the palings, and walls, and crooked fences deep down yonder are artificial. The fetters and traditions, the routine, the dull roundabout, which deadens the spirit like the cold moist earth, are the merest nothing. Here it is easy with the physical eye to look over the highest roof, which must also always be the narrowest. The moment the eye of the mind is filled with the beauty of things natural an equal freedom and width of view comes to it. Step aside from the trodden footpath of personal experience, throwing away the petty cynicism bred of petty hopes disappointed. Step out upon the broad down beside the green corn, and let its freshness become part of life.

The wind passes and it bends—let the wind, too, pass over the spirit. From the cloud-shadow it emerges to the sunshine—let the heart come out from the shadow of roofs to the open glow of the sky. High above, the songs of the larks fall as rain —receive it with open hands. Pure is the colour of the green flags, the slender, pointed blades—let the thought be pure as the light that shines through that colour. Broad are the downs and open the aspect— gather the breadth and largeness of view. Never can that view be wide enough and large enough ; there will always be room to aim higher. As the air of the hills enriches the blood, so let the presence of these beautiful things enrich the inner sense.

A KING OF ACRES

I.—JAMES THARDOVER

A WEATHER-BEATEN man stood by a gateway watching some teams at plough. The bleak March wind rushed across the field, reddening his face ; rougher than a flesh-brush, it rubbed the skin, and gave it a glow as if each puff were a blow with the 'gloves.' His short brown beard was full of dust blown into it. Between the line of the hat and the exposed part of the forehead the skin had peeled slightly, literally worn off by the unsparing rudeness of wintry mornings. Like the early field veronica, which flowered at his feet in the short grass under the hedge, his eyes were blue and grey. The petals are partly of either hue, and so his eyes varied according to the light—now somewhat more grey, and now more blue. Tall and upright, he stood straight as a bolt, though both arms were on the gate, and his ashen walking-stick swung over it. He wore a grey overcoat, a grey felt hat, grey leggings, and his boots were grey with the dust which had settled on them.

He was thinking : 'Farmer Bartholomew is doing the place better this year ; he scarcely hoed a weed last season ; the stubble was a tangle of weeds ; one could hardly walk across it. That second team stops too long at the end of the furrow—idle fellow that. Third team goes too fast; horses will be soon tired. Fourth team—he's getting beyond his work —too old; the stilts nearly threw him over there. This ground has paid for the draining—one, at all events. Never saw land look better. Looks brownish and moist—moist brownish red. Query, what colour is that? Ask Mary—the artist. Never saw it in a picture. Keeps his hedges well; this one is like a board on the top, thorn-boughs molten together; a hare could run along it (as they will sometimes with harriers behind them, and jump off the other side to baffle scent). Now, why is Bartholomew doing his land better this year? Keen old fellow! Something behind this. Has he got that bit of money that was coming to him? Done something, they said, last Doncaster; no one could get anything out of him. Dark as night. Sold the trainer some oats—that I know. Wonder how much the trainer pocketed over that transaction? Expect he did not charge them all. Still, he's a decent fellow. Honesty is uncertain—never met an honest man. Doubt if world could hang together. Bartholomew is honest enough; but either he has won some money, or he really does not want the drawback at audit. Takes care his horses don't look too well. Notice myself that farmers do not let their teams look so glossy as a few years ago. Like them to seem rough and uncared for—can't afford smooth coats these hard times. Don't look very glossy

myself; don't feel very glossy. Hate this wind—
hang kings' ransoms! People who like these winds
are telling falsehoods. That's broken (as one of the
teams stopped); have to send to blacksmith. Knock
off now; no good your pottering there. Next team
stops to go and help potter. Third team stops to
help second. Fourth team comes across to help
third. All pottering. Wants Bartholomew among
them. That's the way to do a morning's work.
Did anyone ever see such idleness! Group about a
broken chain—link snapped. Tie it up with your
leathern garter — not he; no resource. What
patience a man needs to have anything to do with
land! Four teams idle over a snapped link! Rent!
—of course they can't pay rent. Wonder if a gang
of American labourers could make anything out of
our farms? There they work from sunrise to
sunset. Suppose import a gang and try. Did anyone ever see such a helpless set as that yonder?
Depression—of course. No go-ahead in them.'

'Mind opening the gate, you?' said a voice behind; and, turning, the thinker saw a dealer in a
trap, who wanted the gate opened, to save him the
trouble of getting down to do it himself. The
thinker did as he was asked, and held the gate open.
The trap went slowly through.

'Will you come on and take a glass?' said the
dealer, pointing with the butt-end of his whip.
'Crown.' This was sententious for the Crown in the
hamlet. Country-folk speak in pieces, putting the
principal word in a sentence for the entire paragraph.

The thinker shook his head and shut the gate, carefully hasping it.   The dealer drove on.

'Who's that?' thought the grey man, watching the trap jolt down the rough road.   'Wants veal, I suppose.   No veal here—no good.   Now, look!'

The group by the broken chain beckoned to the trap ; a lad went across to it with the chain, got up, and was driven off, so saving himself half a mile on his road to the forge.

'Anything to save themselves exertion.   Nothing will make them move faster—like whipping a cart-horse into a gallop ; it soon dies away in the old jog-trot.   Why, they have actually started again—actually started!'

He watched the teams a little longer, heedless of the wind, which he abused, but which really did not affect him, and then walked along the hedgerow downhill.   Two men were sowing a field on the slope, swinging the hand full of grain from the hip regular as time itself, a swing calculated to throw the seed so far, but not too far, and without jerk.   The next field had just been manured, and he stopped to glance at the crowds of small birds which were looking over the straw—finches and sparrows, and the bluish grey of pied wagtails.   There were hundreds of small birds.   While he stood, a hedge-sparrow uttered his thin, pleading song on the hedge-top, and a meadow-pipit, which had mounted a little way in the air, came down with outspread wings, with a short 'Seep, seep,' to the ground.   Lark and pipit seem near relations ; only the skylark sings rising, descending, anywhere, but the pipits chiefly while slowly descending. There had been a rough attempt at market-gardening in the field after this, and rows of cabbage gone up to seed stood forlorn and ragged. On the top of one of these a skylark was perched, calling at intervals; for though classed as a non-percher, perch he does sometimes. Meadows succeeded on the level ground; one had been covered with the scrapings of roads, a whitish, crumbling dirt, dry, and falling to pieces in the wind. The grass was pale, its wintry hue not yet gone, and the clods seemed to make it appear paler. Among these clods four or five thrushes were seeking their food; on a bare oak a blackbird was perched, his mate no doubt close by in the hedgerow; at the margin of a pond a black-and-white wagtail waded in the water; a blue tit flew across to the corner. Brown thrushes, dark blackbird, blue tit, and wagtail gave a little colour to the angle of the meadow. A gleam of passing sunlight brightened it. Two wood-pigeons came to a thick bush growing over a grey wall on the other side—for ivy-berries, probably.

A cart passed at a little distance, laden with red mangolds, fresh from the pit in which they had been stored; the roots had grown out a trifle, and the root-lets were mauve. A goldfinch perched on a dry dead stalk of wild carrot, a stalk that looked too slender to bear the bird. As the weather-beaten man moved, the goldfinch flew, and the golden wings outspread formed a bright contrast with the dull white clods. Crossing the meadow, and startling the wood-pigeons, our friend scaled the grey walls, putting his foot in a hole left for the purpose. Dark moss lined the interstices between the irregular and loosely placed stones. Above, on the bank, and greener than the grass, grew moss at the roots of ash-stoles and wherever there was shelter. Broad, rank, green arum leaves crowded each other in places. Red stalks of herb-robert spread open. The weather-beaten man gathered a white wild violet from the shelter of a dead dry oak-leaf, and as he placed it in his buttonhole, paused to listen to the baying of hounds. Yowp! yow! The cries echoed from the bank and filled the narrow beechwood within. A shot followed, and then another, and a third after an interval. More yowping. The grey-brown head of a rabbit suddenly appeared over the top of the bank, within three yards of him, and he could see the creature's whiskers nervously working, as its mind estimated its chances of escape. Instead of turning back, the rabbit made a rush to get under an ash-stole, where was a burrow. The yowping went slowly away; the beeches rang again as if the beagles were in cry. Two assistant-keepers were working the outskirts, and shooting the rabbits which sat out in the brushwood, and so were not to be captured by nets and ferrets. The ground-game was strictly kept down; the noise was made by half a dozen puppies they had with them. Passing through the ash-stoles, and next the narrow beechwood, the grey man walked across the open park, and after awhile came in sight of Thardover House. His steps were directed to the great arched porch, beneath which the village folk boasted a waggon-load could pass. The inner door swung open as if by instinct at his approach. The man who had so neighbourly opened the gate to the dealer in the trap was James Thardover, the owner of the property. Historic as was his name and residence, he was utterly devoid of affectation— a true man of the land.

II.—NEW TITLE-DEEDS

Deed, seal, and charter give but a feeble hold compared with that which is afforded by labour. James Thardover held his lands again by right of labour; he had taken possession of them once more with thought, design, and actual work, as his ancestors had with the sword. He had laid hands, as it were, on every acre. Those who work, own. There are many who receive rent who do not own; they are proprietors, not owners; like receiving dividends on stock, which stock is never seen or handled. Their rights are legal only; his right was the right of labour, and, it might be added, of forbearance. It is a condition of ownership in the United States that the settler clears so much and brings so many acres into cultivation. It was just this condition which he had practically carried out upon the Thardover estate. He had done so much, and in so varied a manner, that it is difficult to select particular acts for enumeration. All the great agricultural movements of the last thirty years he had energetically supported. There was the draining movement. The undulating contour of the country, deep vales alternating with moderate brows, gave a sufficient supply of water to every farm, and on the lower lands led to flooding and the formation of marshes. Horley Bottom, where the hay used to be frequently carried into the river by a June freshet, was now safe from flood. Flag Marsh had been completely drained, and made some of the best wheat-land in the neighbourhood. Part of a bark canoe was found in it; the remnants were preserved at Thardover House, but gradually fell to pieces.

Longboro' Farm was as dry now as any such soil could be. More or less draining had been carried out on twenty other farms, sometimes entirely at his expense. Sometimes the tenant paid a small percentage on the sum expended; generally this percentage fell off in the course of a year or two. The tenant found he could not pay it. Except on Flag Marsh, the drainage did not pay him £50. Perhaps it might have done, had the seasons been better; but, as it had actually happened, the rents had decreased instead of increasing. Tile-pipes had not availed against rain and American wheat. So far as income was concerned, he would have been richer had the money so expended been allowed to accumulate at the banker's. The land as land was certainly improved in places, as on Bartholomew's farm. Thardover never cared for the steam-plough; personally, he disliked it. Those who represented agricultural opinion at the farmers' clubs and in the agricultural papers raised so loud a cry for it that he

went half-way to meet them. One of the large
tenants was encouraged to invest in the steam-plough
by a drawback on his rent, on condition that it
should be hired out to others. The steam-plough,
Thardover soon discovered, was not profitable to the
landowner. It reduced the fields to a dead level.
They had previously been thrown into 'lands,' with
a drain-trench on each side. On this dead level
water did not run off quickly, and the growth of
weeds increased. Tenants got into a habit of shirk-
ing the extirpation of the weeds. The best farmers
on the estate would not use it at all. To very large
tenants, and to small tenants who could not keep
enough horses, it was profitable at times. It did
not appear that a single sack more of wheat was
raised, nor a single additional head of stock maintained, since the steam-plough arrived.

Paul of Embersbury, who occupied some of the
best meadow and upland country, a man of some
character and standing, had taken to the shorthorns
before Thardover succeeded to the property. Thardover assisted him in every way, and bought some
of the best blood. There was no home-farm; the
house was supplied from Bartholomew's dairy, and
the Squire did not care to upset the old traditionary
arrangements by taking a farm in hand. What he
bought went to Embersbury, and Paul did well. As
a consequence, there were good cattle all over the
estate. The long prices formerly fetched by Paul's
method had much fallen off, but substantial sums
were still paid. Paul had faced the depression better

than most of them. He was bitter, as was only natural, against the reaction in favour of black cattle. The upland tenants, though, had a good many of the black, in spite of Paul's frowns and thunders after the market ordinary at Barnboro' town. He would put down his pipe, bustle upon his feet, lean his somewhat protuberant person on the American leather of the table, and address the dozen or so who stayed for spirits and water after dinner, without the pretence of a formal meeting. He spoke in very fair language, short, jerky sentences, but well-chosen words. He who had taken the van in improvements thirty years ago was the bitterest against any proposed change now. Black cattle were thoroughly bad.

Another of his topics was the hiring fair, where servant-girls stood waiting for engagements, and which it was proposed to abolish. Paul considered it was taking the bread and cheese out of the poor wenches' mouths. They could stand there and get hired for nothing, instead of having to pay half a crown for advertising, and get nothing then. But though the Squire had supported the shorthorns, even the shorthorns had not prevented the downward course things agricultural were following.

Then there was the scientific movement, the cry for science among the farmers. He founded a scholarship, invited the professors to his place, lunched them, let them experiment on little pieces of land, mournful-looking plots. Nothing came of it. He drew a design for a new cottage himself, a practical plain place. The builders told him it was far dearer to put up than ornamental but inconvenient structures. Thardover sunk his money his own way, and very comfortable cottages they were. Ground-game he had kept down for years before the Act. Farm-buildings he had improved freely. The education movement, however, stirred him most. He went into it enthusiastically. Thardover village was one of the first places to become efficient under the new legislation. This was a piece of practical work after his own heart. Generally, legislative measures were so far off from country people. They affected the condition of large towns, of the Black Country, of the weavers or miners, distant folk. To the villages and hamlets of purely agricultural districts these Acts had no existence. The Education Act was just the reverse. This was a statute which came right down into the hamlets, which was nailed up at the cross-roads, and ruled the barn, the plough, and scythe. Something tangible, that could be carried out and made into a fact—something he could do. Thardover did it with the thoroughness of his nature. He found the ground, lent the money, saw to the building, met the Government inspectors, and organized the whole. A committee of the tenants were the ostensible authority, the motive-power was the Squire. He worked at it till it was completely organized, for he felt as if he were helping to mould the future of this great country. Broad-minded himself, he understood the immense value of education, looked at generally; and he thought, too, that by its aid the farmer and the landowner might be enabled to compete with the foreigner, who was driving them from the market. No speeches and no agitation could equal the power concentrated in that plain school-house; there was nothing from which he hoped so much.

Only one held aloof and showed hostility to the movement, or rather to the form it took. His youngest and favourite daughter, Mary, the artist, rebelled against it. Hitherto she had ruled him as she choose. She had led in every kind act—acts too kind to be called charity. She had been the life of the place. Perhaps it was the strong-minded women whom the cry of education brought to Thardover House that set ajar some chord in her sensitive mind. Strident voices checked her sympathies, and hard rule-and-line work like this repelled her. Till then she had been the constant companion of the Squire's walks; but while the school was being organized she would not go with him. She walked where she could not see the plain angular building; she said it set her teeth on edge.

When the strident voices had departed, when time had made the school-house part and parcel of the place, like the cottages, Mary changed her ways, and occasionally called there. She took a class once a week of the elder girls, and taught them in her own fashion at home—most unorthodox teaching it was —in which the works of the best poets were the chief subjects, and portfolios of engravings were found on the table. Long since father and daughter had resumed their walks together.

It was in this way that James Thardover made his estate his own—he held possession by right of labour. He was resident ten months out of twelve, and after all these public and open works he did far more in private. There was not an acre on the property which he had not personally visited. The farm-houses and farm-buildings were all known to him. He rode from tenancy to tenancy; he visited the men at plough, and stood among the reapers. Neither the summer heat nor the winds of March prevented him from seeing with his own eyes. The latest movement was the silo system, the burying of grass under pressure, instead of making it into hay. By these means the clouds are to be defied, and a plentiful supply of fodder secured. Time alone can show whether this, the latest invention, is any more powerful than steam-plough or guano to uphold agriculture against the shocks of fortune. But James Thardover would have tried any plan that had been suggested to him. It was thus that he laid hold on his lands with the strongest of titles—the work of his own hands. Yet still the tenants were unable to pay the former rent. Some had failed or left, and their farms were vacant; and nothing could be more discouraging than the condition of affairs upon the property.

III.—A RING-FENCE: CONCLUSION

There were great elms in the Out-park, whose limbs or boughs, as large as the trunk itself, came down almost to the ground. They touched the tops of the white wild parsley ; and when sheep were lying beneath, the jackdaws stepped from the sheep's back to the bough and returned again. The jackdaws had their nests in the hollow places of these elms ; for the elm as it ages becomes full of cavities. These great trees often divided into two main boughs, rising side by side, and afar off visible as two dark streaks among the green. For many years no cattle had been permitted in the park, and the boughs of the trees had grown in a drooping form, as they naturally do unless eaten or broken by animals pushing against them. But since the times of agricultural pressure, a large part of the domain had been fenced off, and was now partly grazed and partly mown, being called the Out-park. There were copses at the farther side, where in spring the may flowered ; the purple orchis was drawn up high by the trees and bushes—twice as high as its fellows in the mead, where a stray spindle-tree grew ; and from these copses the cuckoos flew round the park.

But the thinnest hedge about the wheat-fields was as interesting as the park or the covers ; and this is the remarkable feature of English scenery—that its perfection, its beauty, and its interest are not confined to any masterpiece here and there, walled in or enclosed, or at least difficult of access and isolated, but it extends to the smallest portion of the country. Wheatfield hedges are the thinnest of hedges, kept so that the birds may find no shelter, and that the numerous caterpillars may not breed in them more than can be helped. Such a hedge is so low it can

be leaped over, and so narrow that it is a mere
screen of twisted hawthorn branches which can be
seen through, like screens of twisted stone in ancient
chapels. But the sparrows come to it, and the finches,
the mice, and weasles, and now and then a crow, who
searches along, and goes in and out and quests like
a spaniel. It is so tough, this twisted screen of branches,
that a charge of shot would be stopped by it; if a pellet
or two slid through an interstice, the majority would
be held as if by a shield of wicker-work. Old Bartholomew, the farmer, sent his men once or twice
along with reaping-hooks to clear away the weeds
that grew up here under such slight shelter; but other
farmers were not so careful. Then convolvulus
grew over the thin screen, a corncockle stood up
taller than the hedge itself; in time of harvest, yellow
St. John's wort flowered beside it, and later on, bunches
of yellow-weed.

A lark rose on the other side, and so caused the
glance to be lifted and to look farther, and away
yonder was a farm-house at the foot of a hill. Pale
yellow stubble covered the hill, rising like a background to the red-tile roof, and to the elms beside
the house, among whose branches there were pale
yellow spots. Round wheat-ricks stood in a double
row on the left hand—count them, and you counted
the coin of the land, bank-notes in straw—and on
the right and in front were green meads, and horses
feeding—horses who had done good work in plough-
time and harvest-time, and would soon be at plough
again. There were green meads, because some green

meads are a necessity of an English farm-house, and there are few without them, even when in the midst of corn. Meads in which the horses feed, a pony for the children and for the pony-cart, turkeys, two or three cows—all the large and small creatures that live about the place. When the land was torn up and ploughed for corn of old time, these green enclosures were left to stay on, till now it seems as if pressure of low prices for wheat would cause the corn-land to again become pasture. Of old time, golden wheat conquered and held possession, and now the grass threatens to oust the conqueror.

Had anyone studied either of these three—the great elms in the Out-park, or the thin twisted screen of hedge, or the red-tile roof, and the yellow stubble behind it on the hill—he might have found material for a picture in each. There was, in truth, in each far more than anyone could put into a picture, or than anyone could put into a book; for the painter can but give one aspect of one day, and the writer a mere catalogue of things; but Nature refreshes the reality every day with different tints, and as it were new ideas, so that, although it is always there, it is never twice the same. Over that stubble on the hill there were other hills, and among these a combe or valley, in which stood just such another farm-house, but differently placed, with few trees, and those low, somewhat bare in its immediate surroundings, but above, on each side, close at hand, sloping ramparts of green turf rising high, till the larks that sang above seemed to sing in another land, like that found by Jack when he clomb the beanstalk. Along this combe was a cover of gorse, and in spring there was a mile of golden bloom, richer than gold in colour, leading like a broad highway of gold down to the house. From those ramparts in high summer—which is when the corn is ripe and the reapers in it—there could be seen a slope divided into squares of varied grain. This on the left of the fertile undulation was a maize colour, which, when the sunlight touched it, seemed to have a fleeting hue of purple somewhere within. There is no purple in ripe wheat visible to direct and considering vision; look for it specially, and it will not be seen. Purple forms no part of any separate wheat-ear or straw; brown and yellow in the ear, yellow in the upper part of the straw, and still green towards the earth. But when the distant beams of sunlight travelling over the hill swept through the rich ripe grain, for a moment there was a sense of purple on the retina. Beyond this square was a pale gold piece, and then one where the reapers had worked hard, and the shocks stood in diagonal rows; this was a bronze, or brown and bronze, and beside it was a green of clover.

Farther on, the different green of the hill turf, and white sheep, feeding in an extended crescent, the bow of the crescent gradually descending the sward. The hills of themselves beautiful, and possessing views which are their property and belong to them—a two-fold value. The woods on the lower slopes full of tall brake fern, and holding in their shadowy depths the spirit of old time. In the woods it is still the

past, and the noisy mechanic present of this manufacturing century has no place.   Enter in among the
round-boled beeches which the squirrels rush up,
twining round like ivy in ascent, where they nibble
the beech-nuts forty feet aloft, and let the husks drop
to your feet; where the wood-pigeon sits and does not
move, safe in the height and thickness of the spray.
There are jew-berries or dew-berries on a bramble-
bush, which grows where the sunlight and rain fall
direct to the ground, unchecked by boughs.   They
are full of the juice of autumn, black, rich, vine-
like, taken fresh from the prickly bough   Low
down in the hollow is a marshy spot, sedge-grown,
and in the sedge lie yellow leaves of willow already
fallen.   Here in the later months will come a woodcock or two, with feathers so brown and leaf-like of
hue and markings that the plumage might have been
printed in colours from brown leaves of beech.   No
springes are set for the woodcocks now, but the
markings are the same on the feathers as centuries
since; the brown beech-leaves lie in the dry hollows
the year through just as they did then; the large
dew-berries are as rich; and the nuts as sweet.   It
is the past in the wood, and Time here never grows
any older.   Could you bring back the red stag—as
you may easily in fancy—and place him among the
tall brake, and under the beeches, he should not
know that a day had gone by since the stern Round-
heads shot down the last of his race hereabouts in
Charles I.'s days.   For the leaves are turning as they
turned then to the altered colour of the sun's rays as

he declines in his noonday arch, lower and lower every day; his rays are somewhat yellower than in dry hot June; a little of the tint of the ripe wheat floats in the sunshine. To this the woods turn. First, the nut-tree leaves drop, and the green brake is quickly yellow; the slender birch becomes lemon on its upper branches; the beech reddens; by-and-by the first ripe acorn falls, and there's as much cawing of the rooks in the oaks at acorn-time as at their nests in the elms in March.

All these things happened in the old, old time before the red stags were shot down; the leaves changed as the sunbeams became less brilliantly white; the woodcocks arrived; the mice had the last of the acorns which had fallen, and which the rooks and jays and squirrels had spared for them after feasting to the full of their greediness. This ancient oak, whose thick bark, like cast-iron for ruggedness at the base, has grown on steadily ever since the last deer bounded beneath it, utterly heedless of the noisy rattle of machinery in the northern cities, unmoved by any shriek of engine, or hum, or flapping of loose belting, or any volume of smoke drifting into the air —I wish that the men now serving the great polished wheels, and works in iron and steel and brass, could somehow be spared an hour to sit under this ancient oak in Thardover South Wood, and come to know from actual touch of its rugged bark that the past is living now, that Time is no older, that Nature still exists as full as ever, and to see that all the factories of the world have made no difference, and therefore not to pin their faith to any theory born and sprung up among the crush and pale-faced life of modern time ; but to look for themselves at the rugged oak-bark, and up to the sky above the highest branches, and to take an acorn and consider its story and possibilities, and to watch the sly squirrel coming down, as they sit quietly, to play almost at their feet.   That they might gather to themselves some of the leaves—mental and spiritual leaves—of the ancient forest, feeling nearer to the truth and soul, as it were, that lives on in it.   They would feel as if they had got back to their original existence, and had become themselves, as they ought to be, could they live such life, untouched by artificial care.   Then, how hurt they would be if any proposed to cut down that oak ; if any proposed the felling of the forest, and the death of its meaning.   It would be like a blow aimed at themselves.   No picture that could be bought at a thousand guineas could come near that ancient oak ; but you can carry away the memory of it, the picture and thought in your mind for nothing. If the oak were cut down, it would be like thrusting a stick through some valuable painting on your walls at home.

The common below the South Wood, even James Thardover with all his desire for improvement could not do much good with ; the soil, and the impossibility of getting a fall for draining, all checked effort there. A wild, rugged waste, you say, at first, glancing at the rushes, and the gaunt signpost standing up among them, the anthills, and thistles.   Thistles have colour in their bloom, and the prickly leaves are finely cut ; rushes—green rushes—are notes of the season, and with their slender tips point to the days in the book of the year; they are brown now at the tip, and some bent downwards in an angle. The brown will descend the stalk till the snipes come with grey-grass colours in their wings. But all the beatings of the rain will not cast the rushes utterly down ; they will send up fresh green successors for the spring, for the cuckoo to float along over on his way to the signpost, where he will perch a few minutes, and call in the midst of the wilderness. There, too, the lapwings leave their eggs on the ground among the rushes, and rise, and complainingly call. The warm showers of June call up the iris in the corner where the streamlet widens, and under the willows appear large yellow flowers above the flags. Pink and white blossom of the rest-harrow comes on bushy plants where the common is dry, and there is heath, and heather, and fern. The waste has its treasures too—as the song-thrush has his in the hawthorn bush—its treasures of flowers, as the wood its beauties of tree and leaf, and the hills their wheat.

The ring-fence goes farther than this ; it encloses the living creatures, yet without confining them. The wing of the wood-pigeon, as the bird perches, forms a defined curve against its body. The forward edge of the wing—its thickest part—as it is pressed to its side, draws a line sweeping round—a painter's line. How many wood-pigeons are there in the South Wood alone, besides the copses and the fir-plantations? How many turtle-doves in spring in the hedges and outlying thickets, in summer among the shocks of corn? And all these are his—the Squire's —not in the sense of possession, for no true wild creature was ever anyone's yet; it would die first; but still, within his ring-fence, and their destinies affected by his will, since he can cut down their favourite ash and hawthorn, or thin them with shot. Neither of which he does. The robin, methinks, sings sweetest of autumn-tide in the deep woods, when no other birds speak or trill, unexpectedly giving forth his plaintive note, complaining that the summer is going, and the time of love, and the sweet cares of the nest; telling you that the berries are brown, the dew-berries over-ripe, and dropping of over-ripeness like dew as the morning wind shakes the branch; that the wheat is going to the stack, and that the rusty plough will soon be bright once more by the attrition of the earth.

Many of them sing thus in the South Wood, yet scarce any two within sound of each other, for the robin is jealous, and likes to have you all to himself as he tells his tale. Song-thrushes—what ranks of them in April; larks, what hundreds and hundreds of them on the hills above the green wheat; finches of varied species; blackbirds; nightingales; crakes in the meadows; partridges; a whole page might be filled merely with their names.

These, too, are in the ring-fence with the hills and woods, the yellow iris of the common, and the red-roofed farm-houses. Besides which, there are beings infinitely higher—namely, men and women in village and hamlet, and more precious still, those little children with hobnail boots and clean jackets and pinafores, who go a-blackberrying on their way to school. All these are in the ring-fence. Upon their physical destinies the Squire can exercise a powerful influence, and has done so, as the school itself testifies.

Now, is not a large estate a living picture? Or rather, is it not formed of a hundred living pictures? So beautiful it looks, its hills, its ripe wheat, its red-roofed farm-houses, and acres upon acres of oaks; so beautiful, it must be valuable—most valuable; it is visible, tangible wealth. It is difficult to disabuse anyone's mind of that idea; yet, as we have seen, with all the skill, science, and expenditure Thardover could bring to bear upon it, all his personal effort was in vain. It was a possession, not a profit. Had not James Thardover's ancestors invested their wealth in building streets of villas in the outskirts of a great city, he could not have done one-fifth what he had. Men who had made their fortunes in factories—the noisy factories of the present century —paid him high rents for these residences; and thus it was that the labour and time of the many-handed operatives in mill, factory, and workshop really went to aid in maintaining these living pictures. Without that outside income the Squire could not have reduced the rents of his tenants, so that they could push through the depression; without that outside income he could not have drained the lands, put up those good buildings, assisted the school, and in a hundred ways helped the people. Those who watched the polished machinery under the revolving shaft, and tended the loom, really helped to keep the beauties of South Wood, the grain-grown hills, the flower-strewn meadows. These were so beautiful, it seemed as if they must represent money—riches; but they did not. They had a value much higher than that. As the spring rises in the valley at the foot of the hills and slowly increases till it forms a river, to which ships resort, so these fields and woods, meads and brooks, were the source from which the city was derived. If the operative in the factory, or tending the loom, had traced his descent, he would have found that his grandfather, or some scarcely more remote ancestor, was a man of the land. He followed the plough, or tended the cattle, and his children went forth to earn higher wages in the town. For the hamlet and the outlying cottage are the springs whence the sinew and muscle of populous cities are derived. The land is the fountain-head from which the spring of life flows, widening into a river. The river at its broad mouth disdains the spring; the city in its immensity disdains the hamlet and the ploughman. Yet if the spring ceased, the ships could not frequent the river; if the hamlet and the ploughman were wiped out by degrees, the city must run dry of life. Therefore the South Wood and the park, the hamlet and the fields, had a value no one can tell how many times above the actual money rental, and the money earned by the operatives in factory and workshop could not have been better expended than in supporting it.

But it had another value still—which they too helped to sustain—the value of beauty. Parliament has several times intervened to save the Lake District from the desecrating intrusion of useless railways. So, too, the beauty of these woods, and grain-grown hills, of the very common, is worth preservation at the hands and votes of the operatives in factory and mill. If a man loves the brick walls of his narrow dwelling in a close-built city, and the flowers which he has trained with care in the window, how much more would he love the hundred living pictures like those round about Thardover House! After any artificer had once seen such an oak and rested under it, if any threatened to cut it down, he would feel as if a blow had been delivered at his heart. His efforts, therefore, should be not to destroy these pictures, but to preserve them. All the help that they can give is needed to assist a King of Acres in his struggle, and the struggle of the farmers and labourers—equally involved—against the adverse influences which press so heavily on English agriculture.

THE STORY OF SWINDON

WE have all of us passed through Swindon Station, whether *en route* to Southern Wales, to warm Devon — the fern-land — to the Channel Islands, or to Ireland. The ten minutes for refreshment, now in the case of certain trains reduced to five, have made thousands of travellers familiar with the name of the spot. Those who have not actually been there can recall to memory a shadowy tradition which has grown up and propagated itself, that here the soup skins the tongue, and that generally it is a near relative of the famous 'Mugby Junction.' Those who have been there retain at least a confused recollection of large and lofty saloons, velvet sofas, painted walls, and long semicircular bars covered with glittering glasses and decanters. Or it may be that the cleverly executed silver model of a locomotive under a glass case lingers still in their memories. At all events Swindon is a well-known oasis, familiar to the travelling public. Here let us do an act of justice. Much has been done of late to ameliorate many of the institutions which formerly led to bitter things being said against the place. The soup is no longer liquid fire, the beer is not lukewarm, the charges are more moderate ; the lady manager has succeeded in substituting order for disorder, comfort and attention in place of lofty disdain. Passengers have not got to cross the line for a fresh ticket or to telegraph ; the whole place is reformed. So much the better for the traveller. But how little do these birds of passage imagine the varied interest of the strange and even romantic story which is hidden in this most unromantic spot, given over, as it seems, to bricks and mortar !

Not that it ever had a history in the usual sense. There is but a faint, dim legend that the great Sweyn halted with his army on this hill—thence called Sweyn's dune, and so Swindon. There is a family here whose ancestry goes back to the times of the Vikings ; which was in honour when Fair Rosamond bloomed at Woodstock ; which fought in the great Civil War. Nothing further. The real history, written in iron and steel, of the place began forty years ago only. Then a certain small party of gentlemen sat down to luncheon on the greensward which was then where the platform is now. The furze was in blossom around them ; the rabbits frisked in and out of their burrows ; two or three distant farm-houses, one or two cottages, these were all the signs of human habitation, except a few cart-ruts indicating a track used for field purposes. There these gentlemen lunched, and one among them, ay, two among them, meditated great things, which the first planned, and the second lived to see realize the most sanguine anticipations. These two gentle-

men were Isambard Brunel and Daniel Gooch.
Driven away from the original plan, which was to
follow the old coach-road, they had come here to
survey and reconnoitre a possible track running in
the valley at the northern edge of the great range of
Wiltshire Downs. They decided that here should
be their junction and their workshop. Immense
sacrifices, enormous expenditure, the directors of the
new railway incurred in their one great idea of getting it finished! They could not stay to cart the
earth from the cuttings to the places where it was
required for embanking, so where they excavated
thousands of tons of clay they purchased land to
cast it upon out of their way; and where they
required an embankment they purchased a hill, and
boldly removed it to fill up the hollow. They
could not stay for the seasons, for proper weather
to work in, and in consequence of this their clay
embankment, thrown up wet and saturated, swelled
out, bulged at the sides, and could not be made
stable, till at last they drove rows of piles on each
side, and chained them together with chain-cables,
and so confined the slippery soil. They drove these
piles, tall beech-trees, 20 feet into the earth, and at
this day every train passes over tons of chain-cables
hidden beneath the ballast. The world yet remembers the gigantic cost of the Box Tunnel, and how
heaven and earth were moved to get the line open;
and at last it was open, but at what a cost!—a cost
that hung like a millstone round the neck of the
company, till a man rose into power who had the

talent of administration, and that man was the very companion of Brunel whom we saw lunching among the furze-bushes. Reckless as the expenditure was, one cannot but admire the determination which overcame every obstacle. For the great line a workshop was needed, and that workshop was built at Swindon. The green fields were covered with forges, the hedges disappeared to make way for cottages for the workmen. The workmen required food—tradesmen came and supplied that food—and Swindon rose as Chicago rose, as if by magic. From that day to this additions have been made, and other departments concentrated upon this one spot, till at the present time the factory covers a space equal to that of a moderate farm, and employs nearly four thousand workmen, to whom three hundred thousand pounds are yearly paid, whereby to purchase their daily bread. But at that early stage the difficulty was to find experienced workmen, and still greater to discover men who could superintend them. For these it was necessary to go up into the shrewd North, which had already foreseen the demand that must arise, and had partially educated her children in the new life that was about to dawn on the world ; and so it is that to this time the names of those who are in authority over this army of workers carry with them in their sound a strong flavour of the heather and the brae, and seem more in accordance with ideas of 'following the wild deer' than of a dwelling in the midst of the clangour and smoke.

All these new inhabitants of the hitherto deserted fields had to be lodged, and in endeavouring to solve this problem the company were induced to try an experiment which savoured not a little of communism, though not so intended. A building was erected which was locally called the 'barracks,' and it well deserved the name, for at one time as many as perhaps five hundred men found shelter in it. It was a vast place, with innumerable rooms and corridors. The experiment did not altogether answer, and was in time abandoned, when the company built whole streets, and even erected a covered market-place for their labourers. They went further, and bore the chief expense in building a church. A reading-room was started, and grew and grew till a substantial place was required for the accommodation of the members. Finally, the 'barracks' was converted into a place of worship for a Dissenting body, and a grand hall it afforded when the interior was removed and only the shell left. But by this time vast changes had taken place, and great extensions had arisen through private energy. This land was the poorest in the neighbourhood; low-lying, shallow soil on top of an endless depth of stiff clay, worthless for arable purposes, of small value for pasture, covered with furze, rushes, and rowen; so much so that when a certain man with a little money purchased a good strip of it, he was talked of as a fool, and considered to have committed a most egregious error. How vain is human wisdom! In a few years the railway came. Land rose in price, and this very

strip brought its owner thousands; so that the fool
became wise, and the wise was deemed of no account.
Private speculators, seeing the turn things were
taking, ran up rows of houses; building societies
stepped in and laid out streets; a whole town
seemed to start into being at once. Still the company continued to concentrate their works at the
junction, and at last added the culminating stroke
by bringing the carriage department here, which was
like planting a new colony. A fresh impulse was
given to building; fresh blocks and streets arose;
companies were formed to burn bricks—one of these
makes bricks by steam, and can burn a quarter of
a million at once in their kiln. This in a place
where previously the rate of building was five new
houses in twenty years! Sanitary districts were
mapped out; boards of control elected; gas companies; water companies—who brought water out of
the chalk hills three miles distant: all the distinctive
characteristics of a city arose into being. Lastly
came a sewage farm, for so great was the sewage
that it became a burning question how to dispose of
it, and on this sewage farm some most extraordinary
results have been obtained, such as mangolds with
leaves four feet in length—a tropical luxuriance of
growth. One postman had sufficed, then two, then
three, till a strong staff had to be organized, in
regular uniform, provided with bull's-eye lanthorns
to pick their way in and out of the dark and dirty
back-streets. One single constable had sufficed,
and a dark hole had done duty as a prison. Now

a superintendent and other officers, a full staff, and a complete police-station, with cells, justice-room, all the paraphernalia were required; and so preposterous did this seem to other towns, formerly leading towns in the country, but which had remained stagnant while Swindon went ahead, that they bitterly resented the building, and satirized it as a 'Palace of Justice,' though, in good truth, sorely needed. A vast corn exchange, a vaster drill-hall for the workmen—who had formed a volunteer corps—to drill in, chapels of every description, and some of really large size—all these arose.

The little old town on the hill a mile from the station felt the wave of progress strongly. The streets were paved; sewers driven under the town at a depth of 40 feet through solid stone, in order to dispose of the sewage on a second sewage farm of over 100 acres. Shops, banks, and, above all, public-houses, abounded and increased apace, especially in the new town, where every third house seemed to be licensed premises. The cart-track seen by the luncheon-party in the furze was laid down and macadamized, and a street erected, named after the finest street in London, full of shops of all descriptions. Every denomination, from the Plymouth Brethren to the Roman Catholics, had their place of worship. Most of the tradesmen had two branches, one in the upper and one in the lower town, and the banks followed their example. Not satisfied with two railways, two others are now in embryo—one a link in the long-talked-of through communication between North and South, from Manchester to Southampton, the other a local line with possible extensions. A population of barely 2,000 has risen to 15,000, and this does not nearly represent the real number of inhabitants, for there is a large floating population, and, in addition, five or six villages surrounding the town are in reality merely suburbs, and in great part populated by men working in the town. These villages have shared in the general movement, and some of them have almost trebled in size and importance. This population is made up of the most incongruous elements : labouring men of the adjacent counties who have left the plough and the sickle for the hammer and the spade ; Irish in large numbers ; Welshmen, Scotch, and North of England men ; stalwart fellows from York and places in a similar latitude. Yet, notwithstanding all the building that has been going on, despite the rush of building societies and private speculators, the cry is still, ' More bricks and mortar,' for there exists an enormous amount of overcrowding. The high rents are almost prohibitory, and those who take houses underlet them and sublet them, till in six rooms three families may be living. The wages are good, ranging from 18s. for common labourers to 30s., 36s., 40s., and more for skilled mechanics, and the mode in which they live affords an illustrative contrast to the agricultural population immediately surrounding the place. As if to complete the picture, that nothing might be wanting, a music-hall has been opened, where for threepence the workman may listen to the dulcet strains of 'London artistes' while he smokes his pipe.

Can a more striking, a more wonderful and interesting spectacle be seen than this busy, Black-Country-looking town, with its modern associations, its go-ahead ways, in the midst of a purely agricultural country, where there are no coal or iron mines, where in the memory of middle-aged men there was nothing but pasture-fields, furze, and rabbits ? In itself it affords a perfect epitome of the spirit of the nineteenth century.

And much, if not all, of this marvellous transformation, of this abounding life and vigorous vitality, is due to the energy and the forethought, the will of one man. It is notorious that the Swindon of to-day is the creation of the companion of Brunel at the lunch in the furze-bushes. Sir Daniel Gooch has had a wonderful life. Beginning literally at the beginning, he rose from stage to stage, till he became the responsible head of the vast company in whose service he had commenced life. In that position he did not forget the place where his early years were passed, but used his influence to enrich it with the real secret of wealth, employment for the people. In so doing, time has proved that he acted for the best interests of the company, for, apart from monetary matters, the mass of workmen assembled at this spot are possessed of overwhelming political power, and can return the man they choose to Parliament. Thus the company secures a representative in the House of Commons.

Among the institutions which the railway company fostered was the primitive reading-room which has been alluded to. Under their care this grew and grew, until it became a Mechanics' Institute, or, rather, a department of science and art, which at the present day has an intimate connection with South Kensington. Some hundred prizes are here annually distributed to the numerous students, both male and female, who can here obtain the very best instruction, at the very smallest cost, in almost every branch of learning, from sewing to shorthand, from freehand drawing to algebra and conic sections. On one occasion, while distributing the prizes to the successful competitors, Sir Daniel Gooch laid bare some of his early struggles as an incentive to the youth around him. He admitted that there was a time, and a dark hour, when he all but gave up hopes of ultimate success, when it seemed that the dearest wish of his heart must for ever go without fulfilment. In this desponding mood he was slowly crossing a bridge in London, when he observed an inscription upon the parapet—*Nil Desperandum* (Never despair). How he took heart at this as an omen, and went forth and persevered till—— The speaker did not complete the sentence, but all the world knows what ultimately happened, and remembers the man who laid the first Atlantic cable. The great lesson of perseverance, of patience, was never drawn with better effect.

In the Eastern tales of magicians one reads of a town being found one day where there was nothing but sand the day before. Here the fable is fact, and the potent magician is Steam. Here is, perhaps, the greatest temple that has ever been built to that great god of our day. Taking little note of its immense extent, of the vast walls which enclose it, like some fortress, of the tunnel which gives entrance, and through which three thousand workmen pass four times a day, let us enter at once and go straight to the manufacture of those wheels and tires and axles of which we have heard so much since the tragedy at Shipton. To look at a carriage-wheel, the iron carriage-wheel, one would imagine that it was all one piece, that it was stamped out at a blow, so little sign is there of a junction of parts. The very contrary is the fact: the wheel is made of a large number of pieces of iron welded together, and again and again welded together, till at last it forms one solid homogeneous mass. The first of these processes consists in the manufacture of the spokes, which are made out of fine iron. The spoke is made in two pieces, at two different forges, and by two distinct gangs of men. A third forge and a third gang are constantly employed in welding these two detached parts in one continuous piece, forming a spoke. One of these parts resembles a T with the downward stroke very short, and the cross stroke at the top slightly bent, so as to form a section of a curve. The other piece is about the same length, but rather thicker, and at its larger end somewhat wedge-shaped. This last piece forms that part of the spoke which goes nearest to the centre of the wheel. These two parts, when completed, are again heated to a red heat, and in that ductile state hammered with dexterous blows into one, which then resembles the same letter T, only with the downward stroke disproportionately long. Eight or more of these spokes, according to the size of the wheel, and whether it is intended for a carriage, an engine, or tender, are then arranged together on the ground, so that the wedge-shaped ends fit close together, and in that position are firmly fixed by the imposition above them of what is called a 'washer,' a flat circular piece of iron, which is laid red-hot on the centre of the embryo wheel, and there hammered into cohesion. The wheel is then turned over, and a second 'washer' beaten on, so that the partially molten metal runs, and joins together with the particles of the spokes, and the whole is one mass. In the ordinary cart-wheel or gig-wheel the spokes are placed in mortise-holes made in a solid central block ; but in this wheel before us, the ends of the spokes, well cemented together by the two washers, form the central block or boss. The ends of the spokes do not quite touch each other, and so a small circular space is left which is subsequently bored to fit the axle. The wheel now presents a curiously incomplete appearance, for the top strokes of the T's do not touch each other. There is a space between each, and these spaces have now to be filled with pieces of red-hot iron well welded and hammered together. To the uninitiated it would seem that all this work is superfluous ; that the wheel might be made much more quickly in two or three pieces, instead of all these, and that it would be stronger.

But the practical men engaged in the work say differently. It is their maxim that the more iron is hammered, the stronger and better it becomes; therefore all this welding adds to the strength of the wheel. In practice it is found quicker and more convenient to thus divide the labour than to endeavour to form the wheel of fewer component parts. The wheel is now taken to the lathe, and a portion is cut away from its edge, till a groove is left so as to dovetail into the tyre.

The tyres, which are of steel, are not made here; they come ready to be placed upon the wheel, and some care has to be taken in moving them, for, although several inches in thickness and of enormous strength, it has occasionally happened that a sudden jar from other solid bodies has fractured them. One outer edge of the tyre is prolonged, so to say, and forms the projecting flange which holds the rails and prevents the carriage from running off the road. So important a part requires the best metal and the most careful manufacture, and accordingly no trouble or expense is spared to secure suitable tyres. One of the inner edges of the tyre, on the opposite side to the flange, is grooved, and this groove is intended to receive the edge of the wheel itself; they dovetail together here. The tyre is now made hot, and the result of that heating is an expansion of the metal, so that the circle of the tyre becomes larger. The wheel is then driven into the tyre, which fits round it like a band. As it grows cool the steel tyre clasps the iron wheel with enormous force, and the softer metal is driven into the groove of the steel. But this is not all. The wheel is turned over, and the iron wheel is seen to be some little distance sunk, as it were, beneath the surface of the tyre. Immediately on a level with the iron wheel there runs round the steel tyre another deeper groove. The wheel is again heated—not to redness, for the steel will not bear blows if too hot—and when the tyre is sufficiently warm, a long, thin strip of iron is driven into this groove, and so shuts the iron wheel into the tyre as with a continuous wedge. Yet another process has to follow—yet another safeguard against accident. The tyre, once more heated, is attacked with the blows of three heavy sledge-hammers, wielded by as many stalwart smiths, and its inner edge, by their well-directed blows, bent down over the narrow band of iron, or continuous wedge, so that this wedge is closed in by what may be called a continuous rivet. The wheel is now complete, so far as its body is concerned, and to look at, it seems very nearly impossible that any wear or tear, or jar or accident, could disconnect its parts—all welded, overlapped, dovetailed as they are. Practically it seems the perfection of safety ; nor was it to a wheel of this character that *the* accident happened. The only apparent risk is that there may be some slight undiscovered flaw in the solid steel which, under the pressure of unforeseen circumstances, may give way. But the whole design of the wheel is to guard against the ill-effects that would follow the snapping of a tyre. Suppose a tyre to ' fly '—the result would be a small crack ; supposing there were two cracks, or ten cracks, the speciality of this wheel is that not one of those pieces could come off—that the wheel would run as well and as safely with a tyre cracked through in a dozen places as when perfectly sound. The reason of this is that every single quarter of an inch of the tyre is fixed irremovably to the outer edge of the iron wheel, by the continuous dovetail, by the continuous wedge, and by the continuous over-lapping. So that under no condition could any portion of the tyre fly off from the wheel. Close by this wheel thus finished upon this patent process there was an old riveted wheel which had been brought in to receive a new tyre on the new process. This old wheel aptly illustrates the advantages of the new one. Its tyre is fixed to the wheel by rivets or bolts placed at regular intervals. Now, the holes made for these bolts to some extent weaken both tyre and wheel. The bolt is liable, with constant shaking, to wear loose. The bolt only holds a very limited area of tyre to the wheel. If the tyre breaks in two places between the bolts, it comes off. If a bolt breaks, or the tyre breaks at the bolt, it flies. The tyre is, in fact, only fixed on in spots with intervals between. The new fastening leaves no intervals, and instead of spots is fixed everywhere. This is called the Gibson process, and was invented by an employé of the company. Latterly another process has partially come into vogue, particularly for wooden wheels, which are preferred sometimes on account of their noiselessness. By this (the Mansell) process, the tyres, which are similar, are fastened to the wheels by two circular bands which dovetail into the tyre, and are then bolted to the wood.

To return to the wheel—now really and sub-stantially a wheel, but which has still to be turned so as to run perfectly true upon the metals—it is conveyed to the wheel lathe, and affixed to what looks like another wheel, which is set in motion by steam-power, and carries our wheel round with it. A workman sets a tool to plane its edge, which shaves off the steel as if it were wood, and reduces it to the prescribed scale. Then, when its centre has been bored to receive the axle, the genesis of the wheel is complete, and it enters upon its life of perpetual revolution. How little do the innumerable travellers who are carried to their destination upon it imagine the immense expenditure of care, skill, labour, and thought that has been expended before a perfect wheel was produced.

Next in natural order come the rails upon which the wheel must run. The former type of rail was a solid bar of iron, whose end presented a general resemblance to the letter T, which was thick at the top and at the bottom, and smaller in the middle. It was thought that this rail was not entirely satis-factory, for reasons that cannot be enumerated here, and accordingly a patent was taken out for a rail which, it is believed, can be more easily and cheaply manufactured, with a less expenditure of metal, and which can be more readily attached to the sleepers. In reality it is designed upon the principle of the arch, and the end of these rails somewhat resembles the Greek letter Ω, for they are hollow, and formed of a thin plate of metal rolled into this shape. Coming to this very abode of the Cyclops, the rail-mill, the first machine that appears resembles a pair of gigantic scissors, which are employed day and night in snipping off old rails and other pieces of iron into lengths suitable for the manufacture of new rails.

These scissors, or, perhaps, rather pincers, are driven by steam-power, and bite off the solid iron as if it were merely strips of ribbon. There is some danger in this process, for occasionally the metal breaks and flies, and men's hands are severely injured. At a guess, the lengths of iron for manufacture into rails may be about four feet long, and are piled up in flat pieces eight or nine inches or more in height. These pieces are carried to the furnace, heated to an intense heat, and then placed under the resistless blows of a steam-hammer, which welds them into one solid bar of iron, longer than the separate pieces were. The bar then goes back to the furnace, and again comes out white-hot. The swinging-shears seize it, and it is swung along to the rollers. These rollers are two massive cylindrical iron bars which revolve rapidly one over the other. The end of the white-hot metal is placed between these rollers, and is at once drawn out into a long strip of iron, much as a piece of dough is rolled out under the cook's rolling-pin. It is now perfectly flat, and entirely malleable. It is returned to the furnace, heated, brought back, and placed in a second pair of rollers. This second pair have projections upon them, which so impress the flat strip of iron that it is drawn out into the required shape. The rail passes twice through these rollers, once forwards, then backwards. Terrible is the heat in this fiery spot. The experienced workman who guides the long red-hot rails to the mouth of the rollers is protected with a mask, with iron-shod shoes, iron greaves on his legs, an iron apron, and, even further, with a shield of iron. The very floor beneath is formed of slabs of iron instead of slabs of stone, and the visitor very soon finds this iron floor too hot for his feet. The perfect rail, still red-hot or nearly, is run back to the circular saw, which cuts it off in regular lengths; for it is not possible to so apportion the iron in each bundle as to form absolutely identical strips. They are proportioned so as to be a little longer than required, and then sawn off to the exact length. While still hot, a workman files the sawn ends so that they may fit together closely when laid down on the sleepers. The completed rails are then stacked for removal on trucks to their destination. The rollers which turn out these rails in so regular and beautiful a manner are driven by a pair of engines of enormous power. The huge fly-wheel is twenty feet in diameter, and weighs, with its axle, thirty-five tons. When these rails were first manufactured, the rollers were driven direct from the axle of the fly-wheel, and the rails had to be lifted right over the roller—a difficult and dangerous process—and again inserted between them on the side at which it started. Since then an improvement has been effected, by which the rails are sent backwards through the rollers, thus avoiding the trouble of lifting them over. This is managed by reversing the motion of the rollers, which is done in an instant by means of a 'crab.'

Immediately adjacent to these rail-mills are the steam-hammers, whose blows shake the solid earth. The largest descends with the force of seventy tons, yet so delicate is the machinery that visitors are shown how the same ponderous mass of metal and the same irresistible might can be so gently adminis-tered as to crush the shell of a nut without injuring the kernel. These hammers are employed in beat-ing huge masses of iron into cranks for engines, and other heavy work which is beyond the unaided strength of man. Each of the hammers has its own steam-boiler and its furnace close at hand, and over-head there are travelling cranes which convey the metal to and fro. These boilers may be called vertical, and with the structure on which they are supported have a dome-like shape. Hissing, with small puffs of white steam curling stealthily upwards, they resemble a group of volcanoes on the eve of an eruption. This place presents a wonderful and even terrible aspect at night, when the rail-mill and steam-hammers are in full swing. The open doors of the glaring furnaces shoot forth an insupportable beam of brilliant white light, and out from among the glowing fire comes a massive bar of iron, hotter,

whiter than the fire itself—barely to be looked upon.
It is dragged and swung along under the great
hammer; Thor strikes, and the metal doubles up,
and bends as if of plastic clay, and showers of sparks
fly high and far. What looks like a long strip of
solid flame is guided between the rollers, and flattened
and shaped, till it comes out a dull-red-hot rail, and
the sharp teeth of the circular saw cut through it,
throwing out a circle of sparks. The vast fly-wheel
whirls round endless shaftings, and drums are revolving overhead, and the ear is full of a ceaseless
overpowering hum, varied at intervals with the
sharp scraping, ringing sound of the saw. The
great boilers hiss, the furnaces roar, all around there
is a sense of an irresistible power, but just held in
by bars and rivets, ready in a moment to rend all
asunder. Masses of glowing iron are wheeled hither
and thither in wheelbarrows; smaller blocks are slid
along the iron floor. Here is a heap of red-hot
scraps hissing. A sulphurous hot smell prevails, a
burning wind, a fierce heat, now from this side, now
from that, and ever and anon bright streaks of light
flow out from the open furnace doors, casting
grotesque shadows upon the roof and walls. The
men have barely a human look, with the reflection
of the fire upon them; mingling thus with flame and
heat, toying with danger, handling, at it seems, red-
hot metal with ease. The whole scene suggests the
infernal regions. A mingled hiss and roar and thud
fill the building with reverberation, and the glare of
the flames rising above the chimneys throws a re-

flection upon the sky, which is visible miles away, like that of a conflagration.

Stepping out of this pandemonium, there are rows upon rows of gleaming forges, each with its appointed smiths, whose hammers rise and fall in rhythmic strokes, and who manufacture the minor portions of the incipient locomotive. Here is a machine the central part of which resembles a great corkscrew or spiral constantly revolving. A weight is affixed to its inclined plane, and is carried up to the required height by the revolution of the screw, to be let fall upon a piece of red-hot iron, which in that moment becomes a bolt, with its projecting head or cap. Though they do not properly belong to our subject, the great marine boilers in course of construction in the adjoining department cannot be overlooked, even if only for their size—vast cylinders of twelve feet diameter. Next comes the erecting shop, where the various parts of the locomotive are fitted together, and it is built up much as a ship from the keel. These semi-completed engines have a singularly helpless look—out of proportion, without limbs, and many mere skeletons. Close by is the department where engines out of repair are made good. Some American engineer started the idea of a railway thirty feet wide, an idea which in this place is partially realized. The engine to be repaired is run on to what may be described as a turn-table resting upon wheels, and this turn-table is bodily rolled along, like a truck, with the engine on it, to the place where tools and cranes and all the necessary gear are ready for the work upon it. Now by a yard, which seems one vast assemblage of wheels of all kinds—big wheels, little wheels, wheels of all sizes, nothing but wheels; past great mounds of iron, shapeless heaps of scrap, and then, perhaps, the most interesting shop of all, though the least capable of description, is entered. It is where the endless pieces of metal of which the locomotive is composed are filed and planed and smoothed into an accurate fit; an immense building, with shafting overhead and shafting below in endless revolution, yielding an incessant hum like the sound of armies of bees—a building which may be said to have a score of aisles, up which one may walk with machinery upon either side. Hundreds of lathes of every conceivable pattern are planing the solid steel and the solid iron as if it were wood, cutting off with each revolution a more or less thick slice of the hard metal, which curls up like a shaving of deal. So delicate is the touch of some of these tools, so good the metal they are employed to cut, that shavings are taken off three or more feet long, curled up like a spiral spring, and which may be wound round the hand like string. The interiors of the cylinders, the bearings, those portions of the engines which slide one upon the other, and require the most accurate fit, are here adjusted by unerring machinery, which turns out the work with an ease and exactness which the hand of man, delicate and wonderful organ as it is, cannot reach. From the smallest fitting up to the great engine cranks, the lathes smooth them all—reduce them to the precise size which they were intended to be by the draughtsman. These cranks and larger pieces of metal are conveyed to their lathes and placed in position by a steam crane, which glides along upon a single rail at the will of the driver, who rides on it, and which handles the massive metal almost with the same facility that an elephant would move a log of wood with his trunk. Most of us have an inherent idea that iron is exceedingly hard, but the ease with which it is cut and smoothed by these machines goes far to remove that impression.

The carriage department does not offer so much that will strike the eye, yet it is of the highest importance. To the uninitiated it is difficult to trace the connection between the various stages of the carriage, as it is progressively built up, and finally painted and gilded and fitted with cushions. Generally, the impression left from an inspection is that the frames of the carriages are made in a way calculated to secure great strength, the material being solid oak. The brake-vans especially are made strong. The carriages made here are for the narrow gauge, and are immensely superior in every way to the old broad-gauge carriage, being much more roomy, although not so wide. Over the department there lingers an odour of wood. It is common to speak of the scented woods of the East and the South, but even our English woods are not devoid of pleasant odour under the carpenter's hands. Hidden away amongst the piles of wood there is here a triumph of human ingenuity. It is an endless

saw which revolves around two wheels, much in the
same way as a band revolves around two drums.
The wheels are perhaps three feet in diameter, and
two inches in thickness at the circumference. They
are placed — one as low as the workman's feet,
another rather above his head—six or seven feet
apart. Round the wheels there stretches an endless
narrow band of blue steel, just as a ribbon might.
This band of steel is very thin, and almost half an
inch in width. Its edge towards the workman is
serrated with sharp deep teeth. The wheels revolve
by steam rapidly, and carry with them the saw, so
that, instead of the old up and down motion, the
teeth are continually running one way. The band
of steel is so extremely flexible that it sustains the
state of perpetual curve. There are stories in ancient
chronicles of the wonderful swords of famous warriors
made of such good steel that the blade could be bent
till the point touched the hilt, and even till the blade
was tied in a knot. These stories do not seem like
fables before this endless saw, which does not bend
once or twice, but is incessantly curved, and incessantly in the act of curving. A more beautiful
machine cannot be imagined. Its chief use is to cut
out the designs for cornices, and similar ornamental
work in thin wood; but it is sufficiently strong to
cut through a two-inch plank like paper. Every
possible support that can be afforded by runners is
given to the saw; still, with every aid, it is astonishing to see metal, which we have been taught to
believe rigid, flexible as indiarubber. Adjoining are

frame saws, working up and down by steam, and cutting half a dozen or more boards at the same time. It was in this department that the Queen's carriage was built at a great expenditure of skill and money—a carriage which is considered one of the masterpieces of this particular craft.

There rises up in the mind, after the contemplation of this vast workshop, with its endless examples of human ingenuity, a conviction that safety in railway travelling is not only possible, but probable, and even now on the way to us. No one can behold the degree of excellence to which the art of manufacturing material has been brought, no one can inspect the processes by which the wheel, for instance, is finally welded into one compact mass, without a firm belief that, where so much has been done, in a little time still more will be done. That safer plans, that better designs, that closer compacted forms will arise seems as certain and assured a fact as that those forms now in use arose out of the rude beginnings of the past; for this great factory, both in its machine-tools and in its products, the wheels and rails and locomotives, is a standing proof of the development which goes on in the mind of man when brought constantly to bear upon one subject. As with the development of species, so it is with that of machinery: rude and more general forms first, finer and more specialized forms afterwards. There is every reason to hope, for this factory is a proof of the advance that has been made. It would seem that the capability of metal is practically infinite.

But what an enormous amount of labour, what skill, and what complicated machinery must be first employed before what is in itself a very small result can be arrived at! In order that an individual may travel from London to Oxford, see what innumerable conditions have to be fulfilled. Three thousand men have to work night and day that we may merely seat ourselves and remain passive till our destination is reached.

This small nation of workers, this army of the hammer, lathe, and drill, affords matter for deep meditation in its sociological aspect. Though so numerous that no one of them can be personally acquainted with more than a fractional part, yet there is a strong *esprit de corps*, a spirit that ascends to the highest among them; for it is well known that the chief manager has a genuine feeling of almost fatherly affection for these his men, and will on no account let them suffer, and will, if possible, obtain for them every advantage. The influence he thereby acquires among them is principally used for moral and re-ligious ends. Under these auspices have arisen the great chapels and places of worship of which the town is full. Of the men themselves, the majority are intelligent, contrasting strongly with the agri-cultural poor around them, and not a few are well educated and thoughtful. This gleaning of intel-lectual men are full of social life, or, rather, of an interest in the problems of social existence. They eagerly discuss the claims of religion *versus* the allegations of secularism; they are shrewd to detect the weak points of an argument; they lean, in fact, towards an eclecticism : they select the most rational part of every theory. They are full of information on every subject—information obtained not only from newspapers, books, conversation, and lectures, but from travel, for most have at least been over the greater part of England. They are probably higher in their intellectual life than a large proportion of the so-called middle classes. One is, indeed, tempted to declare, after considering the energy with which they enter on all questions, that this class of educated mechanics forms in reality the protoplasm, or living matter, out of which modern society is evolved. The great and well-supplied reading-room of the Mechanics' Institute is always full of readers; the library, now an extensive one, is constantly in use. Where one book is read in agricultural districts, fifty are read in the vicinity of the factory. Social questions of marriage, of religion, of politics, sanitary science, are for ever on the simmer among these men. It would almost seem as if the hammer, the lathe, and the drill would one day bring forth a creed of its own. A characteristic of all classes of these workmen is their demand for meat, of which great quantities are consumed. Nor do they stay at meat alone, but revel in fish and other luxuries at times, though the champagne of the miner is not known here. Notwithstanding the number of public-houses, it is a remarkable fact that there is very little drunkenness in proportion to the population, few crimes of violence, and, what is more singular still, and has been often remarked, very little immorality. Where there are some hundreds, perhaps thousands, of young uneducated girls, without work to occupy their time, there must of course exist a certain amount of lax conduct; but never, or extremely rarely, does a girl apply to the magistrates for an affiliation order, while from agricultural parishes such applications are common. The number of absolutely immoral women openly practising infamy is also remarkably small. There was a time when the work-men at this factory enjoyed an unpleasant notoriety for mischief and drunkenness, but that time has passed away, a most marked improvement having taken place in the last few years.

There appears, however, to be very little prudence amongst them. The man who receives some extra money for extra work simply spends it on unusual luxuries in food or drink; or, if it be summer, takes his wife and children a drive in a hired conveyance. To this latter there can be no objection; but still, the fact remains prominent that men in the receipt of good wages do not save. They do not put by money; this is, of course, speaking of the majority. It would almost seem to be a characteristic of human nature that those who receive wages for work done, so much per week or fortnight, do not contract saving habits. The small struggling tradesman, whose income is very little more than that of the mechanic, often makes great exertions and practises much economy to put by a sum to assist him in difficulty or to extend his business. It may be that

the very certainty of the wages acts as a deterrent—
inasmuch as the mechanic feels safe of his weekly
money, while the shopkeeper runs much risk.   It is
doubtful whether mechanics with good wages save
more than agricultural labourers, except in indirect
ways—ways which are thrust upon them.   First of
all, there is the yard club, to which all are compelled
to pay by their employers, the object being to provide medical assistance in case of sickness.   This is
in some sense a saving.   Then there are the building
societies, which offer opportunities of possessing a
house, and the mechanic who becomes a member has
to pay for it by instalments.   This also may be called
an indirect saving, since the effect is the same.   But
of direct saving—putting money in a bank, or investing it—there is scarcely any.   The quarter of a
million annually paid in wages mostly finds its way
into the pockets of the various trades-people, and at
the end of the year the mechanic is none the better
off.   This is a grave defect in his character.   Much
of it results from a generous, liberal disposition : a
readiness to treat a friend with a drink, to drive the
family out into the country, to treat the daughter
with a new dress.   The mechanic does not set a
value upon money in itself.

The effect of the existence of this factory upon
the whole surrounding district has been marked.   A
large proportion of the lower class of mechanics,
especially the factory labourers, are drawn from the
agricultural poor of the adjacent villages.   These
work all day at the factory, and return at night.

They daily walk great distances to secure this employment: three miles to and three miles back is common, four miles not uncommon, and some have been known to walk six or twelve miles per day. These carry back with them into the villages the knowledge they insensibly acquire from their better-informed comrades, and exhibit an independent spirit. For a radius of six miles round the poorer class are better informed, quicker in perception, more ready with an answer to a question, than those who dwell farther back out of the track of modern life. Wages had materially risen long before the movement among the agricultural labourers took place.

Where there was lately nothing but furze and rabbits there is now a busy human population. Why was it that for so many hundreds of years the population of England remained nearly stationary? and why has it so marvellously increased in this last forty years? The history of this place seems to answer that interesting question. The increase is due to the facilities of communication which now exist, and to the numberless new employments in which that facility of communication took rise, and which it in turn adds to and fosters.

UNEQUAL AGRICULTURE

In the way of sheer, downright force few effects of machinery are more striking than a steam-ploughing engine dragging the shares across a wide expanse of stiff clay. The huge engines used in our ironclad vessels work with a graceful ease which deceives the eye ; the ponderous cranks revolve so smoothly, and shine so brightly with oil and polish, that the mind is apt to underrate the work performed. But these ploughing engines stand out solitary and apart from other machinery, and their shape itself suggests crude force, such force as may have existed in the mastodon or other unwieldy monster of the prehistoric ages. The broad wheels sink into the earth under the pressure ; the steam hissing from the escape valves is carried by the breeze through the hawthorn hedge, hiding the red berries with a strange, unwonted cloud ; the thick dark brown smoke, rising from the funnel as the stoker casts its food of coal into the fiery mouth of the beast, falls again and floats heavily over the yellow stubble, smothering and driving away the partridges and hares. There is a smell of oil, and cotton-waste, and gas, and steam, and smoke, which overcomes the fresh, sweet odour of the earth and green things after a shower. Stray lumps of coal crush the delicate pimpernel and creeping convolvulus. A shrill, short scream rushes forth and echoes back from an adjacent rick—puff! the fly-wheel revolves, and the drum underneath tightens its hold upon the wire rope. Across yonder a curious, shapeless thing, with a man riding upon it, comes jerking forward, tearing its way through stubble and clay, dragging its iron teeth with sheer strength deep through the solid earth. The thick wire rope stretches and strains as if it would snap and curl up like a tortured snake ; the engine pants loudly and quick ; the plough now glides forward, now pauses, and, as it were, eats its way through a tougher place, then glides again, and presently there is a pause, and behold the long furrow with the upturned subsoil is completed. A brief pause, and back it travels again, this time drawn from the other side, where a twin monster puffs and pants and belches smoke, while the one that has done its work uncoils its metal sinews. When the furrows run up and down a slope, the savage force, the fierce, remorseless energy of the engine pulling the plough upwards, gives an idea of power which cannot but impress the mind.

This is what is going on upon one side of the hedge. These engines cost as much as the fee-simple of a small farm ; they consume expensive coal, and water that on the hills has to be brought long distances ; they require skilled workmen to attend to them, and they do the work with a thoroughness which leaves little to be desired. Each puff and pant echoing from the ricks, each shrill whistle rolling along from hill to hill, proclaims as loudly as iron and steel can shout, 'Progress! Onwards!' Now step through this gap in the hedge and see what is going on in the next field.

It is a smaller ground, of irregular shape and uneven surface. Steam-ploughs mean *plains* rather than fields—broad, square expanses of land without awkward corners—and as level as possible, with mounds that may have been tumuli worked down, rising places smoothed away, old ditch-like drains filled up, and fairly good roads. This field may be triangular or some indescribable figure, with narrow corners where the high hedges come close together, with deep furrows to carry away the water, rising here and sinking there into curious hollows, entered by a narrow gateway leading from a muddy lane where the ruts are a foot deep. The plough is at work here also, such a plough as was used when the Corn Laws were in existence, chiefly made of wood—yes, actually wood, in this age of iron—bound and strengthened with metal, but principally made from the tree—the tree which furnishes the African savage at this day with the crooked branch with which to scratch the earth, which furnished the ancient agriculturists of the Nile Valley with their primitive implements. It is drawn by dull, patient oxen, plodding onwards now just as they were depicted upon the tombs and temples, the graves and worshipping places, of races who had their being three thousand years ago. Think of the suns that have shone since then; of the summers and the bronzed grain waving in the wind, of the human teeth that have ground that grain, and are now hidden in the abyss of earth; yet still the oxen plod on, like slow Time itself, here this day in our land of steam and telegraph. Are not these striking pictures, remarkable contrasts? On the one side steam, on the other the oxen of the Egyptians, only a few thorn-bushes between dividing the nineteenth century B.C. from the nineteenth century A.D. After these oxen follows an aged man, slow like themselves, sowing the seed. A basket is at his side, from which at every stride, regular as machinery, he takes a handful of that corn round which so many mysteries have gathered from the time of Ceres to the hallowed words of the great Teacher, taking His parable from the sower. He throws it with a peculiar *steady* jerk, so to say, and the grains, impelled with the exact force and skill, which can only be attained by long practice, scatter in an even shower. Listen! On the other side of the hedge the rattle of the complicated drill resounds as it drops the seed in regular rows—and, perhaps, manures it at the same time—so that the plants can be easily thinned out, or the weeds removed, after the magical influence of the despised clods has brought on the miracle of vegetation.

These are not extreme and isolated instances; no one will need to walk far afield to witness similar contrasts. There is a medium between the two—

a third class—an intermediate agriculture. The pride of this farm is in its horses, its teams of magnificent animals, sleek and glossy of skin, which the carters spend hours in feeding lest they should lose their appetites—more hours than ever they spend in feeding their own children. These noble creatures, whose walk is power and whose step is strength, work a few hours daily, stopping early in the afternoon, taking also an ample margin for lunch. They pull the plough also like the oxen, but it is a modern implement, of iron, light, and with all the latest improvements. It is typical of the system itself—half and half—neither the old oxen nor the new steam, but midway, a compromise. The fields are small and irregular in shape, but the hedges are cut, and the mounds partially grubbed and reduced to the thinnest of banks, the trees thrown, and some draining done. Some improvements have been adopted, others have been omitted.

Upon those broad acres where the steam-plough was at work, what tons of artificial manure, superphosphate, and guano, liquid and solid, have been sown by the progressive tenant! Lavishly and yet judiciously, not once only, but many times, have the fertilizing elements been restored to the soil, and more than restored—added to it, till the earth itself has grown richer and stronger. The scarifier and the deep plough have turned up the subsoil and exposed the hard, stiff under-clods to the crumbling action of the air and the mysterious influence of light. Never before since Nature deposited those earthy atoms there

in the slow process of some geological change has the
sunshine fallen on them, or their latent power been
called forth.   Well-made and judiciously laid drains
carry away the flow of water from the winter rains
and floods—no longer does there remain a species of
reservoir at a certain depth, chilling the tender roots
of the plants as they strike downwards, lowering the
entire temperature of the field.   Mounds have been
levelled, good roads laid down, nothing left undone
that can facilitate operations or aid in the production
of strong, succulent vegetation.   Large flocks of well-
fed sheep, folded on the corn-lands, assist the artificial
manure, and perhaps even surpass it.   When at last
the plant comes to maturity and turns colour under
the scorching sun, behold a widespread ocean of
wheat, an English gold-field, a veritable Yellow Sea,
bowing in waves before the southern breeze—a sight
full of peaceful poetry.   The stalk is tall and strong,
good in colour, fit for all purposes.   The ear is full,
large ; the increase is truly a hundredfold.   Or it
may be roots.   By these means the progressive agriculturist has produced a crop of swedes or mangolds
which in individual size and collective weight per
acre would seem to an old-fashioned farmer perfectly
fabulous.   Now, here are many great benefits.   First,
the tenant himself reaps his reward, and justly adds
to his private store.   Next, the property of the
landlord is improved, and increases in value.   The
labourer gets better house accommodation, gardens,
and higher wages.   The country at large is supplied
with finer qualities and greater quantities of food,

and those who are engaged in trade and manufactures, and even in commerce, feel an increased vitality in their various occupations.

On the other side of the hedge, where the oxen were at plough, the earth is forced to be self-supporting — to restore to itself how it can the elements carried away in wheat and straw and root. Except a few ill-fed sheep, except some small quantities of manure from the cattle-yards, no human aid, so to say, reaches the much-abused soil. A crop of green mustard is sometimes ploughed in to decompose and fertilize, but as it had to be grown first the advantage is doubtful. The one object is to spend as little as possible upon the soil, and to get as much out of it as may be. Granted that in numbers of cases no trickery be practised, that the old rotation of crops is honestly followed, and no evil meant, yet even then, in course of time, a soil just scratched on the surface, never fairly manured, and always in use, must of necessity deteriorate. Then, when such an effect is too patent to be any longer overlooked, when the decline of the produce begins to alarm him, the farmer, perhaps, buys a few hundredweight of artificial manure, and frugally scatters it abroad. This causes 'a flash in the pan'; it acts as a momentary stimulus; it is like endeavouring to repair a worn-out constitution with doses of strong cordial; there springs up a vigorous vegetation one year, and the next the earth is more exhausted than before. Soils cannot be made highly fertile all at once even by superphosphates; it is the inability to discern this fact which leads many to still argue in the face of experience that artificial manures are of no avail. The slow oxen, the lumbering wooden plough, the equally lumbering heavy waggon, the primitive bush-harrow, made simply of a bush cut down and dragged at a horse's tail—these are symbols of a standstill policy utterly at variance with the times. Then this man loudly complains that things are not as they used to be—that wheat is so low in price it will not yield any profit, that labour is so high and everything so dear ; and, truly, it is easy to conceive that the present age, with its competition and eagerness to advance, must really press very seriously upon him.

Most persons have been interested enough, however little connected with agriculture, to at least once in their lives walk round an agricultural show, and to express their astonishment at the size and rotundity of the cattle exhibited. How easy, judging from such a passing view of the finest products of the country centred in one spot, to go away with the idea that under every hawthorn hedge a prize bullock of enormous girth is peacefully grazing ! Should the same person ever go across country, through gaps and over brooks, taking an Asmodeus-like glance into every field, how marvellously would he find that he had been deceived ! He might travel miles, and fly over scores of fields, and find no such animals, nor anything approaching to them. By making inquiries he would perhaps discover in most districts one spot where something of the kind could be seen

—an oasis in the midst of a desert. On the farm he would see a long range of handsome outhouses, tiled or slated, with comfortable stalls and every means of removing litter and manure, tanks for liquid manure, skilled attendants busy in feeding, in preparing food, storehouses full of cake. A steam-engine in one of the sheds—perhaps a portable engine, used also for threshing—drives the machinery which slices up or pulps roots, cuts up chaff, pumps up water, and performs a score of other useful functions. The yards are dry, well paved, and clean; everything smells clean; there are no foul heaps of decaying matter breeding loathsome things and fungi; yet nothing is wasted, not even the rain that falls upon the slates and drops from the eaves. The stock within are worthy to compare with those magnificent beasts seen at the show. It is from these places that the prize animals are drawn; it is here that the beef which makes England famous is fattened; it is from here that splendid creatures are sent abroad to America or the Colonies, to improve the breed in those distant countries. Now step forth again over the hedge, down yonder in the meadows.

This is a cow-pen, one of the old-fashioned style; in the dairy and pasture counties you may find them by hundreds still. It is pitched by the side of a tall hedge, or in an angle of two hedges, which themselves form two walls of the enclosure. The third is the cow-house and shedding itself; the fourth is made of willow rods. These rods are placed upright, confined between horizontal poles, and when new this simple contrivance is not wholly to be despised; but when the rods decay, as they do quickly, then gaps are formed, through which the rain and sleet and bitter wind penetrate with ease. Inside this willow paling is a lower hedge, so to say, two feet distant from the other, made of willow work twisted—like a continuous hurdle. Into this rude manger, when the yard is full of cattle, the fodder is thrown. Here and there about the yard, also, stand cumbrous cribs for fodder, at which two cows can feed at once. In one corner there is a small pond, muddy, stagnant, covered with duckweed, perhaps reached by a steep, 'pitched' descent, slippery, and difficult for the cattle to get down. They foul the very water they drink. The cow-house, as it is called, is really merely adapted for one or two cows at a time, at the period of calving—dark, narrow, awkward. The skilling, or open house where the cows lie and chew the cud in winter, is built of boards or slabs at the back, and in front supported upon oaken posts standing on stones. The roof is of thatch, green with moss; in wet weather the water drips steadily from the eaves, making one long gutter. In the eaves the wrens make their nests in the spring, and roost there in winter. The floor here is hard, certainly, and dry; the yard itself is a sea of muck. Never properly stoned or pitched, and without a drain, the loose stones cannot keep the mud down, and it works up under the hoofs of the cattle in a filthy mass. Over this there is litter and manure a foot deep; or, if the

fogger does clean up the manure, he leaves it in great
heaps scattered about, and on the huge dunghill just
outside the yard he will show you a fine crop of
mushrooms cunningly hidden under a light layer of
litter. It is his boast that the cow-pen was built
in the three sevens; on one ancient beam, worm-
eaten and cracked, there may perhaps be seen the
inscription '1777' cut deep into the wood. Over
all, at the back of the cow-pen, stands a row of tall
elm-trees, dripping in wet weather upon the thatch,
in the autumn showering their yellow leaves into the
hay, in a gale dropping dead branches into the yard.
The tenant seems to think even this shelter effemin-
ate, and speaks regretfully of the old hardy breed
which stood all weathers, and wanted no more cover
than was afforded by a hawthorn bush. From here
a few calves find their way to the butcher, and
towards Christmas one or two moderately fat beasts.

Near by lives a dairy farmer, who, without going
to the length of the famous stock-breeder whose
stalls are the pride of the district, yet fills his
meadows with a handsome herd of productive shorthorns, giving splendid results in butter, milk, and
cheese, and who sends to the market a succession
of animals which, if not equal to the gigantic prize
beasts, are nevertheless valuable to the consumer.
This tenant does good work, both for himself and
for the labourers, the landlord, and the country.
His meadows are a sight in themselves to the experienced eye—well drained, great double mounds
thinned out, but the supply of wood not quite

destroyed—not a rush, a 'bullpoll,' a thistle, or a
'rattle,' those yellow pests of mowing grass, to be
seen. They have been weeded out as carefully as
the arable farmer weeds his plants. Where broad
deep furrows used to breed those aquatic grasses
which the cattle left, drains have been put in and
soil thrown over till the level was brought up to the
rest of the field. The manure carts have evidently
been at work here, perhaps the liquid manure tank
also, and some artificial aid in places where required,
both of seed and manure. The number of stock kept
is the fullest tale the land will bear, and he does no
hesitate to help the hay with cake in the fattening
stalls. For there are stalls, not so elaborately furnished as those of the famous stock-breeder, but
comfortable, clean, and healthy. Nothing is wasted
here either. So far as practicable the fields have
been enlarged by throwing two or three smaller
enclosures together. He does not require so much
machinery as the great arable farmer, but here are
mowing machines, haymaking machines, horse-
rakes, chain harrows, chaff-cutters, light carts
instead of heavy waggons — every labour-saving
appliance. Without any noise or puff this man is
doing good work, and silently reaping his reward.
Glance for a moment at an adjacent field : it is an
old 'leaze' or ground not mown, but used for
grazing. It has the appearance of a desert, a
wilderness. The high, thick hedges encroach upon
the land ; the ditches are quite arched over by the
brambles and briars which trail out far into the grass.

Broad deep furrows are full of tough, grey aquatic grass, 'bullpolls,' and short brown rushes ; in winter they are so many small brooks. Tall bennets from last year and thistle abound—half the growth is useless for cattle ; in autumn the air here is white with the clouds of thistle-down. It is a tolerably large field, but the meadows held by the same tenant are small, with double mounds and trees, rows of spreading oaks and tall elms ; these meadows run up into the strangest nooks and corners. Sometimes, where they follow the course of a brook which winds and turns, actually an area equal to about half the available field is occupied by the hedges. Into this brook the liquid sewage from the cow-pens filtrates, or, worse still, accumulates in a hollow, making a pond, disgusting to look at, but which liquid, if properly applied, is worth almost its weight in gold. The very gateways of the fields in winter are a Slough of Despond, where the wheels sink in up to the axles, and in summer great ruts jolt the loads almost off the waggons.

Where the steam-plough is kept, where first-class stock are bred, there the labourer is well housed, and his complaints are few and faint. There cottages with decent and even really capital accommodation for the families spring up, and are provided with extensive gardens. It is not easy, in the absence of statistics, to compare the difference in the amount of money put in circulation by these contrasted farms, but it must be something extraordinary. First comes the capital expenditure upon machinery—ploughs, engines, drills, what not—then the annual expenditure upon labour, which, despite the employment of machinery, is as great or greater upon a progressive farm as upon one conducted on stagnant principle. Add to this the cost of artificial manure, of cake and feeding-stuffs, etc., and the total will be something very heavy. Now, all this expenditure, this circulation of coin, means not only gain to the individual, but gain to the country at large. Whenever in a town a great manufactory is opened and gives employment to several hundred hands, at the same time increasing the production of a valuable material, the profit—the *outside* profit, so to say—is as great to others as to the proprietors. But these half-cultivated lands, these tons upon tons of wasted manure, these broad hedges and weed-grown fields, represent upon the other hand an equal loss. The labouring classes in the rural districts are eager for more work. They may popularly be supposed to look with suspicion upon change, but such an idea is a mistaken one. They anxiously wait the approach of such works as new railways or extension of old ones in the hope of additional employment. Work is their gold-mine, and the best mine of all. The capitalist, therefore, who sets himself to improve his holding is the very man they most desire to see. What scope is there for work upon a stagnant dairy farm of one hundred and fifty acres? A couple of foggers and milkers, a hedger and ditcher, two or three women at times, and there is the end. And such work!—mere animal labour, leading to so little result. The effect of constant, of lifelong application in such labour cannot but be deteriorating to the mind. The master himself must feel the dull routine. The steam-plough teaches the labourer who works near it something; the sight must react upon him, utterly opposed as it is to all the traditions of the past. The enterprise of the master must convey some small spirit of energy into the mind of the man. Where the cottages are built of wattle and daub, low and thatched—mere sheds, in fact—where the gardens are small, and the allotments, if any, far distant, and where the men wear a sullen, apathetic look, be sure the agriculture of the district is at a low ebb.

Are not these few pictures sufficient to show beyond a cavil that the agriculture of this country exhibits the strangest inequalities? Anyone who chooses can verify the facts stated, and may perhaps discover more curious anomalies still. The spirit of science is undoubtedly abroad in the homes of the English farmers, and immense are the strides that have been taken; but still greater is the work that remains to be done. Suppose anyone had a garden, and carefully manured, and dug over and over again, and raked, and broke up all the larger clods, and well watered one particular section of it, leaving all the rest to follow the dictates of wild nature, could he possibly expect the same amount of produce from those portions which, practically speaking, took care of themselves? Here are men of intellect and energy employing every possible means to develop the latent powers of the soil, and producing extraordinary results in grain and meat. Here also are others who, in so far as circumstances permit, follow in their footsteps. But there remains a large area in the great garden of England which, practically speaking, takes care of itself. The grass grows, the seed sprouts and germinates, very much how they may, with little or no aid from man. It does not require much penetration to arrive at the obvious conclusion that the yield does not nearly approach the possible production. Neither in meat nor corn is the tale equal to what it well might be. All due allowance must be made for barren soils of sand or chalk with thinnest layers of earth ; yet then there is an enormous area, where the soil is good and fertile, not properly productive. It would be extremely unfair to cast the blame wholly upon the tenants. They have achieved wonders in the past twenty years; they have made gigantic efforts and bestirred themselves right manfully. But a man may wander over his farm and note with discontented eye the many things he would like to do—the drains he would like to lay down, the manure he would like to spread abroad, the new stalls he would gladly build, the machine he so much wants—and then, shrugging his shoulders, reflect that he has not got the capital to do it with. Almost to a man they are sincerely desirous of progress ; those who cannot follow in great things do in little. Science and invention have done almost all that they can be expected to do ; chemistry and research have supplied powerful fertilizers. Machinery has been made to do work which at first sight seems incapable of being carried on by wheels and cranks. Science and invention may rest awhile : what is wanted is the universal application of their improvements by the aid of more capital. We want the great garden equally highly cultivated everywhere.

VILLAGE ORGANIZATION

THE great centres of population have almost entirely occupied the attention of our legislators of late years, and even those measures which affect the rural districts, or which may be extended to affect them at the will of the residents, have had their origin in the wish to provide for large towns. The Education Act arose out of a natural desire to place the means of learning within the reach of the dense population of such centres as London, Birmingham, Manchester, and others of that class; and although its operation extends to the whole country, yet those who have had any experience of its method of working in agricultural parishes will recognize at once that its designers did not contemplate the conditions of rurul life when they were framing their Bill. What is reasonable enough when applied to cities is often extremely inconvenient when applied to villages. It would almost seem as if the framers of the Bill left out of sight the circumstances which obtain in agricultural districts. It was obviously drawn up with a view to cities and towns, where an organization exists which can be called in to assist the new institution. This indifference of the Bill to the conditions of

country life is one of the reasons why it is so re-
luctantly complied with.   The number of School
Boards which have been called into existence in the
country is extremely small, and even where they do
exist they cannot be taken as representing a real
outcome of opinion on the part of the inhabitants.
They owe their establishment to certain causes which,
in process of time, bring the parish under the operation of the Act, with or without the will of the residents. This is particularly the case in parishes where
there is no large landlord, no one to take the initiative, and no large farmers to support the clergyman
in his attempt to obtain, or maintain, an independent
school. The matter is distinct from political feelings.
It arises in a measure from the desultory village life,
which possesses no organization, no power of combination.   Here is a large and fairly populous parish
without any great landowners, and, as a natural consequence, also without any large farmers.   The
property of the parish is in the hands of some score
of persons; it may be split up into almost infinitesimal holdings in the village itself. Now, everyone knows the thoroughly independent character of
an English farmer. He will follow what he considers
the natural lead of his landlord, if he occupy a
superior social position. He will follow his landlord
in a sturdy, independent way, but he will follow no
one else. Let there be no great landowner in the
parish, and any combination on the part of the agriculturists becomes impossible.   One man has one
idea, another another, and each and all are determined

not to yield an inch. Most of them are decidedly against the introduction of a School Board, and are quite ready to subscribe towards an independent school; but, then, when it comes to the administration of the school funds, there must be managers appointed to carry the plan into execution, and these managers must confer with the clergyman. Now here are endless elements of confusion and disagreement. One man thinks he ought to be a manager, and does not approve of the conduct of those who are in charge. Another dislikes the tone of the clergyman. A third takes a personal dislike to the schoolmaster who is employed. One little discord leads to further complication ; someone loses his temper, and personalities are introduced; then it is all over with the subscription, and the school ceases, simply because there are no funds. Finally, the Imperial authorities step in, and finding education at a dead-lock, a School Board is presently established, though in all probability nine out of ten are against it, but hold their peace in the hope of at last getting some kind of organization. So it will be found that the few country School Boards which exist are in parishes where there is no large landowner, or where the owner is a non-resident, or the property in Chancery. In other words, they exist in places where there is no natural chief to give expression to the feelings of the parish.

Agriculturists of all shades of political opinions are usually averse to a School Board. An ill-defined feeling is very often the strongest rule of conduct.

Now there is an ill-defined but very strong feeling that the introduction of a School Board means the placing of the parish more or less under imperial rule, and curtailing the freedom that has hitherto existed. This has been much strengthened by the experience gained during the last few years of the actual working of the Bill with respect to schools which are not Board Schools, but which come under the Government inspection. Every step of the proceedings shows only too plainly the utter unfitness of the clauses of the Bill to rural conditions. One of the most important clauses is that which insists upon a given amount of cubic space for each individual child. This has often entailed the greatest inconveniences, and very unnecessary expense. It was most certainly desirable that overcrowding and the consequent evolution of foul gases should be guarded against; and in great cities, where the air is always more or less impure, and contaminated with the effluvia from factories as well as from human breath, a large amount of cubic feet of space might properly be insisted upon; but in villages where the air is pure and free from the slightest contamination, villages situated often on breezy hills, or at worst in the midst of sweet meadow land, the hard-and-fast rule of so many cubic feet is an intolerable burden upon the supporters of the school. Still, that would not be so objectionable were it confined to the actual number of attendants at the school; but it would appear that the Government grant is not applicable to schools, unless they are large enough to allow to all children in the parish a certain given cubic space.

Now, as a matter of fact, nothing like all the children of the parish attend the school. In rural districts, especially, where the distance of cottages from the school is often very great, there will always be a heavy percentage of absentees. There will also be a percentage who attend schools in connection with a Dissenting establishment, and even a certain number who attend private schools, to say nothing of the numbers who never attend at all. It is, then, extremely hard that the subscribers to a school should be compelled to erect a building sufficiently large to allow of the given quantity of space to each and every child in the parish. Matters like these have convinced the residents in rural districts that the Act was framed without any consideration of their peculiar position, and they naturally feel repugnant to its introduction amongst them, and decline to make it in any way a foundation of village organization. The Act regulating the age at which children may be employed in agriculture was also an extension of an original Act, passed to protect the interest of children in cities and manufacturing districts. There is no objection to the Act except that it is a dead-letter. How many prosecutions have taken place under it? No one ever hears of anything of the kind, and probably no one ever will. The fact is, that since the universal use of machinery there is not so ready an employment for boys and children of that tender age as formerly. They are not by any means so greatly in demand, neither do they pay so well, on account of the much larger wages they now ask for. In addition, the farmers are strongly in favour of the education of their labourers' children, and place every facility in the way of those attending school. In many parishes a very strong moral pressure is voluntarily put upon the labouring poor to induce them to send their children, and the labouring poor themselves have awakened in a measure to the advantages of education. The Act, therefore, is practically a dead-letter, and bears no influence upon village life. These two Acts, and the alteration of the law relating to sanitary matters—by which the Guardians of the Poor become the rural sanitary authority—are the only legislation of modern days that goes direct to the heart of rural districts. The rural sanitary authority possesses great powers, but rarely exercises them. The constitution of that body forbids an active supervision. It is made up of one or two gentlemen from each parish, who are generally elected to that office without any contest, and simply because their brother farmers feel confidence in their judgment. The principal objects to which their attention is directed while at the board is to see that no unnecessary expenditure is permitted, so as to keep the rates at the lowest possible figure, and to state all they know of the conduct and position of the poor of their own parishes who apply for relief, in which latter matter they afford the most valuable assistance, many of the applicants having been known to them for a score of years or more. But if there is one thing a farmer dislikes more than another it is meddling and interfering with other persons' business. He would sooner put up with any amount of inconvenience, and even serious annoyance, than take an active step to remove the cause of his grumbling, if that step involves the operation of the law against his neighbours. The guardian who rides to the board meeting week after week may be perfectly well aware that the village which he represents is suffering under a common nuisance : that there is a pond in the middle of the place which emits an offensive odour; that there are three or four cottages in a dilapidated condition and unfit for human habitation, or crowded to excess with dirty tenants; or that the sewage of the place flows in an open ditch into the brook which supplies the inhabitants with water. He has not got power to deal with these matters personally, but he can, if he chooses, bring them before the notice of the board, which can instruct its inspector (probably also its relieving officer) to take action at law against the nuisance. But it is not to be expected that a single person will do anything of the kind.

There is in all properly-balanced minds an instinctive dislike to the office of public prosecutor, and nothing more unpopular could be imagined. The agriculturist who holds the office of guardian does not feel it his duty to act as common spy and informer, and he may certainly be pardoned if he neglects to act contrary to his feelings as a gentleman.

Therefore he rides by the stinking pond, the over-crowded cottages, the polluted water, week by week, and says nothing whatever. It is easy to remark that the board has its inspector, who is paid to report upon these matters; but the inspector has, in the first place, to traverse an enormous extent of country, and has no opportunity of becoming acquainted with nuisances which are not unbearably offensive. He has usually other duties to perform which occupy the greater part of his time, and he is certainly not overpaid for the work he does and the distance he travels. He also has his natural feelings upon the subject of making himself disagreeable, and he shrinks from interference, unless instructed by his superiors. His position is not sufficiently inde-pendent to render him, in all cases, a free agent; so it happens that the rural sanitary authority is prac-tically a nullity. It is too cumbrous, it meets at too great a distance, and its powers, after all, even when at last set in motion, are too limited to have any appreciable effect in ameliorating the condition of village life. But even if this nominal body were actively engaged in prosecuting offenders, the desired result would be far from being attained. One of the most serious matters is the supply of water for public use in villages. At the present moment there exists no authority which can cause a parish to be supplied with good drinking water. While the great centres of population have received the most minute attention from the Legislature, the large population which resides in villages has been left to its own devices, with the exception of the three measures, the first of which is unsuitable and strenuously opposed, the second a dead-letter, and the third cumbrous and practically inoperative.

Let us now examine the authorities which act under ancient enactments, or by reason of long standing, immemorial custom. The first of these may be taken to be the Vestry. The powers of the vestries appear to have formerly been somewhat extended, but in these latter times the influence they exercise has been very much curtailed. At the time when each parish relieved its own poor, the Vestry was practically the governing authority of the village, and possessed almost unlimited power, so far as the poor were concerned. That power was derived from its control over the supply of bread to the destitute. As the greater part of the working population received relief, it followed that the Vestry, composed of the agriculturists and landowners, was practically autocratic. Still longer ago, when the laws of the land contained certain enactments as to the attendance of persons at church, the Vestry had still greater powers. But at present, in most parishes, the Vestry is a nominal assembly, and frequently there is a difficulty in getting sufficient numbers of people together to constitute a legal authority. The poor rate is no longer made at the Vestry; the church rate is a thing of the past; and what is then left? There is the appointment of overseers, churchwardens, and similar formal matters; but the power has departed. In all probability they will never be resuscitated, because in all authorities of the kind there is a suspicion of Church influence; and there seems to be almost as much dislike to any shadow of that as against the political and temporal claims of the Roman Pontiff. The Vestry can never again become a popular vehicle of administration. The second is the Board of Guardians—though this is not properly a village or local authority at all, but merely a representative firm for the supervision of certain funds in which a number of villages are partners, and which can only be applied to a few stated purposes, under strictly limited conditions. There is no popular feeling involved in the expenditure of this fund, except that of economy, and almost any ratepayer may be trusted to vote for this; so that the office of guardian is a most routine one, and offers no opportunity of reform. Often one gentleman will represent a village for twenty years, being simply nominated, or even not as much as nominated, from year to year. If at last he grows tired of the monotony, and mentions it to his friends, they nominate another gentleman, always chosen for his good-fellowship and known dislike to change or interference—a man, in fact, without any violent opinions. He is nominated, and takes his seat. There is no emulation, no excitement. The Board of Guardians would assume more of the character of a local authority if it possessed greater freedom of action. But its course is so rigidly bound down by minute regulations and precedents that it really has no volition of its own, and can only deal with circumstances as they arise, according to a code laid down at a distance. It is not permitted to discriminate; it can neither relax nor repress; it is absolutely inelastic. In consequence it does not approach to the idea of a real local power, but rather resembles an assembly of unpaid clerks doling out infinitesimal sums of money to an endless stream of creditors, according to written instructions left by the absent head of the firm. Next there is the Highway Board; but this also possesses but limited authority, and deals only with roads. It has merely to see that the roads are kept in good repair, and that no encroachments are made upon them. Like the Board of Guardians, it is a most useful body; but its influence upon village life is indirect and indeterminate. There only remains the Court Leet. This, the most ancient and absolute of all, nevertheless approaches in principle nearest to the ideal of a local village authority. It is supposed to be composed of the lord of the manor, and of his court or jury of tenants, and its object is to see that the rights of the manor are maintained. The Court Leet was formerly a very important assembly, but in our time its offices are minute, and only apply to small interests. It is held at long intervals of time—as long, in some instances, as seven years—and is summoned by the steward of the lord of the manor, and commonly held at an inn, refreshments being supplied by the lord. Here come all the poor persons who occupy cottages or garden grounds on quit-rent, and pay their rent, which may amount in seven years

to as much as fourteen shillings.   A member of the
court will, perhaps, draw the attention of the court
to the fact that a certain ditch or watercourse has
become choked up, and requires clearing out or
diverting; and if this ditch be upon the manor, the
court can order it to be attended to.   On the manor
they have also jurisdiction over timber, paths, and
similar matters, and can order that a cottage which
is dilapidated shall be repaired or removed.   In point
of fact, however, the Court Leet is merely a jovial
assembly of the tenants upon the estate of the landowner, who drink so many bottles of sherry at his
expense, and set to right a few minute grievances.

In many places—the vast majority, indeed—there
is no longer any Court Leet held, because the
manorial rights have become faint and indistinct
with the passage of time; the manor has been sold,
split up into two or three estates, the entail cut off;
or the manor as a manor has totally disappeared
under the changes of ownership, and the various
deeds and liabilities which have arisen.   But this
merely general gathering of the farmers of the village
—where Court Leets are still held, all farmers are
invited, irrespective of their supposed allegiance to
the lord of the manor or not—this pleasant dinner
and sherry party, which meets to go through obsolete
customs, and exercise minute and barely legal rights,
contains nevertheless many of the elements of a
desirable local authority.   It is composed of gentlemen of all shades of opinion; no politics are introduced.   It meets in the village itself, and under the

direct sanction of the landowner. Its powers are confined to strictly local matters, and its members are thoroughly acquainted with those matters. The affairs of the village are discussed without acrimony, and a certain amount of understanding arrived at. It regulates disputes and grievances arising between the inhabitants of cottage property, and can see that that property is habitable. It acts more by custom, habit, more by acquiescence of the parties than by any imperious, hard-and-fast law laid down at a distance from the scene. But any hope of the resuscitation of Court Leets must not be entertained, because in so many places the manor is now merely 'reputed,' and has no proper existence; because, too, the lord of the manor may be living at a distance, and possess scarcely any property in the parish, except his 'rights.' The idea, however, of the agriculturists and principal residents in a village meeting in a friendly manner together, under the direct leadership of the largest landowner, to discuss village matters, is one that may be revived with some prospect of success. At present, who, pray, has the power of so much as convening a meeting of the parishioners, or of taking the sense of the village? It may be done by the churchwardens convening a Vestry, but a Vestry is extremely limited in authority, unpopular, and without any cohesion. Under the new Education Acts the signatures of a certain number of ratepayers to a requisition compels the officer appointed by law to call a meeting, but only for objects connected with the school. Upon consideration it appears that there

really is no village authority at all ; no recognized
place or time at which the principal inhabitants can
meet together and discuss the affairs of the parish
with a prospect of immediate action resulting. The
meetings of the magistrates at petty sessions, quarter
sessions, and at various other times are purposely
omitted from this argument, because there is rarely
more than one magistrate resident in a village, or at
most two, and the assemblies of these gentlemen at
a distance from their homes cannot be taken to form
a village council in any sense of the term.

The places where agriculturists and the principal
inhabitants of the parish do meet together and discuss
matters in a friendly spirit are the churchyard, before
service, the market dinner, the hunting-field, and the
village inn. The last has fallen into disuse. It used
to be the custom to meet at the central village inn
night after night to hear the news, as well as for con-
vivial purposes. In those days of slow travelling and
few posts, the news was communicated from village
to village by pedlars, or carriers' carts calling, as they
went, at each inn. But now it is a rare thing to find
farmers at the inn in their own village. The old
drinking habits have died out. It is not that there
is any prejudice against the inn ; but there is a cessation of the inducement to sit there night after night.
People do not care to drink as they used to, and they
can get the news just as well at home. The parlour
at the inn has ceased to be the village parliament.
The hunting-field is an unfavourable place for discussion, since in the midst of a remark the hounds may

start, and away go speaker and listener, and the subject is forgotten. The market dinner is not so general and friendly a meeting as it was. There is a large admixture of manure and machinery agents, travellers for seed-merchants, corn-dealers, and others who have no interest in purely local matters, and the dinner itself is somewhat formal, with its regular courses of fish and so forth, till the talk is more or less constrained and general. The churchyard is a singular place of meeting, but it is still popular. The agriculturist walks into the yard about a quarter to eleven, sees a friend; a third joins; then the squire strolls round from his carriage, and a pleasant chat ensues, till the ceasing bell reminds them that service is about to commence. But this is a very narrow representation of the village, and is perhaps never made up on two occasions of the same persons. The duration of the gathering is extremely short, and it has no cohesion or power of action.

It is difficult to convey an adequate idea of the desultory nature of village life. There is an utter lack of any kind of cohesion, a total absence of any common interest, or social bond of union. There is no *esprit de corps*. In old times there was, to a certain extent—in the days when each village was divided against its neighbour, and fiercely contested with it the honour of sending forth the best backsword player. No one wishes those times to return. We have still village cricket clubs, who meet each other in friendly battle, but there is no enthusiasm over it. The players themselves are scarcely excited, and it is often difficult to get sufficient together to fulfil an engagement. There is the dinner of the village benefit club, year after year. The object of the club is of the best, but its appearance upon club-day is a woeful spectacle to eyes that naturally look for a little taste upon an occasion of supposed festivity. What can be more melancholy than a procession of men clad in ill-fitting black clothes, in which they are evidently uncomfortable, with blue scarves over the shoulder, headed with a blatant brass band, and going first to church, and then all round the place for beer ? They eat their dinner and disperse, and then there is an end of the matter. There is no social bond of union, no connection.

It is questionable whether this desultoriness is a matter for congratulation. It fosters an idle, slow, clumsy, heedless race of men—men who are but great children, who have no public feeling whatever —without a leading idea. This fact was most patently exhibited at the last General Election, when the agricultural labourers for the first time exercised the franchise freely to any extent. The great majority of them voted plump for the candidate favoured by the squire or by the farmer. There was nothing unreasonable· in this ; it is natural and fit that men should support the candidate who comes nearest to their interest ; but, then, let there be some better reason for it than the simple fact 'that master goes that way.' Whether it be for Liberal or Conservative, whatever be the party, surely it is desirable that the labourer should possess a leading idea, an independent conviction of what is for the public good. Let it be a mistaken conviction, it is better than an absence of all feeling ; but politics are no part of the question. Politics apart, the villager might surely have some conception of what is best for his own native place, the parish in which he was born and bred, and with every field in which he is familiar. But no, nothing of the kind. He goes to and fro his work, receives his wages, spends them at the ale-house, and wanders listlessly about. The very conception of a public feeling never occurs to him ; it is all desultory. A little desultory work —except in harvest, labourer's work cannot be called downright *work*—a little desultory talk, a little desultory rambling about, a good deal of desultory drinking : these are the sum and total of it ; no, add a little desultory smoking and purposeless mischief to make it complete. Why should not the labourer be made to feel an interest in the welfare, the prosperity, and progress of his own village? Why should he not be supplied with a motive for united action? All experience teaches that united action, even on small matters, has a tendency to enlarge the minds and the whole powers of those engaged. The labourer feels so little interest in his own progress, because the matter is only brought before him in its individual bearing. You can rarely interest a single person in the improvement of himself, but you can interest a number in the progress of that number as a body. The vacancy of mind, the absence of any ennobling aspiration, so noticeable in the agricultural labourer, is a painful fact. Does it not, in great measure, arise from this very desultory life—from this procrastinating dislike to active exertion? Supply a motive—a general public motive—and the labourer will wake up. At the present moment, what interest has an ordinary agricultural labourer in the affairs of his own village ? Practically none whatever. He may, perhaps, pay rates ; but these are administered at a distance, and he knows nothing of the system by which they are dispensed. If his next-door neighbour's cottage is tumbling down, the thatch in holes, the doors off their hinges, it matters nothing to him. Certainly, he cannot himself pay for its renovation, and there is no fund to which he can subscribe so much as a penny with that object in view. A number of cottages may be without a supply of water. Well, he cannot help it ; probably he never gives a thought to it. There is no governing body in the place responsible for such things—no body in the election of which he has any hand. He puts his hands in his pockets and slouches about, smoking a short pipe, and drinks a quart at the nearest ale-house. He is totally indifferent. To go still further, there can be no doubt that the absence of any such ruling body, even if ruling only on sufferance, has a deteriorating effect upon the minds of the best-informed and broadest-minded agriculturist. He sees a nuisance or a grievance, possibly something that may approach the nature of a calamity. 'Ah, well,' he sighs, 'I can't help it ; I've no power to interfere.' He walks round his farm, examines his sheep, pats his horses, and rides to market, and naturally forgets all about it. Were there any ready and available means by which the nuisance could be removed, or the calamity in some measure averted, the very same man would at once put it in motion, and never cease till the desired result was attained ; but the total absence of any authority, any common centre, tends to foster what appears an utter indifference.   How can it be otherwise ?   The absence of such a body tends, therefore, in two ways to the injury of the labourer : first, because he has no means of helping himself ; and, secondly, because those above him in social station have no means of assisting him.   But why cannot the squire step in and do all that is wanted?   What is there that the landowner is not expected to do? He is compelled by the law to contribute to the maintenance of roads by heavy subscriptions, while men of much larger income, but no real property, ride over them free of cost.   He is expected by public opinion to rebuild all the cottages on his estate, introducing all the modern improvements, to furnish them with large plots of garden ground, to supply them with coal during the winter at nominal cost, to pay three parts of the expense of erecting schools, and what not.   He is expected to extend the farm-buildings upon the farms, to rebuild the farmsteads, and now to compensate the tenants for improvements, though he may not particularly care for them, knowing full well by experience that improvements are a long time before they pay any interest on the principal invested.   Now we expect him to remove all nuisances in the village, to supply water, to exercise a wise paternal authority, and all

at his own cost. The whole thing is unreasonable.
Many landowners have succeeded to heavily-burdened
estates. The best estates pay, it must be remembered,
but a very small comparative interest upon their value
—in some instances not more than two and a half per
cent. Moreover, almost all landowners do take an
interest in improvements, and are ready to forward
them ; but can a gentleman be expected to go round
from cottage to cottage performing the duties of an
inspector of nuisances? and, if he did so, would it be
tolerated for an instant? The outcry would be raised
of interference, tyranny, overbearing insolence, intolerable intrusion. It is undoubtedly the landowner's duty to forward all reasonable schemes of
improvement ; but if the inhabitants are utterly
indifferent to progress of any kind, it is not his duty
to issue an autocratical ukase. Let the inhabitants
combine, in however loose and informal a manner,
and the landowner will always be ready to assist
them with purse and moral support.

Granting, then, that there is at present no such
local authority, and that it is desirable—what are the
objects which would come within its sphere of operation ? In an article which had the honour of ap-
pearing in a former number of this magazine,* the
writer pointed out that the extension of the allotment system was only delayed because there was no
body or authority which had power to increase the
area under spade cultivation. Throughout the
country there is an undoubted conviction that such

* See 'Toilers of the Field,' by Richard Jefferies.—ED.

extension is extremely desirable, but who is to take the initiative? There is an increasing demand for these gardens—a demand that will probably make itself loudly felt as time goes on and the population grows larger. Even those villages that possess allotment grounds would be in a better position if there were some body who held rule over the gardens, and administered them according to varying circumstances. Some of these allotments are upon the domain of the landowner, and have been broken up for the purpose under his directions; but it is not every gentleman who has either the time or the inclination to superintend the actual working of the gardens, and they are often left pretty much to take care of themselves. Other allotment grounds are simply matters of speculation with the owner, and are let out to the highest bidder in order to make money, without any species of control whatever. This is not desirable for many reasons, and such owners deprecate the extension of the system, because if a larger area were offered to the labourer, the letting value would diminish, since there would be less competition for the lots. There can be very little doubt that the allotment garden will form an integral part of the social system of the future, and, as such, will require proper regulation. If it is to be so, it is obviously desirable that it should be in the hands of a body of local gentlemen with a perfect knowledge of the position and resource of the numerous small tenants, and a thorough comprehension of the practical details which are essential to success in such cultivation. It may be predicted that the first step which would ensue upon the formation of such a body would be an extension of allotments. There would be no difficulty in renting a field or fields for that purpose. The village council, as we may for convenience term it, would select a piece of ground possessing an easily-moved soil, avoiding stiff clay on the one hand, and too light, sandy ground on the other. For this piece they would give a somewhat higher rent than it would obtain for agricultural purposes—say £3 per acre—which they would guarantee to the owner after the manner of a syndicate. They would cause the hedges to be pared down to the very smallest proportions, but the mounds to be somewhat raised, so as to avoid harbouring birds, and at the same time safely exclude cattle, which in a short time would play havoc with the vegetables. If possible, a road should run right across the plot, with a gateway on either side, so that a cart might pass straight through, pick up its load, and go on and out without turning. Each plot should have a frontage upon this road, or to branch roads running at right angles to it, so that each tenant could remove his produce without trespassing upon the plot of his neighbour. Such trespasses often lead to much ill-will. The narrow paths dividing these strips should be sufficiently wide to allow of wheeling a barrow down them, and should on no account be permitted to be overgrown with grass. Grass-paths are much prettier, but are simply reservoirs of couch, weeds, and slugs, and therefore to be avoided. The whole field should be accurately mapped, and each plot numbered on the map, and a strong plug driven into the plot with a similar number upon it—a plan which renders identification easy, and prevents disputes. A book should be kept, with the name of every tenant entered into it, and indexed, like a ledger, with the initial letter. Against the name of the tenant should be placed the area of his holdings, and the numbers of his plots upon the map; and in this book the date of his tenancy, and any change of holding, should be registered. There should be a book of printed forms (not to be torn out) of agreement, with blank spaces for name, date, and number, which should be signed by the tenant. In a third book all payments and receipts should be entered. This sounds commercial, and looks like serious business; but as the rent would be payable half-yearly only, there would be really very little trouble required, and the saving of disputes very great. During the season of cropping, the payment of a small gratuity to the village policeman would insure the allotment being well watched, and if pilferers were detected they should invariably be prosecuted. As many of the tenants would come from long distances, and would not frequent their plots every evening, there might possibly be a small lock-up tool-house in which to deposit their tools, the key being left in charge of some old man living in an adjacent cottage. The rules of cultivation would depend in some measure upon the nature of the soil, but such a village council would be composed of practical men, who would have no difficulty whatever in drawing up concise and accurate instructions. The council could depute one or more members to receive the rent-money and to keep the books, and if any labour were required, there are always bailiffs and trustworthy men who could be employed to do it. At a small expense the field should be properly drained before being opened, and even though let at a very low charge per perch, there would still remain an overplus above the rent paid by the council for the field, sufficient in a short time to clear off the debt incurred in draining.

It is very rarely that allotment gardens are sufficiently manured, and this is a subject that would come very properly under the jurisdiction of the allotment committee of our village council. Some labourers keep a pig or two, but all do not; and many living at a considerable distance would find, and do find, a difficulty in conveying any manure they may possess to the spot. So it often happens that gardens are cropped year after year without any substances being restored to the soil, which gradually becomes less productive. Means should be devised of supplying this deficiency. Manure is valuable to the farmer, but still he could spare a little—quite sufficient for this purpose. Suppose the allotment gardens consisted of twelve acres, then let one-fourth, or three acres, be properly manured every year. This would be no strain upon the product of manure in the vicinity, and in four years—four years' system—

the whole of the field would receive a proper amount, in addition to the small quantities the labourer's pig produced. Every tenant, in his agreement, could be caused to pay, in addition to his rent, once every four years, a small sum in part-payment for this manuring, and also for the hauling of the material to the field. This payment would not represent the actual value of the manure, but it would maintain the principle of self-help ; and, as far as possible, the allotments should be self-supporting. In cases of dispute, the committee would simply have to refer the matter to the council, and the thing would be definitely settled ; but under a regular system of this kind, as it were mapped down and written out, no obstinate disputes could arise. In this one matter of allotment-gardens alone there is plenty of scope for the exertions of a village council, and incalculable good might be attained. The very order and systematic working of the thing would have a salutary effect upon the desultory life of the village.

Next comes the water-supply of the village. This is a matter of vital importance. There are, of course, villages where water is abundant, even too abundant, as in low-lying meadow-land by the side of rivers which are liable to overflow. There are villages traversed throughout the whole of their length by a brook running parallel with the road, so that to gain access to each cottage it is necessary to cross a 'drock,' or small bridge, and in summer-time such villages are very picturesque. In the colder months, the mist on the water and damp air are not so pleasant or healthy. Many villages, situated at the edge of a range of hills—a most favourite position for villages—are supplied with good springs of the clearest water rising in those hills. But there are also large numbers of villages placed high up above the water-level on the same hills, which are most scantily supplied with water ; and there are also villages far away down in the valley which are liable to run short in the summer or dry time, when the 'bourne,' or winter watercourse, fails them. Such places, situated in the midst of rich meadows, can sometimes barely find water enough for the cattle, who are not so particular as to quality. Even in places where there is a good natural spring, or a brook which is rarely dry, the cottagers experience no little difficulty in conveying it to their homes, which may be situated a mile away. It is not uncommon in country places to see the water trickling along in the ditch by the roadside bayed up with a miniature dam in front of a cottage, and from the turbid pool thus formed the woman fills her kettle. People who live in towns, and can turn on the water in any room of their houses without the slightest exertion, have no idea of the difficulty the poor experience in the country in procuring good water, despite all the beautiful rivers and springs and brooks which poetry sings of. After a man or woman has worked all day in the field, perhaps at a distance of two miles from home, it is weary and discouraging work to have to trudge with the pail another weary half-mile or so to the pool for water.

It is harder still, after trudging that weary half-mile, pail in hand, to find the water almost too low to dip, muddied by cattle, and diminished in quantity to serve the pressing needs of the animals living higher up the stream. Now, in starting, it may be assumed that the nearest source of water in a village is certain to be found upon the premises of some agriculturist. He will, doubtless, be perfectly willing to allow free access to his stream or pool; but he cannot be expected to construct conveniences for the public use, and he may even feel naturally annoyed if continual use by thirty people, twice a day, finally breaks his pump. He naturally believes that other gentlemen in the village should take an equal interest with himself in the public welfare, but they do not appear to do so. It may be that the path to the pump leads through the private garden, right before his sitting-room window, and the constant passage of women and children for water, particularly children, who are apt to lounge and stare about them, becomes a downright nuisance. This, surely, ought not to be. A very little amount of united action on the part of the principal inhabitants of the village would put this straight. The pump could be repaired, a new path made, and the water conveyed to a stone trough by a hose, or something of the kind, and the owner would be quite willing to sanction it, but he does not see why it should all be done at his expense. The other inhabitants of the village see the difficulty, recognize it, perhaps talk about remedying it, but nothing is done, simply because there exists no body, no council to undertake it. Spontaneous combination is extremely uncertain in its action ; the organization should exist before the necessity for utilizing it arises. In other places what is wanted is a well, but cottagers cannot afford to dig a deep well, and certainly no combination can be expected from them alone and unassisted. Village wells require also to be under some kind of supervision. At intervals they require cleaning out. The machinery for raising water must be prepared ; the cover to prevent accidents to children renewed. A well that has no one to look after it quickly becomes the receptacle of all the stones and old boots and dead cats in the place. But if there is a terror of prosecution, the well remains clear and useful. The digging of a deep well is an event of national importance, so to say, to a village. It may happen that a noble spring of water bursts out some little distance from the village, but is practically useless to the inhabitants because of its distance. What more easy than to run a hose from it right to a stone trough, or dipping-place, in the centre of the village ? In most cases, very simple engineering ability would be sufficient to supply the hamlet. The hose, or whatever the plan might be, need not take half nor a quarter of the water thrown out by the spring. The owner might object ; certainly he would object to any forcible carrying away of his water ; but if he were himself a party to the scheme, and to receive compensation for any injury, he would not do so.

Water has been the cause of more disputes,

probably, than anything else between neighbouring agriculturists. One wishes it for his water-meadows, another for his cattle, a third for his home-consumption ; then there is, perhaps, the miller to be consulted. After all, there is, in most cases, more than enough water for everybody, and a very little mutual yielding would accommodate all, and supply the village in the bargain. But each party being alone in his view, without any mediator, the result may be a lawsuit, or ill-blood, lasting for years ; the cutting down of bays and dams, the possible collision of the men employed.

Between these parties, between agriculturists themselves, the establishment of a species of village council would often lead to peace and harmony. The advice and expressed wishes of their neighbour, the influence of the clergyman and the resident landlord, and the existence of a common public want in the village, would have an irresistible effect ; and what neither would yield to his opponent, all would yield to a body of friends. Taken in this way it may safely be considered that there would be no difficulty in obtaining access to water. In places which are still less fortunate and, especially in dry times, are at a greater distance from the precious element, there still remains a plan by which sufficient could be secured, and that is the portable water-tank. Our agricultural machinists now turn out handsome and capacious iron tanks which are coming into general use. Now, no one farmer can be expected to send water-tank and team three or four times every evening to fetch up water for the use of cottagers, not one-twentieth of whom work for him. But why should there not be a tank, the public property of the village, and why should not teams take it in turn ? Undoubtedly something of the kind would immediately spring into existence were there any village organization whatever. In a large number of villages, the natural supply would be sufficient during three parts of the year, and it would be only in summer that any assistance would be necessary.

While on the subject of water, another matter may as well be dealt with, and that is the establishment of bathing-places near villages. This is, of course, impossible over considerable areas of country where water is scarce, and especially scarce in the bathing season. Even in many places, however, where water is comparatively deficient in quantity, there are usually some great ponds, which for part of the season could be made applicable for bathing purposes. There then remain an immense number of villages situated on or near a stream, and wherever there is a stream a bathing-place is practicable. At the present moment it would be difficult to find one such place,. unless on the banks of a large river, and rivers are far between. The boys and young men who feel a natural desire to bathe in the warm weather resort to muddy ponds, with a filthy bottom of black slush, or paddle about in shallow brooks no more than knee-deep, or in the water-carriers in water meadows. This species of bathing is practically useless ; it does not answer any purposes of cleanliness, and learning to swim is out of the question.   The formation of a proper bathing-place presents few difficulties.   A spot must be chosen near to the village, but far enough away for decency.   The bottom of the stream should be covered with a layer of sand and small gravel, carefully avoiding large stones and sharp-edged flints. Much of the pleasure of bathing depends upon a good bottom, and nothing is more likely to deter a young beginner than the feeling that he cannot place his feet on the ground without the danger of lacerating them.   For this reason, also, care should be taken to exclude all boughs and branches, and particularly the prickly bushes cut from hedges, which are most annoying to bathers.   The stream should be bayed up to a depth at the deepest part of about five feet, which is quite deep enough for ordinary swimming, and reduces the danger to a minimum.   If possible, a strong smooth rail should run across the pool, or partly across.   This is for the encouragement of boys and young bathers, who like something to catch hold of, and it is also an adjunct in learning to swim, for the boy can stand opposite to it, and after two or three strokes place his hand on it, and so gradually increasing the distance, he can swim without once losing confidence.   Those who cannot swim can hold to the rail and splash about and enjoy themselves. Such a bathing-place will sound childish enough to strong swimmers, who have learnt to go long distances with ease in the Thames or in the sea, but it must be remembered that we are dealing with an inland population who are timid of water.   A boy who can cross such a small pool without touching the bottom with his feet, would soon feel at home in broader waters, if ever circumstances should bring him near them.   If there is no stream a large pond could be cleaned out, and sand and gravel placed upon the bottom—almost anything is better than the soft oozy mud, which, once stirred up, will not settle for hours, and destroys all pleasure or benefit from bathing.   No building is necessary to dress in, or anything of that kind.   The place selected would be, of course, at a distance from any public footpath, and even if it were near there are so few passing in rural outlying districts that no one need be shocked. But if it was considered necessary an older man could be paid a small sum to walk down every evening, or at the stated hours for bathing, and see that no irregularity occurred.   A loose pole or two always kept near the stream or pond, and ready to hand, would amply provide against any little danger there might be.   Bathing is most important to health, and if a really good swim is possible there is nothing so conducive to an elasticity of frame.   Our labourers are notoriously strong and muscular, and possess considerable power of endurance (though they destroy their 'wind,' in running phraseology, by too much beer), but their strength is clumsy, their gait ungainly, their run heavy and slow.   The freedom of motion in the water, the simultaneous use of arms and limbs, the peculiar character of the exercise, renders it one, above all others, calculated to give an ease and grace to the body.   In a good physical education, swimming must form an important part; and the labourer requires a physical education quite as much as a mental. The bathing-place, as a means of inducing personal cleanliness, would have its uses. The cottages of the labouring poor are often models of cleanliness, but the persons of the inhabitants precisely the reverse. The expense of such a bathing-place need be but very small. If it was situated in a cow-leaze, the bathing could begin the moment the spring became warm enough; if in a meadow usually mown, as soon as the grass has been cut, which would be early in June. It would perhaps be necessary to have stated hours of bathing; but no other regulation—the less restriction the better the privilege would be appreciated. Exercises of this character could not be too much encouraged. Every accomplishment of the kind adds a new power to the man, and gives him a sense of superiority.

There should be a rough kind of gymnasium for the villagers. Almost always a piece of waste ground could be found, and the requisite materials are very simple and inexpensive. A few upright poles for climbing; horizontal bars; a few ropes, and a ladder would be sufficient. In wet weather some large open cow-house could be utilized for such purposes. In summer such outbuildings are empty, the cattle being in the fields. A few pairs of quoits also could be added at a small cost. Wrestling, perhaps, had better be avoided, as liable to lead to quarrels; but jumping and running should be fostered, and prizes presented for excellence. It is not the value of the prize, it is the fact that it is a prize. A good strong pocket-knife with four or five blades would be valued by a ploughboy, and a labourer would be pleased with an ornamental pipe costing five shillings, or a hoe or spade could be substituted as more useful.

The institution of such annual village games, the bathing-place, the gymnasium in the open air, the running match, the quoits, would have a tendency to awaken the emulation of the labouring class; and once awaken the emulation, an increase of intelligence follows. A man would feel that he was not altogether a mere machine, to do so much work and then trudge home and sleep. Lads would have something better to do than play pitch-and-toss, and slouch about the place, learning nothing but bad language. A life would be imparted to the village, there would be a centre of union, a gathering-place, and a certain amount of proper pride in the village, and an *esprit de corps* would spring up. In all these things the labourer should be encouraged to carry them out as much as possible in his own way, and without interference or supervision. Make the bathing-place, erect the poles and horizontal bars, establish the pocket-knife and hoe prizes, present the quoits, but let him use them in his own way. There must be freedom, liberty, or the attempt would certainly fail.

How many villages have so much as a reading-room? Such a local council as has been indicated would soon come to discuss the propriety of establishing such an institution. If managed strictly with a view to the real wants and ideas of the people, and not in accordance with any preconceived principles of so-called instruction, it would be certain to succeed. The labouring poor dislike instruction being forced down their throats quite as much, or more, than the upper classes. The very worst way to induce a man to learn is to begin by telling him he is ignorant, and thereby insulting his self-esteem. A village reading-room should be open to all, and not to subscribers only. From six till nine in the evening would be long enough for it to be open, and the key could be kept by some adjacent cottager. With every respect for the schoolmaster, let the schoolmaster be kept away from it. If there is a night-school, keep it distinct from the reading-room; let the reading-room be a voluntary affair, without the slightest suspicion of *drill* attaching to it. It should be a place where a working man could come in, and sit down and *spell* over a book, without the consciousness that someone was watching him, ready to snap him up at a mistake. Exclude all 'goody' books; there are sects in villages as well as towns, and the presence of an obnoxious work may do much harm. To the Bible itself, in clear print, no sect will object; but let it be the Bible only. A collection of amusing literature can easily be made. For £5 enough books could be bought on an old bookstall in London to stock a village library; such as travels, tales—not despising Robinson Crusoe—and a few popular expositions of science. There should be one daily paper. It could be brought by one of the milk-carts from the nearest railway-station. This daily paper would form a very strong counteraction to the ale-house. Of course, the ale-house would start a daily in opposition; but at the reading-room the labourer would soon learn that he need not purchase a glass of beer in order to pay for his news. The daily paper would be a most important feature, for such papers are rare in villages. Very few farmers even take them. The rent of a room for this purpose in a village would be almost nominal. A small room would be sufficient, for only a few would be present at a time. Cricket clubs may be left to establish themselves.

The next suggestion the writer is about to make will be thought a very bold one; but is it not rational enough when the first novelty of the idea has subsided? It is, that an annual excursion should be arranged for the villagers. It is common to see in the papers appeals made on behalf of the poor children of crowded districts in London, for funds to give them a day in the country. It is stated that they never see anything but stone pavements; never breathe anything but smoky air. The appeal is a proper and good one, and should be generously responded to. Now, the position of the villager is the exact antithesis. He, or she, sees nothing but green fields or bare fields all the year round. They hear nothing but a constant iteration of talk about cattle, crops, and weather—important matters, but apt to grow monotonous. It may be, that for thirty years they never for one day lose sight of the hills overhanging the village. Their subjects of conversation are consequently extremely narrow. They want a change quite as much as the dwellers in cities; but it is a change of another character—a change to bustle and excitement. Factories and large tradesmen arrange trips for their work-people once or twice a year. Why should not the agricultural labourers have a trip? A trip of the simplest kind would satisfy them, and afford matter of conversation for months. All railway lines now issue tickets at reduced rates for parties above a certain number. For instance, to the population of an inland village, what would be more delightful than a few hours on the sea-beach? Where the sea is not within easy reach, take them to a great town — if possible, London—but if not London, any large town will be a change. There is no great difficulty in the plan. Perhaps twenty or thirty would be the largest number who would wish to go. Let these assemble at a stated hour and place, and take them down to the railway-station with two or three waggons and teams, which should also meet them on their return. The expense would not be great, and might be partly borne by the excursionists themselves. All that is wanted is some amount of leadership, a little organization. Such enterprises as these would go far to create a genuine mutual understanding and pleasant feeling between employer and employed. There may be outlying places where such an excursion would be very difficult. Then harness the horses to the waggons, and take them to a picnic ten miles off on a noted hill or heath, or by the side of a river—somewhere for a change.

To return to more serious matters. Perhaps it would be as well if the first endeavour of such a local authority were addressed to the smaller matters that have been just alluded to, so that the public mind might become gradually accustomed to change, and prepared for greater innovations. Village drainage is notoriously defective. Anyone who has walked through a village or hamlet must be perfectly well aware that there is no drainage, from the unpleasant odours that constantly assail the nostrils. It seems absurd, that with such an expanse of open country around, and with such an exposure to the fresh air, such foul substances should be permitted to contaminate the atmosphere. Each cottager either throws the sewage right into the road, and allows it to find its way as it can by the same channel as the rain-water; or, at best, flings it into the ditch at the back, which parts the garden from the agricultural land. Here it accumulates and soaks into the soil till the first storm of rain, which sweeps it away, but at the same time causes an abominable smell. It is positively unbearable to pass some cottages after a fresh shower.

Not unfrequently this ditch at the back of the garden runs down to the stream from which the cottagers draw their water, and the dipping-place may be close to the junction of the two. In places where there is a fall—when the cottages are built upon a slope—there can be little difficulty about drainage; but here steps in the question of water-supply, for drains of this character require flushing.

The supply of water must, therefore, in such places, precede the attempt at drainage. The disposal of the sewage, when collected, offers no difficulty. Its value is well understood, and it would be welcomed upon agricultural land. In the case of villages where there is no natural fall, and small hamlets and out-lying cottages, the Moule system should be en-couraged, especially as it affords a valuable product that can be transported to the allotment garden. A certain amount of most unreasonable prejudice exists against the introduction of this useful contrivance, which every means should be used to overcome. Now, most farm-houses stand apart, and in their own grounds, where any system of sewer is almost im-possible. These are the very places where the Moule plan is available; and if agriculturists were to employ it, the poor would quickly learn its advantages. It would, perhaps, be even better than a public sewer in large villages, for a sewer entails an amount of super-vision, repairs, and must have an outfall, and other difficulties, such as flushing with water, and, if neglected, it engenders sewer-gas, which is more dangerous than the sewage itself. The plan to be pursued depends entirely upon the circumstances of the place and the configuration of the ground. The subject of drainage connects itself with that of nuisances. This is, perhaps, the most difficult matter with which a local authority would have to deal. Nuisances are comparative. One man may not consider that to be a nuisance which may be an intolerable annoyance to his neighbour. The keeping of pigs, for instance, is a troublesome affair. The cottager cannot be requested to give up so reasonable a habit; but there can be no doubt that the presence of a number of pigs in a village, in their dirty sties, and with their accompanying heaps of decaying garbage, is very offensive, and perhaps unhealthy. The pig itself, though commonly called a dirty animal, is not anything near so bad as has been represented. To convince oneself of that it is only necessary to visit farm-buildings which are well looked after. The pigsties have no more smell than the stables, because the manure is removed, and no garbage is allowed to accumulate. It is the man who keeps the pig that makes it filthy and repulsive, and not the animal itself. Regular and *clean* food has also much to do with it, such as barley-meal. Cottagers cannot afford barley-meal, but they certainly could keep their sties much cleaner. It does not seem possible to attack the nuisance with any other means than that of persuasion, unless some plan could be devised of keeping pigs in a common building outside the village; or at any rate, of having the manure taken outside at short intervals. Such nuisances as stagnant ponds and mud-filled ditches are more easily dealt with, because they are public, and interference with them would not touch upon any man's liberty of action. Stagnant ponds are of no use to anyone—even horses will not drink at them. The simple plan is to remove the mud, and then fill them up level with the ground, laying in drain-pipes to carry off the water which accumulated there. But some of these ponds could be utilized for the benefit of passing horses and cattle. They are fed with a running stream, but, being no man's property, the pond becomes choked with mud and manure, and the small inflow of pure water is not enough to overcome the noisome exhalations. These should be cleaned out now and then, and, if possible, the bottom laid down with gravel or small stones, making the pond shallow at the edges, and for some distance in. Nothing is more valuable upon a country road than ponds of this character, into which a jaded horse can walk over his fetlock, and cool his feet at the same time that he refreshes his thirst. They are most welcome to cattle driven along the road.

The moral nuisances of drunkenness, gambling, and bad language at the corners of the streets and cross-roads had best be left to the law to deal with, though the influence of a local council in reproof and caution would undoubtedly be considerable. But if a bathing-place, an out-of-doors gymnasium, and such things, were established, these evils would almost disappear, because the younger inhabitants would have something to amuse themselves with; at present they have nothing whatever.

A local authority of this kind would confer a great boon upon the agricultural poor if they could renovate the old idea of a common. Allotment grounds are most useful, but they do not meet every want. The better class of cottagers, who have contrived to save a little money, often try to keep a cow, and before the road surveyors grew so strict, they had little difficulty in doing so.   But now the roads are so jealously and properly preserved purely for traffic, the cottager has no opportunity of grazing a cow or a donkey.   It would not be possible in places where land is chiefly arable, nor in others where the meadow-land is let at a high rent, but still there are places where a common could be provided.   It need not be the best land.   The poorest would do. Those who graze should pay a small fee—so much per head per week.   Such a field would be a great benefit, and an encouragement to those who were inclined to save.

In almost every parish there are a number of public charities.   Many of these are unfortunately expressly devised for certain purposes, from which they cannot be diverted without much trouble and resorting to high authorities.   But there are others left in a loose manner for the good of the poor, and the very origin of which is doubtful.   Such are many of the pieces of land scattered about the country, the rent of which is paid to the church-wardens for the time being, in trust for the poor.   At present these charities are dissipated in petty alms-giving, such as so much bread and a fourpenny-piece on a certain day of the year, a blanket or cloak at Christmas, and so on, the utility of which is more than doubtful.   Stories are currently believed of such fourpenny-pieces purchasing quarts of ale, and of such blankets being immediately sold to raise money for the same end.   A village council would be able to suggest many ways in which the income of these charities could be far better employed. The giving of coal has already been substituted in some places for the fourpenny-piece and blanket, which is certainly a sensible change; but if possible it would be better to avoid so-called charity altogether. Why should not the income of half a dozen villages lying adjacent to each other be concentrated upon a cottage hospital, or upon a hospital for lying-in women, which is one of the great desiderata in country places. Such institutions afford charity of the highest and best character, without any degradation to the recipient. At the present moment the woman who has lost her reputation, and is confined with an illegitimate child, simply proceeds to the workhouse, where she meets with every attention skilled nurses and science can afford. The labourer's wife is left to languish in a close overcrowded room, and permitted to resume her household labours before she has properly recovered. There is nothing more wretched than the confinement of an agricultural labourer's wife.

The health of villagers, notwithstanding the pure air, is often prejudiced by the overcrowding of cottages. This overcrowding may not be sufficiently great to render an appeal to the legal authorities desirable, and yet may be productive of very bad effects, both moral and physical. It is particularly the case where the cottages are the property of the labourer himself, and are held at a low quit-rent. The labourer cannot afford to rebuild the cottage, which has descended to him from his father, or possibly grandfather, and which was originally designed for one small family, but, in the course of years, three or four members of that family have acquired a right of residence in it. Of this right they are extremely tenacious, though it may be positively injurious to them. As many as two married men, with wives and children, may crowd themselves into this dirty hovel, with a result of quarrelling and immorality that cannot be surpassed; in fact, some things that have happened in such places are not to be mentioned. Under the best circumstances it often happens that there are not sufficient cottages in a parish for the accommodation of the necessary workmen. Complaints are continually arising, from no one so much as from the agriculturists, who can never depend upon their men remaining because of the deficiency of lodging. It is not often that the entire parish belongs to one landlord; frequently, there are four or five landlords, and a large number of freehold properties let to tenants. Nor even where parishes are more or less the property of one person, is it always practicable for the estate to bear the burden of additional cottage building. The cost of a cottage varies more, perhaps, than any other estimate, according to the size, the materials to be employed, and their abundance in the neighbourhood. But it may be safely believed that the estimates given to landowners and others desirous of erecting cottages, very much exceed the sum at which they can be built. Deduct the hauling of materials—a considerable item—which could be done by the farmers themselves at odd times.

In some places the materials may be found upon an adjacent farm, and for such purposes might be had for a nominal sum. Altogether, a very fair cottage might be built for £100 to £150, according to the circumstances. These, of course, would not be ornamental houses with Gothic porches and elaborate gables; but plain cottages, and quite as comfortable. In round figures, four such places might be erected for £500.* For a large parish will contain as many as twenty farmers, and some more than that: £500 distributed between twenty is but £25 apiece, and this sum could be still further reduced if the landlords, the clergy, and the principal inhabitants are calculated to take an interest in the matter. Let it be taken at £20 each, and the product four cottages. As there are supposed to be twenty farms, it may be reckoned that eight or ten new cottages would be welcome. This would vary with circumstances. In some places five would be sufficient. Ten would be the very highest number; and may be considered quite exceptional. Now for the repayment of the investment of £20. Four cottages at 2s. per week equals £20 per annum. At this rate in five-and-twenty years, each subscriber would be paid back his principal; say, after the manner of bonds, one redeemable every year, and drawn for by lot. An agriculturist who invests

* This, of course, is upon the supposition that the materials are obtained at a nominal cost, and the hauling not charged for.

£100 or £150 in a cottage expects some interest upon his money; but he can afford to sink £20 for a few years in view of future benefit. But there are means by which the repayment could be much accelerated; *i.e.*, by inducing the tenant of a cottage to pay a higher rent, and so become, after a time, the possessor of the tenement, in the same way as with building societies.

It may, however, be considered preferable that the cottages should remain the property of the village council—each member receiving back his original payment. This is thrown out merely as a suggestion; but this much is clear, that were there an organization of this kind there would be no material difficulty in the way of increasing the cottage accommodation. A number of gentlemen working together would overcome the want with ease. At all events, if they did not go so far as to erect new cottages, they might effect a great deal of improvement in repairing dilapidated places, and enlarging existing premises.

In thus rapidly sketching out the various ways in which a local village authority might encourage the growth and improvement of the place, it has been endeavoured to indicate, in a suggestive manner, the way in which such an authority might be established. It is not for one moment proposed that an application should be made to the Legislature for a special enactment enabling such councils to act with legal force. To such a course there would certainly arise the most vigorous opposition on the part of all classes of the agricultural community, from landlord, tenant, and labourer alike. There exists an irresistible dislike to any form of 'imperial' interference, as is amply proved by the resistance offered to the School Board system, and by the comparative impotence of the rural sanitary authorities. People would rather suffer annoyance than call in an outside power. The species of local authority here indicated must be founded entirely upon the will of the inhabitants themselves; and its power be derived rather from acquiescence than from inherent force. In fact, the major part of its duties would not require any legal power. The allotment-garden, the cottage repair, the common, the bathing-place, reading-room, etc., would require no legal authority to render them useful and attractive. Neither is it probable that any serious opposition would be made to a system of drainage, and certainly none whatever to an improved water supply. No force would be necessary, and the whole moral influence of landlord, and tenant, and clergy, would sway in the proposed direction. It has often been remarked that the agricultural class— the tenant farmer—is the one least capable of combination, and there is a great deal of truth in the assertion of the lack of all cohesion, and united action. It must, however, be remembered that until very lately no kind of combination has been proposed, no attempt made to organize action. That, at least in local matters, agriculturists are capable of combination and united action has been proved by the strenuous exertions made to retain the voluntary school system, and also by the endeavours made for the restoration of village churches. If the total of the sums obtained for schools and for village church restoration could be ascertained, it would be found to amount to something very great; and in the case of the schools, at any rate, and to some degree in the case of restorations, the administration of the funds has rested upon the leading farmers assembled in committees. When once a number of agriculturists have formed a combination with an understood object, they are less liable to be thrown into disorder by factious differences amongst themselves than any other class of men. They are willing to agree to anything reasonable, and do not persist in amendments just in order that a favourite crotchet may be gratified. In other words, they are amenable to common sense and practical arguments.

There would be very little doubt of harmonious action if once such a combination was formed. It could be started in many ways—by the clergyman asking the tenants of the parish to meet him in the village school-room, and there giving a rapid sketch of the proposed organization; and if any landlord, or magistrate, or leading gentleman was present, the thing would be set on its legs on the spot. In most parishes there are one or more large tenant farmers who naturally take the lead in their own class, and they would speedily obtain adherents to the movement. It would be as well, perhaps, if the attempt were made, for the promoters to draw up a species of circular for distribution in every house and cottage in the parish, explaining the objects of the association, and inviting co-operation on the part of rich and poor alike. Once a meeting was called together, and a committee appointed, the principal difficulty would be got over.

The next matter—in fact, the first matter for the consideration of such a committee—would be the method of raising funds. All legally-established bodies have powers of obtaining money, as by rates ; but the example of the independent schools and church restorations has amply proved that money will be forthcoming for proper purposes without resort to compulsion. The abolition of Church-rates has not in any way tended to the degradation of the Church ; perhaps, on the contrary, more has been done towards Church extension since that date than before. A voluntary rate is still collected in many places, and produces a considerable sum, the calculation being made upon the basis of the poor-rate assessment. The objects of such a village association being eminently practical, devoid of any sectarian bearing and thoroughly local in application, there would probably be little difficulty in collecting a small voluntary rate for its support, even amongst the poorest of the population. The cottager would not grudge a few pence for objects in which he has an obvious interest, and which are close at home ; but in the formation of the association it would, perhaps, be practicable to begin with a subscription of one guinea each from every member, the subscription of one guinea per annum endowing the giver with voting power at the meetings. If there were five-and-twenty farmers in a parish, there would be five-and-twenty guineas (it is not probable that any farmer would stand out from such a society), and five-and-twenty guineas would be quite sufficient to start the thing. Suppose the society commence with supplying additional allotment-grounds. They rent, say, eight acres at £2 10s. per acre, equalling £20 per annum ; but they only expend £10 on rent for one half-year, because the other half will be paid by incoming tenants. The labour to be expended on the plot in making it tenable can hardly be reckoned, because, in all probability, it would be done by their own men at odd times. Many places would not require draining at all, and it need not be done at starting, and the generality of fields are already drained. So that about £15 would suffice to start the allotment-grounds, leaving £10 in hand to make a bathing-place with, or to erect a pump, or purchase hose or tank for water-supply. Here we have a considerable progress arrived at with one year's subscription only, not counting on any sub-scription from the landlord, or clergy, or resident gentlemen. The funds required are, in fact, not nearly so large as might be imagined. Most of these improvements, when once started, would last for some years without further outlay ; the allotments would probably return a small income. It is not so necessary to do everything in one year. Add the sums collected on the low rate to the yearly subscription of the members, and there would probably be sufficient for every purpose, except that of cottage repairs or the erection of new cottages. Such more expensive matters would require shareholders investing larger sums ; but the income already mentioned would probably enable all ordinary improvements to be carried out, even draining ; and, after a year or two, a small reserve fund would even accumulate. It would, however, be important to bring the poorer class to feel that these matters, in a manner, depended upon their own exertions. There might be a subscription of twopence a month for certain given objects, as the bathing-place, the water-tank, or other things in hand at the time ; and it would probably be well responded to. They should also be invited to give their labour free of charge after farm work. In the case of important alterations affecting the whole village, such as drainage, they might be asked to meet the society in the school-room, and then let the matter be put to the vote. After a few months, there can be no doubt the labouring population would come to take a very animated interest in such proceedings. There is a great deal of common sense in the labourer, and once let him see the practical as opposed to the theoretical benefit, and his co-operation is certain.

The members of the society would have no trouble in electing a committee. There might be more than one committee to attend to different matters, as the allotment and the water-supply, because it would happen that one gentleman would have more practical knowledge of gardening, and another would have more acquaintance with the means of dealing with water, from the experience gained in his own water meadows. There should be a president of the society, a treasurer, and secretary ; and a general meeting might take place once every two months, the committee meeting as circumstances dictated. Any member having a scheme to propose could draw up a short outline of his plan in writing, and submit it to the general meeting, when, if it met with favour, it could be handed over to a committee for execution.

Such an association might call itself the village Local Society. It would be distinct from all party politics ; it would have nothing to do with individual disputes or grievances between landlord and tenant ; it would most carefully disclaim all sectarian objects. It would meet in a friendly genial manner, and if a few bottles of sherry could be placed on the table the better. A formal, hard, entirely business-like meeting is undesirable and to be avoided. The affairs in progress should be discussed in a free, open manner, and without any attempt at set speeches, though to prevent mistakes propositions would have to be moved and seconded, and entered in a minute-book. Such a society would be the means of bringing gentlemen together from distant parts of the parish, and would lead to a more intimate social connection. It would have other uses than those for which it was formally instituted.

In the event of a serious outbreak of fever in the village, or any infectious disease, it might be of the very greatest utility in affording assistance to the poor, and in making arrangements for preventing the spread of infection by the plan of isolation. It might set apart a cottage for the reception of patients, and engage additional medical assistance. The influence it would exercise in the village and parish would be very great, and might produce a decided improvement in the moral tone of the place. In the event of disaffection and agitation arising among the labouring classes, it might be enabled to establish a reasonable compromise, and, in time, a good many little petty disputes among the poor would be referred to the society for arbitration.

In large villages it might be found advantageous to establish a ladies' committee in connection with such a society.   There are many matters in which the ladies are better agents, and possess a special knowledge.   It may, perhaps, be thought rather an advanced idea ; but would not some instruction in cookery be extremely useful to the agricultural girl just growing up into womanhood ?   The cooking she learns at home is simply no cooking at all.   It is hardly possible to induce the elder women to change the habits of a lifetime, but the girls, fast growing up, would be eager to learn.   With the increase of wages, the labourer has obtained a certain addition to his fare, and can occasionally afford some of the cheaper pieces of butcher's meat.   But the women have no idea of utilizing these pieces in the

most economical and savoury ways. Plentiful as
vegetables are at times, they are only used in the
coarsest manner. The ladies' committee would also
have important work before them in boarding out
the orphan children from the Union, and also in
endeavouring to find employment for the great girls
who play about the village, getting them into service,
and so on. In the distribution of charities (if charities there must be), ladies are far more efficient than
men, and they may exercise an influence in moral
matters where no one else could interfere. If there
is any charity which deserves to be assisted by this
local society, it is the cheapening of coals in the
winter. Already in some villages the principal
farmers combine to purchase a good stock of coal at
the beginning of winter, and as they buy it in large
quantities they get it somewhat cheaper. Their
teams and waggons haul it to the village, and in the
dead of winter it is retailed to the cottagers at less
than cost price. This is a most useful institution,
and can hardly be called a charity. The fact that
this has been done is a proof that organization for
objects of local benefit is quite possible in rural
parishes. Landowners and resident gentlemen would
naturally take an interest in such proceedings, and
may very properly be asked to subscribe; but the
actual execution of the plans decided on should be
left in the hands of tenant-farmers, who have a
direct interest, and who come into daily contact with
the lower class. As a means of adding to their
funds, the society could give popular entertainments

of reading and singing, which have often been found effective in raising money for the purchase of a new harmonium, and which, at the same time, afford a harmless gratification. It would, perhaps, be better if such a society were to keep itself distinct from any project of church restoration, or even from the school question, because it is most essential that they should be free from the slightest suspicion of leaning towards any party. Their authority must be based upon universal consent. They might perform a useful task if they could induce the cottagers to insure their goods and chattels, or in any way assist them to do so. Cottages are exceptionally liable to conflagration, and after the place is burnt, there is piteous weeping and wailing, and general begging to replace the lost furniture and bedding. There is much to be done also in the matter of savings. It seems to be pretty well demonstrated by the history of benefit clubs and the calculations of actuaries, that the agricultural labourer, out of his amount of wages, cannot put by a sufficient monthly contribution to enable him to receive a pension when he becomes old and infirm. But that is not the slightest reason why he should not save small sums year by year, which, in course of time, would amount to a nice little thing to fall back upon in case of sickness or accident. There are many aged and deserving men who have worked all their lives in one place and almost upon one farm, and, at last, are reduced to the pitiful allowance of the parish, occasionally supplemented by a friendly gift. These cases are very painful to witness, and are felt to be wrong by the tenant-farmers. But one person cannot entirely support them ; and often it happens that the man who would have done his best is dead—the old employer for whom they worked so many years is gone before them to his rest. If there were but a little organization such cases would not pass unnoticed.

Certain it is that the tendency of the age, and the progress of recent events, indicates the coming of a time when organization of some kind in rural districts will be necessary. The labour-agitation was a lesson of this kind. There are upheaving forces at work among the agricultural lower class as well as in the lower class of towns ; a flow of fresh knowledge, and larger aspirations, which require guidance and supervision, lest they run to riot and excess. An organization of the character here indicated would meet the difficulties of the future, and meet them in the best of ways; for while possessing power to improve and to reform, it would have no hated odour of compulsion. The suggestions here put forth are, of course, all more or less tentative. They sketch an outline, the filling up of which must fall upon practical men, and which must depend greatly upon the circumstances of the locality.

THE IDLE EARTH

THE bare fallows of a factory are of short duration, and occur at lengthened intervals. There are the Saturday afternoons—four or five hours' shorter time; there are the Sundays—fifty-two in number; a day or two at Christmas, at Midsummer, at Easter. Fifty-two Sundays, plus fifty-two half-days on Saturdays; eight days more for *bonâ-fide* holidays—in all, eighty-six days on which no labour is done. This is as near as may be just one quarter of the year spent in idleness. But how fallacious is such a calculation! for overtime and night-work make up far more than this deficient quarter; and therefore it may safely be said that man works the whole year through, and has no bare fallow. But earth—idle earth—on which man dwells, has a much easier time of it. It takes nearly a third of the year out in downright leisure, doing nothing but inchoating; a slow process indeed, and one which all the agricultural army have of late tried to hasten, with very indifferent success. Winter seed sown in the fall of the year does not come to anything till the spring; spring seed is not reaped till the autumn is at hand. But it will be argued that this land is not idle, for during those months the seed is slowly growing—absorbing its constituent parts from the atmosphere, the earth, the water; going through astonishing metamorphoses; outdoing the most wonderful laboratory experiments with its untaught, instinctive chemistry. All true enough; and hitherto it has been assumed that the ultimate product of these idle months is sufficient to repay the idleness ; that in the *coup* of the week of reaping there is a dividend recompensing the long, long days of development. Is it really so? This is not altogether a question which a practical man used to City formulas of profit and loss might ask. It is a question to which, even at this hour, farmers themselves—most unpractical of men—are requiring an answer. There is a cry arising throughout the country that farms do not pay; that a man with a moderate 400 acres and a moderate £1,000 of his own, with borrowed money added, cannot get a reasonable remuneration from those acres. These say they would sooner be hotel-keepers, tailors, grocers—anything but farmers. These are men who have tried the task of subduing the stubborn earth, which is no longer bountiful to her children. Much reason exists in this cry, which is heard at the market ordinary, in the lobby, at the club meetings—wherever agriculturists congregate, and which will soon force itself out upon the public. It is like this. Rents have risen. Five shillings per acre makes an enormous difference, though nominally only an additional £100 on 400 acres. But as in agricultural profits one must not reckon more than 8 per cent., this 5s. per acre represents nearly another £1,000 which must be invested in the business, and which must be made to return interest to pay the additional rent. If that cannot be done, then it represents a dead £100 per annum taken out of the agriculturist's pocket.

Then—labour, the great agricultural *crux*. If the occupier pays 3s. per week more to seven men, that adds more than another £50 per annum to his outgoings, to meet which you must somehow make your acres represent another £500. Turnpikes fall in, and the roads are repaired at the ratepayers' cost. Compulsory education—for it is compulsory in reality, since it compels voluntary schools to be built—comes next, and as generally the village committee mull matters, and have to add a wing, and rebuild, and so forth, till they get in debt, there grows up a rate which is a serious matter, not by itself, but added to other things. Just as in great factories they keep accounts in decimals because of the vast multitude of little expenses which are in the aggregate serious —each decimal is equivalent to a rusty nail or so— here on our farm threepence or fourpence in the pound added to threepence or sixpence ditto for voluntary Church-rate, puts an appreciable burden on the man's back. The tightness, however, does not end here; the belt is squeezed closer than this. No man had such long credit as the yeoman of yore (thirty years ago is 'of yore' in our century). Butcher and baker, grocer, tailor, draper, all gave him unlimited credit as to *time*. As a rule, they got paid in the end; for a farmer is a fixture, and does

not have an address for his letters at one place and
live in another. But modern trade manners are
different. The trader is himself pressed. Competition galls his heel. He has to press upon his
customers, and in place of bills sent in for payment
once a year, and actual cash transfer in three, we
have bills punctually every quarter, and due notice
of county court if cheques are not sent at the half-
year. So that the agriculturist wants more ready
cash ; and as his returns come but once a year, he
does not quite see the fairness of having to swell
other men's returns four times in the same period.
Still a step further, and a few words will suffice to
describe the increased cost of all the materials supplied
by these tradesmen. Take coals, for instance. This
is a fact so patent that it stares the world in the face.
A farmer, too, nowadays has a natural desire to live
as other people in his station of life do. He cannot
reconcile himself to rafty bacon, cheese, radishes,
turnip-tops, homespun cloth, smock frocks. He
cannot see why his girls should milk the cows or
wheel out manure from the yards any more than the
daughters of tradesmen ; neither that his sons should
say 'Ay' and 'Noa,' and exhibit a total disregard of
grammar and ignorance of all social customs. The
piano, he thinks, is quite as much in its place in his
cool parlour as in the stuffy so-called drawing-room
at his grocer's in the petty town hard by, where they
are so particular to distinguish the social ranks of
'professional tradesmen' from common tradesmen.
Here in all this, even supposing it kept down to

economical limits, there exists a considerable margin of expenditure greater than in our forefathers' time. True, wool is dearer, meat dearer ; but to balance that put the increased cost of artificial manure and artificial food—two things no farmer formerly bought —and do not forget that the seasons rule all things, and are quite as capricious as ever, and when there is a bad season the loss is much greater than it used to be, just as the foundering of an ironclad costs the nation more than the loss of a frigate.

Experience every day brings home more and more the fatal truth that moderate farms do not pay, and there are even ominous whispers about the 2,000 acres system. The agriculturist says that, work how he may, he only gets 8 per cent. per annum ; the tradesman, still more the manufacturer, gets only 2 per cent. each time, but he turns his money over twenty times a year, and so gets 40 per cent. per annum. Eight per cent. is a large dividend on one transaction, but it is very small for a whole year—a year, the one-thirtieth of a man's whole earning period, if we take him to be in a business at twenty-five, and to be in full work till fifty-five, a fair allowance. Now, why is it that this cry arises that agriculture will not pay? and why is it that the farmer only picks up 8 per cent.? The answer is simple enough. It is because the earth is idle a third of the year. So far as actual cash return is concerned, one might say it was idle eleven out of the twelve months. But that is hardly fair. Say a third of the year.

The earth does not continue yielding a crop day by day as the machines do in the manufactory. The nearest approach to the manufactory is the dairy, whose cows send out so much milk per diem ; but the cows go dry for their calves. Out of the tall chimney shaft there floats a taller column of dark smoke hour after hour ; the vast engines puff and snort and labour perhaps the whole twenty-four hours through ; the drums hum round, the shafts revolve perpetually, and each revolution is a penny gained. It may be only steel-pen making—pens, common pens, which one treats as of no value and wastes by dozens ; but the iron-man thumps them out hour after hour, and the thin stream of daily profit swells into a noble river of gold at the end of the year. Even the pill people are fortunate in this : it is said that every second a person dies in this huge world of ours. Certain it is that every second somebody takes a pill ; and so the millions of globules disappear, and so the profit is nearer 8 per cent. per hour than 8 per cent. per annum. But this idle earth takes a third of the year to mature its one single crop of pills ; and so the agriculturist with his slow returns cannot compete with the quick returns of the trades-man and manufacturer. If he cannot compete, he cannot long exist ; such is the modern law of business. As an illustration, take one large meadow on a dairy farm ; trace its history for one year, and see what an idle workshop this meadow is. Call it twenty acres of first-class land at £2 15s. per acre, or £55 per annum. Remember that twenty acres is a large piece on which some millions multiplied by millions of cubic feet of air play on a month, and on which an incalculable amount of force in the shape of sunlight is poured down in the summer. January sees this plot of a dull, dirty green, unless hidden by snow ; the dirty green is a short, juiceless herbage. The ground is as hard as a brick with the frost. We will not stay now to criticize the plan of carting out manure at this period, or dwell on the great useless furrows. Look carefully round the horizon of the twenty acres, and there is not an animal in sight, not a single machine for making money, not a penny being turned. The cows are all in the stalls. February comes, March passes ; the herbage grows slowly ; but still no machines are introduced, no pennies roll out at the gateways. The farmer may lean on the gate and gaze over an empty workshop, twenty acres big, with his hands in his pockets, except when he pulls out his purse to pay the hedge-cutters who are clearing out the ditches, the women who have been stone-picking, and the carters who took out the manure, half of which stains the drains, while the volatile part mixes with the atmosphere. This is highly profitable and gratifying. The man walks home, hears his daughter playing the piano, picks up the paper, sees himself described as a brutal tyrant to the labourer, and ten minutes afterwards in walks the collector of the voluntary rate for the village school, which educates the labourers' children. April arrives ; grass grows rapidly. May comes ; grass is now long. But still not one farthing has

been made out of that twenty acres. Five months
have passed, and all this time the shafts in the
manufactories have been turning, and the quick
coppers accumulating. Now it is June, and the
mower goes to work ; then the haymakers, and in a
fortnight if the weather be good, a month if it be
bad, the hay is ricked. Say it cost £1 per acre to
make the hay and rick it—*i.e.*, £20—and by this
time half the rent is due, or £27 10s. = total
expenditure (without any profit as yet), £47 10s.,
exclusive of stone-picking, ditch-cleaning, value of
manure, etc. This by the way. The five months'
idleness is the point at present. June is now gone.
If the weather be showery the sharp-edged grass may
spring up in a fortnight to a respectable height ; but
if it be a dry summer—and if it is not a dry summer
the increased cost of haymaking runs away with
profit—then it may be fully a month before there is
anything worth biting. Say at the end of July (one
more idle month) twenty cows are turned in, and
three horses. One cannot estimate how long they
may take to eat up the short grass, but certain it is
that the beginning of November will see that field
empty of cattle again ; and fortunate indeed the
agriculturist who long before that has not had to
' fodder' (feed with hay) at least once a day. Here,
then, are five idle months in spring, one in summer,
two in winter ; total, eight idle months. But, not
to stretch the case, let us allow that during a part
of that time, though the meadow is idle, its produce
—the hay—is being eaten and converted into milk,

cheese and butter, or meat, which is quite correct ;
but, even making this allowance, it may safely be
said that the meadow is absolutely idle for one-third
of the year, or four months. That is looking at the
matter in a mere pounds, shillings, and pence light.
Now look at it in a broader, more national view.
Does it not seem a very serious matter that so large
a piece of land should remain idle for that length of
time ? It is a reproach to science that no method of
utilizing the meadow during that eight months has
been discovered. To go further, it is very hard to
require of the agriculturist that he should keep pace
with a world whose maxims day by day tend to
centralize and concentrate themselves into the one
canon, Time is Money, when he cannot by any
ingenuity get his machinery to revolve more than once
a year. In the old days the farmer belonged to a
distinct class, a very isolated and independent class,
little affected by the progress or retrogression of any
other class, and not at all by those waves of social
change which sweep over Europe. Now the farmer
is in the same position as other producers : the fall
or rise of prices, the competition of foreign lands,
the waves of panic or monetary tightness, all tell
upon him quite as much as on the tradesman. So
that the cry is gradually rising that the idle earth
will not pay.

On arable land it is perhaps even more striking.
Take a wheat crop, for instance. Without going
into the cost and delay of the three years of preparation under various courses for the crop, take the field

just before the wheat year begins. There it lies in November, a vast brown patch, with a few rooks here and there hopping from one great lump to another ; but there is nothing on it—no machine turning out materials to be again turned into money. On the contrary, it is very probable that the agriculturist may be sowing money on it, scarifying it with steam ploughing-engines, tearing up the earth to a great depth in order that the air may penetrate and the frost disintegrate the strong, hard lumps. He may have commenced this expensive process as far back as the end of August, for it is becoming more and more the custom to plough up directly after the crop is removed. All November, December, January, and not a penny from this broad patch, which may be of any size from fifteen to ninety acres, lying perfectly idle. Sometimes, indeed, persons who wish to save manure will grow mustard on it and plough it in, the profit of which process is extremely dubious. At the latter end of February or beginning of March, just as the season is early or late, dry or wet, in goes the seed—another considerable expense. Then April, May, June, July are all absorbed in the slow process of growth—a necessary process, of course, but still terribly slow, and not a penny of ready-money coming in. If the seed was sown in October, as is usual on some soils, the effect is the same—the crop does not arrive till next year's summer sun shines. In August the reaper goes to work, but even then the corn has to be threshed and sent to market before there is any return. Here is a whole year spent in elaborating one single crop, which may, after all, be very unprofitable if it is a good wheat year, and the very wheat over which such time and trouble have been expended may be used to fat beasts, or even to feed pigs. All this, however, and the great expense of preparation, though serious matters enough in themselves, are beside our immediate object. The length of time the land is useless is the point. Making every possible allowance, it is not less than one-third of the year—four months out of the twelve. For all practical—*i.e.*, monetary—purposes it is longer than that. No wonder that agriculturists aware of this fact are so anxious to get as much as possible out of their one crop—to make the one revolution of their machinery turn them out as much money as possible. If their workshop must be enforcedly idle for so long, they desire that when in work there shall be full blast and double tides. Let the one crop be as heavy as it can. Hence the agitation for compensatory clauses, enabling the tenant to safely invest all the capital he can procure in the soil. How else is he to meet the increased cost of labour, of rent, of education, of domestic materials; how else maintain his fair position in society? The demand is reasonable enough; the one serious drawback is the possibility that, even with this assistance, the idle earth will refuse to move any faster.

We have had now the experience of many sewage-farms where the culture is extremely 'high.' It has been found that these farms answer admirably where the land is poor—say, sandy and porous—but on fairly good soil the advantage is dubious, and almost limited to growing a succession of rye-grass crops. After a season or two of sewage soaking the soil becomes so soft that in the winter months it is unapproachable. Neither carts nor any implements can be drawn over it; and then in the spring the utmost care has to be exercised to keep the liquid from touching the young plants, or they wither up and die. Sewage on grass lands produces the most wonderful results for two or three years, but after that the herbage comes so thick and rank and 'strong' that cattle will not touch it; the landlord begins to grumble, and complains that the land, which was to have been improved, has been spoilt for a long time to come. Neither is it certain that the employment of capital in other ways will lead to a continuous increase of profit. There are examples before our eyes where capital has been unsparingly employed, and upon very large areas of land, with most disappointing results. In one such instance five or six farms were thrown into one; straw, and manure, and every aid lavishly used, till a fabulous number of sheep and other stock was kept; but the experiment failed. Many of the farms were again made separate holdings, and grass laid down in the place of glowing cornfields. Then there is another instance, where a gentleman of large means and a cultivated and business mind, called in the assistance of the deep plough, and by dint of sheer subsoil ploughing grew corn profitably several years in succession. But after a while he began to pause, and to turn his attention to stock and other aids. It is not for one moment contended that the use of artificial manure, of the deep plough, of artificial food, and other improvements will not increase the yield, and so the profit of the agriculturist. It is obvious that they do so. The question is, Will they do so to an extent sufficient to repay the outlay? And, further, will they do so sufficiently to enable the agriculturist to meet the ever-increasing weight which presses on him? It would seem open to doubt. One thing appears to have been left quite out of sight by those gentlemen who are so enthusiastic about compensation for unexhausted improvements, and that is, if the landlord is to be bound down so rigidly, and if the tenant really is going to make so large a profit, most assuredly the rents will rise very considerably. How then? Neither the sewage system, nor the deep plough, nor the artificial manure has, as yet, succeeded in overcoming the *vis inertiæ* of the idle earth. They cause an increase in the yield of the one revolution of the agriculturist machine per annum; but they do not cause the machine to revolve twice or three times. Without a decrease in the length of this enforced idleness any very great increase of profit does not seem possible. What would any manufacturer think of a business in which he was compelled to let his engines rest for a third of the year? Would he be eager to sink his capital in such an enterprise?

The practical man will, of course, exclaim that all

this is very true, but Nature is Nature, and must have
its way, and it is useless to expect more than one crop
per annum, and any talk of three or four crops is
perfectly visionary. 'Visionary,' by the way, is a very
favourite word with so-called practical men. But the
stern logic of figures, of pounds, shillings, and pence,
proves that the present condition of affairs cannot
last much longer, and they are the true 'visionaries'
who imagine that it can. This enormous loss of time,
this idleness, must be obviated somehow. It is a
question whether the millions of money at present
sunk in agriculture are not a dead loss to the country;
whether they could not be far more profitably
employed in developing manufacturing industries, or
in utilizing for home consumption the enormous
resources of Southern America and Australasia;
whether we should not get more to eat, and cheaper,
if such was the case. Such a low rate of interest as
is now obtained in agriculture—and an interest by no
means secure either, for a bad season may at any
time reduce it, and even a too good season—such a
state of things is a loss, if not a curse. It is questionable whether the million or so of labourers
representing a potential amount of force almost
incalculable, and the thousands of young farmers
throbbing with health and vigour, eager *to do*, would
not return a far larger amount of good to the world
and to themselves if, instead of waiting for the idle
earth at home to bring forth, they were transported
bodily to the broad savannahs and prairies, and were
sending to the mother-country innumerable shiploads

of meat and corn—unless, indeed, we can discover some method by which our idle earth shall be made to labour more frequently. This million or so of labourers and these thousands of young, powerfully made farmers literally do nothing at all for a third the year but wait, wait for the idle earth. The of strength, the will, the vigour latent in them is wasted. They do not enjoy this waiting by any means. The young agriculturist chafes under the delay, and is eager *to do*. They can hunt and course hares, 'tis true, but that is feeble excitement indeed, and feminine in comparison with the serious work which brings in money.

The idleness of arable and pasture land is as nothing compared to the idleness of the wide, rolling downs. These downs are of immense extent, and stretch through the very heart of the country. They maintain sheep, but in how small a proportion to the acreage ! In the spring and summer the short herbage is cropped by the sheep; but it is short, and it requires a large tract to keep a moderate flock. In the winter the down is left to the hares and field-fares. It has just as long a period of absolute idleness as the arable and pasture land, and when in work the yield is so very, very small.

After all, the very deepest ploughing is but scratching the surface. The earth at five feet beneath the level has not been disturbed for countless centuries. Nor would it pay to turn up this subsoil over large areas, for it is nothing but clay, as many a man has found to his cost who, in the hope of a heavier crop, has dug up his garden half a spade deeper than usual. But when the soil really is good at that depth, we cannot get at it so as to turn it to practical account. The thin stratum of artificial manure which is sown is no more in comparison than a single shower after a drought of months; yet to sow too much would destroy the effect. No blame, then, falls upon the agriculturist, who is only too anxious to get a larger produce. It is useless charging him with incompetency. What countless experiments have been tried to increase the crop : to see if some new system cannot be introduced ! With all its progress, how little real advance has agriculture made ! All because of the stubborn, idle earth. Will not science some day come to our aid, and show how two crops or three may be grown in our short summers ; or how we may even overcome the chill hand of winter ? Science has got as far as this : it recognizes the enormous latent forces surrounding us—electricity, magnetism ; some day, perhaps, it may be able to utilize them. It recognizes the truly overwhelming amount of force which the sun of summer pours down upon our fields, and of which we really make no use. To recognize the existence of a power is the first step towards employing it. Till it was granted that there was a power in steam the locomotive was impossible.

It would be easy to swell this notice of idle earth by bringing in all the waste lands, now doing nothing—the parks, deer forests, and so on. But that is not to the purpose. If the wastes were reclaimed and the parks ploughed up, that would in nowise solve the problem how to make the cultivated earth more busy. It is no use for a man who has a garden to lean on his spade, look over his boundary wall, and say, ' Ah, if neighbour Brown would but dig up his broad green paths how many more potatoes he would grow!' That would not increase the produce of the critic's garden by one single cabbage. Certainly it is most desirable that all lands capable of yielding crops should be reclaimed, but one great subject for the agriculturist to study is, how to shorten the period of idleness in his already cultivated plots. At present the earth is so very idle.

AFTER THE COUNTY FRANCHISE

THE money-lender is the man I most fear to see in the villages after the extension of the county franchise—the money-lender both in his private and public capacity, the man who has already taken a grasp of most little towns that have obtained incorporation in some form. Like Shylock he demands what is in his bond : he demands his interest, and that means a pull at every man's purse—every man, rich or poor—who lives within the boundary. Borrowing is almost the ruin of many such little towns ; rates rise nearly as high as in cities, and people strive all they can to live anywhere outside the limit. Borrowing is becoming one of the curses of modern life, and a sorrowful day it will be when the first village takes to it. The name changes—now it is a local board, now it is commissioners, sometimes a town council : the practice remains the same. These authorities exist but for one purpose—to borrow money, and as any stick will do to beat a dog with, so any pretence will do to exact the uttermost farthing from the inhabitants. Borrowing boards they are, one and all, and nothing else, from whom no one obtains benefit except the solicitor, the surveyor, the lucky architect, and those who secure a despicable living in the rear of the county court. Nothing could better illustrate the strange supineness of the majority of people than the way in which they pay, pay, pay, and submit to every species of extortion at the hands of these incapable blunderers, without so much as a protest. The system has already penetrated into the smallest of the county towns which groan under the incubus; let us hope, let us labour, that it may not continue its course and enter the villages.

It may reasonably be supposed that when once the extension of the franchise becomes an established fact, some kind of local government will soon follow. At present country districts are either without any local government at all—I mean practically, not theoretically—or else they are ruled without the least shadow of real representation. When men are admitted to vote and come to be enlightened as to the full meaning and force of such rights, it is probable that they will shortly demand the power to arrange their own affairs. They will have something to say as to the administration of the poor-law, over which at present they do not possess the slightest control, and they are not at all unlikely to set up a species of self-government in every separate village. I think, in short, that the parish may become the unit in the future to the disintegration of the artificial divisions drawn to facilitate the poor-law. Such divisions, wherein many parishes of the most diverse description and far apart are thrown together anyhow as the gardener pitches weeds into his basket, have done serious harm in the past. They have injured the sense of personal responsibility, they have created a bureaucracy absolutely without feeling, and they have tended to shift great questions out of sight. The shifting of things out of sight—round the corner—is a vile method of dealing with them. Send your wretched poor miles away into a sort of alien workhouse, and then congratulate yourself that you have tided over the difficulty! But the difficulty has not been got over.

A man who can vote, and who is told—as he certainly will be told—that he bears a part in directing the great affairs of his nation, will ask himself why he should not be capable of managing the little affairs of his own neighbourhood. When he has asked himself this question, it will be the first step towards the downfall of the inhuman poor - law. He will go further and say, 'Why should I not settle these things at home? Why should I not walk up to the village from my house in the country lane, and there and then arrange the business which concerns me? Why should I any longer permit it to be done over my head and without my consent by a body of persons in whom I have no confidence, for they do not represent me—they represent property?'

In his own village the voter will observe the school—his own village then is worthy to possess its own school; possibly he may even remotely have some trifling share in the control of the school if there is a board. If that great interest, the children of the parish, can be administered at home, why not the other and much less important interests? Here may be traced a series of reflections, and a succession of steps by which ultimately the whole system of boards of guardians with their attendant powers, as the rural sanitary authority and so forth, may ultimately be swept away. Government will come again to the village.

Then arises the money-lender, and no time should be lost by those who have the good and the genuine liberty of the countryside at heart in labouring to prevent his entry into the village. Whatsoever constitution the village obtains in future, let us strive to strictly limit the borrowing powers of its council. No borrowing powers at all would be best —government without loans would be almost ideal —if that cannot be accomplished, then .at least lay down a stringent regulation putting a firm and impassable limit. Were every one of my way of thinking, government without loans would be imperative. It would be done if it had to be done. Rugged discomfort is preferable to borrowing.

I dread, in a word, lest the follies perpetrated in towns should get into the villages and hamlets, and want to say a word betimes of warning. Imagine a new piece of roadway required, then to get the money let a penny be added to the rates, and the amount produced laid by at interest year after year, till the sum be made up. Better wait a few years and walk half a mile round than borrow the five or six hundred pounds, and have to pay that back and all the interest on it. Shift somehow, do not borrow.

In the discussions upon the agricultural franchise it has been generally assumed that the changes it portends will be shown in momentous State affairs and questions of principle. But perhaps it will be rather in local and home concerns that the alterations will be most apparent. The agricultural labourer voters—and the numerous semi-agricultural voters, not labourers—are more than likely to look at their own parish as well as at the policy of the Foreign Office. Gradually the parish—that is, the village—must become the centre to men who feel at last that they are their own masters. Under some form or other they will take the parish into their own hands, and insist upon their business being managed at home. Some shape of village council must come presently into existence.

Shrewd people are certain to appear upon the scene, pointing out to the cottager that if he desires to rule himself in his own village, he must insist upon one most important point. This is the exclusion of property representation. Instead of property having an overwhelming share, as now, in the direction of affairs, the owner of the largest property must not weigh any heavier in the village council than the wayside cottager. If farmer or landowner sit there he must have one vote only, the same as any other member. The council, if it is to be independent, must represent men and not land in the shape of landowners, or money in the shape of tenant-farmers.

Shrewd people will have no difficulty in explaining
the meaning of this to the village voters, because
they can quote so many familiar instances.   There is
the Education Act in part defeated by the combination of property, landowners and farmers paying to
escape a school-board —a plan temporarily advantageous to them, but of doubtful benefit, possibly
injurious, to the parish at large.   Leaving that
question alone, the fact is patent that the cottager
has no share in the government of his school, because
land and money have combined.   It may be governed
very well ; still it is not *his* government, and will
serve to illustrate the meaning.   There is the board
of guardians, nominally elected, really selected, and
almost self-appointed.   The board of guardians is
land and money simply, and in no way whatever
represents the people.   A favourite principle continually enunciated at the present day is that the
persons chiefly concerned should have the management.   But the lower classes who are chiefly concerned with poor relief, as a matter of fact, have not
the slightest control over that management.   Besides
the guardians, there is still an upper row, and here
the rulers are not even invested with the semblance
of representation, for magistrates are not elected, and
they are guardians by virtue of their being magistrates.
The machinery is thus complete for the defeat of representation and for the despotic control of those who,
being principally concerned, ought by all rule and
analogy to have the main share of the management.
We have seen working men's representatives sit in

the House of Commons; did anyone ever see a
cottage labourer sit as administrator at the board
before which the wretched poor of his own neighbourhood appear for relief?

But it may be asked, Is the village council, then,
composed of small proprietors, to sit down and vote
away the farmer's or landowner's money without
farmer or landowner having so much as a voice in
the matter? Certainly not. The idea of village
self-government supposes a distinct and separate
existence, as it were; the village apart from the
farmer or landowner, and the latter apart from the
village. At present the money drawn in rates from
farmer or landowner is chiefly expended on poor-law
purposes. But, as will presently appear, village self-
government proposes the entire abolition of the poor-
law system, and with it the rates which support it, or
at least the heaviest part of them. Therefore, as this
money would not be concerned, they could receive no
injury, even if they did not sit at the village council
at all.

Imagine the village, figuratively speaking, surrounded by a high wall like a girdle, as towns
were in ancient times, and so cut off altogether
from the large properties surrounding it—on the
one hand the village supporting and governing
itself, and on the other the large properties equally
independent.

The probable result would be a considerable reduction in local burdens on land. A self-supporting
and self-governing moral population is the first step

towards this relief to land so very desirable in the interest of agriculture.

In practice there must remain certain more or less imperial questions, as lines of through road, police, etc., some of which are already managed by the county authority. As these matters affect the farmer and landowner even more than the cottager, clearly they must expect to contribute to the cost, and can rightly claim a share in the management.

Having advanced so far as a village council, and arrived at the stage of managing their own affairs, having, in fact, emerged from pupilage, next comes a question for the council. We now govern our village ourselves; why should we not possess our village? Why should we not live in our own houses? Why should we not have a little share in the land, as much, at least, as we can pay for? At this moment the village, let us say, consists of a hundred cottages, and perhaps there are another hundred scattered about the parish. Of these three-fourths belong to two or three large landowners, and those who reside in them, however protected by enactment, can never have a sense of complete independence. We should own these cottages, so that the inhabitants might practically pay rent to themselves. We must purchase them, a few at a time; the residents can repurchase from us and so become freeholders. For a purchaser there must be a seller, and here one of the questions of the future appears: Can an owner of this kind of property be permitted to refuse to sell? Must he be compelled to sell?

It is clear that if the village voter thoroughly addresses himself to his home affairs there is room for some remarkable incidents. There is reason now, is there not, to dread the appearance of the money-lender ?

About this illustrative parish there lie many hundred acres of good land all belonging to one man, while we, the said village council, do not possess a rood apiece, and our constituents not a square yard. Rightfully we ought to have a share, yet we do not agitate for confiscation. Shall we then say that every owner of land should be obliged to sell a certain fixed percentage—a very small percentage would suffice—upon proffer of a reasonable amount, the proffer being made by those who propose to personally settle on it ? Of one thousand acres suppose ten or twenty liable to forcible purchase at a given and moderate price. After all it is not a much more overbearing thing than the taking by railways of land in almost any direction they please, and not nearly so tyrannous, so stupidly tyrannous, as some of the acts of folly committed by local boards in towns. Not long since the newspapers reported a case where a local authority actually ran a main sewer across a gentleman's park, and ventilated it at regular intervals, completely destroying the value of an historic mansion, and utterly ruining a beautiful domain. This was fouling their own nest with a vengeance. They should have cherished that park as one of their chiefest glories, their proudest possession. Parks and woods are daily becoming of almost priceless value to the nation; nothing could be so mad as to destroy these last homes of nature. Just conceive the inordinate folly of marking such a property with sewer ventilators. This is a hundred times more despotic than a proposal that say two per cent. of land should be forcibly purchasable for actual settlement. Even five per cent. would not make an appreciable difference to an estate, though every fraction of the five per cent. were taken up.

For such proposals to have any effect, the transfer of real property must be greatly simplified and cheapened. From time to time, whenever a discussion occurs upon this subject, and there are signs that the glacier-like movements of government will be hastened by public stir, up rises some great lawyer and explains to the world that really nothing could be simpler or cheaper than such transfer. All that can be wished in that direction has been accomplished already; there is not the slightest ground for agitation; every obstruction has been removed, and the machinery is now perfect. He quotes a long list of Acts to demonstrate the progress that has been made, and so winds up a very effective speech. Facts, however, are not in accordance with these gracious words. Here is an instance. A cottage in a village was recently sold for seventy pounds; the costs, legal expenses, parchments, all the antiquated formalities absorbed *thirty-two pounds*, only three pounds less than half the value of the little property. Could anything be more obviously wrong than such a system.

The difficulties in the way of simplification are created difficulties, entirely artificial, owing their existence to legal ingenuity. How often has the question been asked and never answered : Why should there be any more expense in transferring the ownership of an acre of land than of £100 stock ?

The village council coming into contact with this matter is likely to agitate continuously for its rectification, since otherwise its movements will be seriously hampered. If they succeed in obtaining the abolition of these semi-feudal survivals, they will have conferred a substantial benefit upon the community. County franchise would be worth the granting merely to secure this.

Let us take the case for a moment of a labourer at this day and consider his position. What has he before him? He has a hand-to-mouth, nomad existence, ending in the inevitable frozen misery of the workhouse. Men with votes and political power are hardly likely to endure this for many more years, and it is much to be hoped that they will not endure it. A labourer may be never so hard-working, so careful, so sober, and yet let his efforts be what they may, his old age finds him helpless. I am sure there is no class of men among whom may be found so many industrious, plodding, sober folk, economical to the verge of starvation. Their straightforward lives are thrown away. Their sons and daughters, warned by example, go to the cities, and there lose the virtues that rendered their forefathers so ad-

mirable even in their wretchedness. It will indeed
be a blessing if, as I hope, the outcome of the
franchise is the foundation of solid inducements to
the countryman to stay in the country. I use the
phrase countryman purposely, intending it to include
small farmers and small farmers' sons; the latter are
likewise driven away from the land year by year as
much as the young labourers, and are as serious a
loss to it. Did the possibility exist of purchasing a
cottage and a plot of ground of moderate size, it is
more than probable that the labourer's son would
remain in the village, or return to it, and his
daughter would come back to the village to be
married. We hear how the poor Italian or the poor
Swiss leaves his native country for our harder climate,
how he works and saves, and by-and-by returns to
his village and purchases some corner of earth. This
seems a legitimate and worthy object. We do not
hear of our own sturdy labourers returning to their
village with a pocketful of money and purchasing a
plot of ground or a cottage. They do not attempt
it, because they know that under present conditions
it is nearly impossible. There is no land for them
to buy. Why not, when the country is nothing but
land? Because the owner of ten thousand acres is
by no means obliged to part with the minutest frag-
ment of it. If by chance a stray portion be somewhere for sale, the expenses, the costs, the parchments,
the antiquated formalities, the semi-feudal routine
delay and possibly prevent transfer altogether. If
land were accessible, and the cost of transferring

cottage property reduced to reasonable proportions, the labourer would have the soundest of all inducements to practise self-denial in his youth. Cities might attract him temporarily for the advantage of higher wages, but he would put the excess by and ultimately bring it home. Even the married cottager with a family would try his hardest to save a little with such a hope before him.

The existing circumstances deny hope altogether. Neither land nor cottages are to be had, there are no sellers, and the cost of transfer is prohibitive; men are shifted on, they have no security of tenure, they are passed on from farm to farm and can settle nowhere. The competition for a house in some districts is keen to the last degree; it seems as if there were eager crowds waiting for homes. Recently while roaming on the Sussex hills I met an ancient shepherd whose hair was white as snow, though he stood upright enough. I inquired the names of the hills there, and he replied that he did not know; he was a stranger, he had only been moved there lately. How strangely changed are things when a grey-headed shepherd does not know the names of his hills! At a time of life when he ought to have been comfortably settled he had had to shift.

Sentiment is more stubborn than fact. People will face the sternest facts, dire facts, stubborn facts, and stay on in spite of all; but once let sentiment alter and away they troop. So I think that some part of the distaste for farming visible about us is due to change of sentiment—to feeling repelled—as well as to unfruitful years. Men have stood out against weary weather in all ages of agriculture, but lately they have felt hurt and repelled, the sentiment of attachment to home has been rudely torn up, and so now the current sets against farming, though farms are often offered on advantageous terms. In the same way, besides the stubborn facts that drive the labourer from the village and prevent his return to settle, there is a yet more stubborn sentiment repelling him. Made a man of by education—not only of books, but the unconscious education of progressive times—the labourer and his son and daughter have thoughts of independence. To be humbly subservient to the will of those above them, to be docilely obedient, not only to the employer, but to all in some sort of authority, is not attractive to them. Plainly put, the rule of parson and squire, tenant and guardian, is repellent to them in these days. They would rather go away. If they do save money in cities, they do not care to return and settle under the thumb of these their old masters. Besides more attractive facts, the sentiment of independence must be called into existence before the labourer, or, for the matter of that, the small farmer's son, will willingly settle in the village. That sense of independence can only arise when the village governs itself by its own council, irrespective of parson, squire, tenant, or guardian. Towards that end the power to vote is almost certain to drift slowly.

Nothing can be conceived more harshly antagonistic to the feelings of a naturally industrious race of men than the knowledge that as a mass they are looked upon as prospective 'paupers.' I detest this word so much that it is painful to me to write it; I put it between inverted commas as a sort of protest, so that it may appear a hated intruder, and not native to the text. The local government existing at this day in country districts is practically based upon the assumption that every labouring man will one day be a 'pauper,' will one day come to the workhouse. By the workhouse and its board the cottage is governed; the workhouse is the centre, the bureau, the *hôtel de ville*. The venue of local government must be changed before the labourer can feel independent, and it will be changed doubtless as he becomes conscious of the new power he has acquired. Shall the bitterness of the workhouse at last pass away? Let us hope so let us be thankful indeed if the franchise leads to the downfall of those cruel walls. Yet what is the cruelty of cold walls to the cruelty of 'system'? A workhouse in the country is usually situated as nearly as possible in the centre of the Union, it may be miles from the outlying parishes. Thither the worn-out cottager is borne away from the fields, his cronies, his little helps to old age such as the corner where the sun shines, the friend who allows little amenities, to dwindle and die. The workhouse bureau extends its unfeeling hands into every detail of cottage life. No wonder the labourer does not deny himself to save money in order to settle where these things are done. A happy day it will be when the workhouse door is shut and the building sold for materials. A gentleman not long since wrote to me a vindication of his workhouse— I cannot at the moment place my hand on the figures he sent me, but I grant that they were conclusive from his point of view; they were not extravagant, the administration appeared correct. But this is not my point of view at all. Figures are not humanity. The workhouse and the poor-law system are inhuman, debasing, and injurious to the whole country, and the better they are administered, the worse it really is, since it affords a specious pretext for their continuance. What would be the use of a captain assuring his passengers that the ship was well found, plenty of coal in the bunkers, the engines oiled and working smoothly, when they did not want to go to the port for which he was steering? An exact dose of poison may be administered, but what comfort is it to the victim to assure him that it was accurately measured to a minim? What is the value of informing me that the 'paupers' are properly looked after when I do not want any 'paupers'?

But how manage without the poor-law system? There are several ways. There is the insurance method: space will not permit of discussion in this paper, but one fact which speaks volumes may be alluded to. Two large societies exist in this country called the 'Oddfellows' and the 'Foresters'; they number their members by the million; they assist their members not only at home, but all over the world (which is what no poor-law has ever done); they govern themselves by their own laws, and they prosper exceedingly—an honour to the nation. They have solved the difficulty for themselves.

When the village governs itself and takes all matters into its own hands, in time the sentiment of independence may grow up and men begin to work and strive and save, that they may settle at home. It would be a very noble thing indeed if the true English feeling for home life should become the dominant passion of the country once again. By home life I mean that which gathers about a house, however small, standing in its own grounds. Something comes into existence about such a house, an influence, a pervading feeling, like some warm colour softening the whole, tinting the lichen on the wall, even the very smoke-marks on the chimney. It is home, and the men and women born there will never lose the tone it has given them. Such homes are the the strength of a land. The emigrant who leaves us for the backwoods hopes to carve out a home for himself there, and we consider that an ambition to be admired. I hope the day will come when some at least of our people may be able to set up homes for themselves in their own country. To-day, if they would live, they must crowd into the city, often to dwell in the midst of hideous squalor, or they must cross the ocean. They would rather endure the squalor, rather say farewell for ever and sail for America, than stay in the village where everyone is master, and none of their class can be independent. The village must be its own master before it becomes popular. County government may be reformed with advantage, but that is not enough, because it must necessarily be too far off. People in the country are scattered, and each little centre is naturally only concerned with itself. A government having its centre at the county town is too far away, and is likely to bear too much resemblance to the boards of guardians and present authorities, to be representative of land and money rather than of men. Progress can only be made in each little centre separately by means of village councils, genuinely representative of the village folk, unswayed by mansion, vicarage, or farm. Then by degrees we may hope to see the re-awakening of English home-life in contradistinction to that unhappy restlessness which drives so many to the cities.

Men will then wake up and work with energy because they will have hope. The slow, plodding manner of the labourer—the dull ways even of the many industrious cottagers—these will disappear, giving place to push and enterprise. Why does a lawyer work as no navvy works? Why does a cabinet minister labour the year through as hard as a miner? Because they have a mental object. So will the labourer work when he has a mental object —to possess a home for himself.

Whenever such homes become numerous and the new life of the country begins to flow, pressure will soon be brought to bear for the removal of the mediæval law which prevents the use of steam on common roads. Modern as the law is, it is mediæval in its tendency as much as a law would be for the restriction of steam on the ocean. Suppose a statute compelling all ships to sail, or, if they steamed, not to exceed four miles an hour ! One of the greatest drawbacks to agriculture is the cost and difficulty of transit ; wheat, flour, and other foods come from America at far less expense in proportion than it takes to send a waggon-load to London. This cost of transit in the United Kingdom will ultimately, one would think, become the question of the day, concerning as it does every individual. Agriculture on a large scale finds it a heavy drawback ; to agriculture on a small scale it is often prohibitory. A man may cultivate his two-acre plot and produce vegetables and fruit, but if he cannot get his produce to London (or some great city), the demand for it is small, and the value low in proportion. As settlers increase, as the village becomes its own master, and men pass part at least of their time labouring on their own land, the difficulty will be felt to be a very serious one. Transit they must have, and steam alone can supply it. Engines and cars can be built to run on common roads almost as easily as on rails, and as for danger it is merely the interested outcry of those who deal in horses. There is no danger. Fine smooth roads exist all over the country ; they have been kept up from coaching days as if in a prophetic spirit for their future use by steam. Upon these roads engines and cars can travel at a good fair pace, collecting produce, and either delivering it to the through lines of rail, or passing it on from road-train to road-train till it reaches the city. This is a very important matter indeed, for in the future easier and quicker transit will become imperative for agriculture. The impost of extraordinary tithe—the whole system of tithe—again, is doomed when once the country begins to live its new life. Freedom of cultivation is ten times more needful to the small than to the large proprietor.

These changes closely examined lose their threatening aspect, so much so that the marvel is they did not commence fifty years ago instead of waiting till now, and even now to be only potential. What is there in the present condition of agriculture to make farmer or landowner anxious that the existing system of things should continue ? Surely nothing ; surely every consideration points in favour of moderate change. Those who quote the example of France, and would argue that dissatisfaction must, as there, increase with efforts to allay it, must know full well in their hearts that there is no comparison whatever with France. The two peoples are so entirely different. So little contents our race that the danger is rather the other way, that they will be too easily satisfied. Such changes as I have indicated, when examined closely, are really so mild that in full operation they would scarcely make any difference in the relation of the classes. Such village councils would be very anxious for the existence of the farmer, and for his interests to be respected, for the sufficient reason that they know the value of wages. Perhaps they might even, under certain conditions, become almost too willing partisans of the farmer for their best interests to be served. I can imagine such conditions easily enough, and the possibility of the three sections, labourer, farmer, and owner, becoming more closely welded together than ever. There is far more stolidity to be regretted than revolution to be feared. The danger is lest the new voters should stolidify—crystallize—in tacit league with existing conditions ; not lest we should go hop, skip, and jump over Niagara.

A probable result of these changes is an increase in the value of land : if thousands of people should ever really begin to desire it, and to work and save for the object of buying it, analogy would suppose a rise in value. Instead of a loss there would be a gain to the landowner, and I think to the farmer, who would have a larger supply of labour, and possibly a strong posse of supporters at the poll in their men. Instead of division coalescence is more probable. The greater his freedom, the greater his attachment to home, the more settled the labourer, the firmer will become the position of all three classes. The landowner has nothing whatever to fear for his park, his mansion, his privacy, his shooting, or anything else. What is taken will be paid for, and no more will be taken than needful. Parks and woods are becoming of priceless value ; we should have to preserve a few landlords if only to have parks and woods. Perfect rights of possession are not at all incompatible with enjoyment by the people. There are domains to be found where people wander at their will, and enjoy themselves as much as they please, and yet the owner retains every right. It is true that there are also numerous parks rigidly closed to the public, demonstrating the folly of the proprietors—square miles of folly. The use of a little compulsion to open them would not be at all deplorable. But it must stop there and not encroach farther. Having obtained the use, be careful not to destroy.

The one great aim I have in all my thoughts is the acquisition of public and the preservation of private liberty. Freedom is the most valuable of all things, and is to be sought with all our powers of mind and hand. Freedom does not mean injustice, but neither will it put up with injustice. A singular misapprehension seems to be widely spread in our time; it is that there are two great criminals, the poor man or 'pauper' and the landlord. At opposite extremes of the scale they are regarded as equally guilty. Every right—the right to vote, the right to live in his native village, the right to be buried decently—is taken from the unhappy poor man or 'pauper.' He is a criminal. To own land is to be guilty of unpardonable sin, nothing is so bad; as criminals are ordered to be searched and everything taken from them, so everything is to be taken from the landowner. The injustice to both is equally evident. Anyone by chance of circumstances, uncontrollable, may be reduced to extreme poverty; how cruel to punish the unfortunate with the loss of civil rights! Anyone by good fortune and labour may acquire wealth, and would naturally wish to purchase land : is he then guilty ? In equity both the poor and the rich should enjoy the same civil rights.

Let the new voter then bear in mind above all things the value of individual liberty, and not be too anxious to destroy the liberty of others, an action that invariably recoils. Let him, having obtained his freedom, beware how he surrenders it again either to local influence in the shape of land or money, or to the outside orator who may urge him on for his own ends. Efforts will be made no doubt to use the new voter for the purposes of cliques and fanatics. He can always test the value of their object by the question of wages and food—'How will it affect my wages and food?'—and probably that is the test he will apply. A little knot of resolute and straightforward men should be formed in every village to see that the natural outcome of the franchise is obtained. They can begin as vigilance committees, and will ultimately reach to legal status as councils.

THE WILTSHIRE LABOURER

TEN years have passed away,* and the Wiltshire labourers have only moved in two things—education and discontent. I had the pleasure then of pointing out in 'Fraser' that there were causes at work promising a considerable advance in the labourers' condition. I regret to say now that the advance, which in a measure did take place, has been checkmated by other circumstances, and there they remain much as I left them, except in book-learning and mental restlessness. They possess certain permanent improvements—unexhausted improvements in agricultural language—but these, in some way or other, do not seem now so valuable as they looked. Ten years since important steps were being taken for the material benefit of the labouring class. Landowners had awakened to the advantage of attaching the peasantry to the soil, and were spending large sums of money building cottages. Everywhere cottages were put up on sanitary principles, so that to-day few farms on great estates are without homes for the men. This substantial improvement remains, and cannot fade away. Much building, too, was progressing about the farmsteads; the cattle-sheds were

* Written in 1887.

undergoing renovation, and this to some degree concerned the labourer, who now began to do more of his work under cover. The efforts of every writer and speaker in the country had not been without effect, and allotments, or large gardens, were added to most cottage homes. The movement, however, was slow, and promised more than it performed, so that there are still cottages which have not shared in it. But, on the whole, an advance in this respect did occur, and the aggregate acreage of gardens and allotments must be very considerably larger now than formerly. These are solid considerations to quote on the favourable side. I have been thinking to see if I could find anything else. I cannot call to mind anything tangible, but there is certainly more liberty, an air of freedom and independence—something more of the 'do as I please' feeling exhibited. Then the sum ends. At that time experiments were being tried on an extended scale in the field : such as draining, the enlargement of fields by removing hedges, the formation of private roads, the buildings already mentioned, and new systems of agriculture, so that there was a general stir and bustle which meant not only better wages but wages for more persons. The latter is of the utmost importance to the tenant-labourer, by which I mean a man who is settled, because it keeps his sons at home. Common experience all over the world has always shown that three or four or more people can mess together, as in camps, at a cheaper rate than they can live separately. If the father of the family can find work for his boys within a reasonable distance of home, with their united contributions they can furnish a very comfortable table, one to which no one could object to sit down, and then still have a sum over and above with which to purchase clothes, and even to indulge personal fancies. Such a pleasant state of things requires that work should be plentiful in the neighbourhood. Work at that time was plentiful, and contented and even prosperous homes of this kind could be found. Here is just where the difficulty arises. From a variety of causes the work has subsided. The father of the family—the settled man, the tenant-labourer—keeps on as of yore, but the boys cannot get employment near home. They have to seek it afar, one here, one yonder—all apart, and the wages each separately receives do but just keep them in food among strangers. It is this scarcity of work which in part seems to have counterbalanced the improvements which promised so well. Instead of the progress naturally to be expected you find the same insolvency, the same wearisome monotony of existence in debt, the same hopeless countenances and conversation.

There has been a contraction of enterprise everywhere, and a consequent diminution of employment. When a factory shuts its doors, the fact is patent to all who pass. The hum of machinery is stopped, and smoke no longer floats from the chimney ; the building itself, large and regular—a sort of emphasized plainness of architecture—cannot be overlooked. It is evident to everyone that work has ceased, and the least reflection shows that hundreds of men, perhaps hundreds of families, are reduced from former comparative prosperity. But when ten thousand acres of land fall out of cultivation, the fact is scarcely noticed. There the land is just the same, and perhaps some effort is still made to keep it from becoming altogether foul, so that a glance detects no difference. The village feels it, but the world does not see it. The farmer has left, and the money he paid over as wages once a week is no longer forthcoming. Each man's separate portion of that sum was not much in comparison with the earnings of fortunate artisans, but it was money. Ten, twelve, or as much as fifteen shillings a week made a home ; but just sufficient to purchase food and meet other requirements, such as clothes ; yet still a home. On the cessation of the twelve shillings where is the labourer to find a substitute for it ? Our country is limited in extent, and it has long been settled to its utmost capacity. Under present circumstances there is no room anywhere for more than the existing labouring population. It is questionable if a district could be found where, under these present circumstances, room could be found for ten more farmers' men. Only so many men can live as can be employed ; in each district there are only so many farmers ; they cannot enlarge their territories ; and thus it is that every agricultural parish is full to its utmost. Some places among meadows appear almost empty. No one is at work in the fields as you pass ; there are cattle swishing their tails in the shadow of the elms, but not a single visible person ; acres upon acres of grass, and no human being. Towards the latter part of the afternoon, if the visitor has patience to wait, there will be a sound of shouting, which the cattle understand, and begin in their slow way to obey by moving in its direction. Milking time has come, and one or two men come out to fetch in the cows. That over, for the rest of the evening and till milking time in the morning the meadows will be vacant. Naturally it would be supposed that there is room here for a great number of people. Whole crowds might migrate into these grassy fields, put up shanties, and set to work. But set to work at what? That is just the difficulty. Whole crowds could come here and find plenty of room to walk about—and starve! Cattle require but few to look after them. Milch cattle need most, but grazing beasts practically no one, for one can look after so many. Upon inquiry it would be found that this empty parish is really quite full. Very likely there are empty cottages, and yet it is quite full. A cottage is of no use unless the occupier can obtain regular weekly wages. The farmers are already paying as many as they can find work for, and not one extra hand is wanted ; except, of course, in the press of hay-harvest, but no one can settle on one month's work out of twelve. When ten or fifteen thousand acres of land fall out of cultivation, and farmers leave, what is to become of the labouring families they kept? What has become of them?

It is useless blinking the fact that what a man wants in our time is good wages, constant wages,

and a chance of increasing wages. Labouring men
more and more think simply of work and wages.
They do not want kindness—they want coin.   In
this they are not altogether influenced by self-
interest ; they are driven rather than go of their
own movement.   The world pushes hard on their
heels, and they must go on like the rest.   A man
cannot drift up into a corner of some green lane,
and stay in his cottage out of the tide of life, as was
once the case.   The tide comes to him.   He must
find money somehow ; the parish will not keep him
on out-relief if he has no work ; the rate-collector
calls at his door ; his children must go to school
decently clad with pennies in each little hand.   He
must have wages.   You may give him a better
cottage, you may give him a large allotment, you
may treat him as an equal, and all is of no avail.
Circumstance—the push of the world—forces him to
ask you for wages.   The farmer replies that he has
only work for just so many and no more.   The
land is full of people.   Men reply in effect, ' We
cannot stay if a chance offers us to receive wages
from any railway, factory, or enterprise ; if wages
are offered to us in the United States, there we must
go.'   If they heard that in a town fifty miles distant
twenty shillings could be had for labour, how many
of the hale men do you suppose would stay in the
village ?   Off they would rush to receive the twenty
shillings per week, and the farmers might have the
land to themselves if they liked.   Eighteen shillings
to a pound a week would draw off every man from

agriculture, and leave every village empty. If a vast industrial combination announced regular wages of that amount for all who came, there would not be a man left in the fields out of the two millions or more who now till them.

A plan to get more wages out of the land would indeed be a wonderful success. As previously explained, it is not so much the amount paid to one individual as the paying of many individuals that is so much to be desired. Depression in agriculture has not materially diminished the sum given to a particular labourer, but it has most materially diminished the sum distributed among the numbers. One of the remarkable features of agricultural difficulties is, indeed, that the quotation of wages is nominally the same as in the past years of plenty. But then not nearly so many receive them. The father of the family gets his weekly money the same now as ten years since. At that date his sons found work at home. At the present date they have to move on. Some farmer is likely to exclaim, 'How can this be, when I cannot get enough men when I want them ?' Exactly so, but the question is not when you want *them*, but when they want you. You cannot employ them, as of old, all the year round, therefore they migrate, or move to and fro, and at harvest time may be the other side of the county.

The general aspect of country life was changing fast enough before the depression came. Since then it has continued to alter at an increasing rate—a rate accelerated by education ; for I think education increases the struggle for more wages. As a man grows in social stature so he feels the want of little things which it is impossible to enumerate, but which in the aggregate represent a considerable sum. Knowledge adds to a man's social stature, and he immediately becomes desirous of innumerable trifles which, in ancient days, would have been deemed luxuries, but which now seem very commonplace. He wants somewhat more fashionable clothes, and I use the word fashion in association with the plough-man purposely, for he and his children do follow the fashion now in as far as they can, once a week at least. He wants a newspaper—only a penny a week, but a penny is a penny. He thinks of an excursion like the artisan in towns. He wants his boots to shine as workmen's boots shine in towns, and must buy blacking. Very likely you laugh at the fancy of shoe-blacking having anything to do with the farm labourer and agriculture. But I can assure you it means a good deal. He is no longer satisfied with the grease his forefathers applied to their boots; he wants them to shine and reflect. For that he must, too, have lighter boots, not the heavy, old, clod-hopping watertights made in the village. If he retains these for week-days, he likes a shiny pair for Sundays. Here is the cost, then, of an addi-tional pair of shoes; this is one of the many trifles the want of which accompanies civilization. Once now and then he writes a letter, and must have pen, ink, and paper; only a pennyworth, but then a penny is a coin when the income is twelve or fourteen shillings a week.   He likes a change of hats—a felt at least for Sunday.   He is not happy till he has a watch.   Many more such little wants will occur to anyone who will think about them, and they are the necessary attendants upon an increase of social stature. To obtain them the young man must have money— coins, shillings, and pence.   His thoughts, therefore, are bent on wages ; he must get wages somewhere, not merely to live, for bread, but for these social necessaries.   That he can live at home with his family, that in time he may get a cottage of his own, that cottages are better now, large gardens given, that the labourer is more independent—all these and twenty other considerations—all these are nothing to him, because they are not to be depended on.   Wages paid weekly are his aim, and thus it is that education increases the value of a weekly stipend, and increases the struggle for it by sending so many more into the ranks of competitors.   I cannot see myself why, in the course of a little time, we may not see the sons of ploughmen competing for clerk- ships, situations in offices of various kinds, the numerous employments not of a manual character. So good is the education they receive, that, if only their personal manners happen to be pleasant, they have as fair a chance of getting such work as others.

Ceaseless effort to obtain wages causes a drifting about of the agricultural population.   The hamlets and villages, though they seem so thinly inhabited, are really full, and every extra man and youth, find- ing himself unable to get the weekly stipend at home, travels away. Some go but a little distance, some across the width of the country, a few emigrate, though not so many as would be expected. Some float up and down continually, coming home to their native parish for a few weeks, and then leaving it again. A restlessness permeates the ranks ; few but those with families will hire for the year. They would rather do anything than that. Family men must do so because they require cottages, and four out of six cottages belong to the landowners and are part and parcel of the farms. The activity in cottage building, to which reference has been made, as prevailing ten or twelve years since, was solely on the part of the landowners. There were no independent builders ; I mean the cottages were not built by the labouring class. They are let by farmers to those labourers who engage for the year, and if they quit this employment they quit their houses. Hence it is that even the labourers who have families are not settled men in the full sense, but are liable to be ordered on if they do not give satisfaction, or if cause of quarrel arises. The only settled men—the only fixed population in villages and hamlets at the present day—are that small proportion who possess cottages of their own. This proportion varies, of course, but it is always small. Of old times, when it was the custom for men to stay all their lives in one district, and to work for one farmer quite as much for payment in kind as for the actual wages, this made little difference. Very few men once settled in regular employment moved again ; they and their families remained for many years as stationary as if the cottage was their property, and frequently their sons succeeded to the place and work. Now in these days the custom of long service has rapidly disappeared. There are many reasons, the most potent, perhaps, the altered tone of the entire country. It boots little to inquire into the causes. The fact is, then, that no men, not even with families, will endure what once they did. If the conditions are arbitrary, or they consider they are not well used, or they hear of better terms elsewhere, they will risk it and go. So, too, farmers are more given to changing their men than was once the case, and no longer retain the hereditary faces about them. The result is that the fixed population may be said to decline every year. The total population is probably the same, but half of it is nomad. It is nomad for two reasons—because it has no home, and because it must find wages.

Farmers can only pay so much in wages and no more ; they are at the present moment really giving higher wages than previously, though nominally the same in amount. The wages are higher judged in relation to the price of wheat ; that is, to their profits. If coal falls in price, the wages of coal-miners are reduced. Now, wheat has fallen heavily in price, but the wages of the labourer remain the same, so that he is, individually, when he has employment, receiving a larger sum. Probably, if farming accounts were strictly balanced, and farming like any other business, that sum would be found to be more than the business would bear. No trace of oppression in wages can be found. The farmer gets allowances from his landlord, and he allows something to his labourers, and so the whole system is kept up by mutual understanding. Except under a very important rise in wheat, or a favourable change in the condition of agriculture altogether, it is not possible for the farmers to add another sixpence either to the sum paid to the individual or to the sum paid in the aggregate to the village.

Therefore, as education increases—and it increases rapidly — as the push of the world reaches the hamlet; as the labouring class increase in social stature, and twenty new wants are found ; as they come to look forth upon matters in a very different manner to their stolid forefathers ; it is evident that some important problems will arise in the country. The question will have to be asked : Is it better for this population to be practically nomad or settled ? How is livelihood—*i.e.*, wages—to be found for it? Can anything be substituted for wages ? Or must we devise a gigantic system of emigration, and in a twelvemonth (if the people took it up) have every farmer crying out that he was ruined, he could never get his harvest in. I do not think myself that the people could be induced to go under any temptation. They like England in despite of their troubles. If the farmer could by any happy means find out some new plant to cultivate, and so obtain a better profit and be able to give wages to more hands, the nomad population would settle itself somehow, if in mud

huts.   No chance of that is in sight at present, so
we are forced round to the consideration of a substitute for wages.

Now, ten or twelve years since, when much
activity prevailed in all things agricultural, it was
proposed to fix the labouring population to the soil
by building better cottages, giving them large gardens
and allotments, and various other privileges.   This
was done; and in 'Fraser' I did not forget to credit
the good intent of those who did it.   Yet now we
see, ten years afterwards, that instead of fixing the
population, the population becomes more wandering.
Why is this?   Why have not these cottages and
allotments produced their expected effect?   There
seems but one answer—that it is the lack of fixity
of tenure.   All these cottages and allotments have
only been held on sufferance, on good behaviour,
and hence they have failed.   For even for material
profit in the independent nineteenth century men do
not care to be held on their good behaviour.   A
contract must be free and equal on both sides to be
respected.   To illustrate the case, suppose that some
large banking institution in London gave out as a
law that all the employés must live in villas belonging to the bank, say at Norwood.   There they could
have very good villas, and gardens attached, and on
payment even paddocks, and there they could dwell
so long as they remained in the office.   But the
instant any cause of disagreement arose they must
quit not only the office but their homes.   What an
outcry would be raised against bank managers'

tyranny were such a custom to be introduced ! The extreme hardship of having to leave the house on which so much trouble had been expended, the garden carefully kept up and planted, the paddock ; to leave the neighbourhood where friends had been found, and which suited the constitution, and where the family were healthy. Fancy the stir there would be, and the public meetings to denounce the harsh interference with liberty ! Yet, with the exception that the clerk might have £300 a year, and the labourer 12s. or 14s. a week, the cases would be exactly parallel. The labourer has no fixity of tenure. He does not particularly care to lay himself out to do his best in the field or for his master, because he is aware that service is no inheritance, and at any moment circumstances may arise which may lead to his eviction. For it is really eviction, though unaccompanied by the suffering associated with the word—I was going to write 'abroad' for in Ireland. So that all the sanitary cottages erected at such expense, and all the large gardens and the allotments offered, have failed to produce a contented and settled working population. Most people are familiar by this time with the demand of the tenant farmers for some exalted kind of compensation, which in effect is equivalent to tenant-right, *i.e.*, to fixity of tenure. Without this, we have all been pretty well informed by now, it is impossible for farmers to flourish, since they cannot expend capital unless they feel certain of getting it back again. This is precisely the case with the labourer. His labour is his capital, and he cannot expend it in one district unless he is assured of his cottage and garden —that is, of his homestead and farm. You cannot have a fixed population unless it has a home, and the labouring population is practically homeless. There appears no possibility of any real amelioration of their condition until they possess settled places of abode. Till then they must move to and fro, and increase in restlessness and discontent. Till then they must live in debt, from hand to mouth, and without hope of growth in material comfort. A race for ever trembling on the verge of the work-house cannot progress and lay up for itself any saving against old age. Such a race is feeble and lacks cohesion, and does not afford that backbone an agricultural population should afford to the country at large. At the last, it is to the countryman, to the ploughman, and 'the farmer's boy,' that a land in difficulty looks for help. They are the last line of defence—the reserve, the rampart of the nation. Our last line at present is all unsettled and broken up, and has lost its firm and solid front. Without homes, how can its ranks ever become firm and solid again?

An agricultural labourer entering on a cottage and garden with his family, we will suppose, is informed that so long as he pays his rent he will not be disturbed. He then sets to work in his off hours to cultivate his garden and his allotment; he plants fruit-trees; he trains a creeper over his porch. His boys and girls have a home whenever out of service, and when they are at home they can assist in cultivating their father's little property. The family has a home and a centre, and there it will remain for generations. Such is certainly the case wherever a labourer has a cottage of his own. The family inherit it for generations ; it would not be difficult to find cases in which occupation has endured for a hundred years. There is no danger now of the younger members of the family staying too much at home. The pressure of circumstances is too strong, as already explained ; all the tendencies of the time are such as would force them from home in search of wages. There is no going back, they must push forwards.

The cottage-tenure, like the farm-tenure, must come from the landlord, of course. All movements must fall on the landlord unless they are made imperial questions. It is always the landowner who has to bear the burden in the end. As the cottages belong to the landowners, fixity or certainty of tenure is like taking their rights from them. But not more so than in the case of the exalted compensation called tenant-right. Indeed, I think I shall show that the change would be quite trifling beside measures which deal with whole properties at once, of five, ten, or twenty thousand acres, as the case may be. For, in the first place, let note be taken of a most important circumstance, which is that at the present time these cottages let on sufferance do not bring in one shilling to the landlord. They are not the least profit to him. He does not receive the nominal rent, and if he did, of what value would be so insignificant a sum, the whole of which for a year would not pay a tenth part of the losses sustained by the failure of one tenant farmer. As a fact, then, the cottages are of no money value to the landowner. A change, therefore, in the mode of tenure could not affect the owner like a change in the tenure of a great farm, say at a rental of £1,500. Not having received any profit from the previous tenure of cottages, he suffers no loss if the tenure be varied. The advantage the landowner is supposed to enjoy from the possession of cottages scattered about his farms is that the tenants thereby secure men to do their work. This advantage would be much better secured by a resident and settled population. Take away the conventional veil with which the truth is usually flimsily hidden, and the fact is that the only objection to a certain degree of fixity in cottage tenure is that it would remove from the farmer the arbitrary power he now possesses of eviction. What loss there would be in this way it is not easy to see, since, as explained, the men must have wages, and can only get them from farmers, to whom therefore they must resort. But then the man knows the power to give such notice is there, and it does not agree with the feelings of the nineteenth century. No loss whatever would accrue either to landowner or tenant from a fixed population. A farmer may say, ' But suppose the man who has my cottage will not work for me?' To this I reply, that if the district is so short of cottages that it is possible for a farmer to be short of hands, the sooner pressure is applied in some way, and others built, the better for landowner, tenant, and labourer. If there is sufficient habitation for the number of men necessary for cultivating the land, there will be no difficulty, because one particular labourer will not work for one particular farmer. That labourer must then do one of two things, he must starve or work for some other farmer, where his services would dispossess another labourer, who would immediately take the vacant place. The system of employing men on sufferance, and keeping them, however mildly, under the thumb, is a system totally at variance with the tenets of our time. It is a most expensive system, and ruinous to true self-respect, insomuch as it tends to teach the labourer's children that the only way they can show the independence of their thought is by impertinent language. How much better for a labourer to be perfectly free —how much better for an employer to have a man to work for him quite outside any suspicion of sufferance, or of being under his thumb! I should not like men under my thumb; I should like to pay them for their work, and there let the contract end, as it ends in all other businesses. As more wages cannot be paid, the next best thing, perhaps the absolutely necessary thing, is a fixed home.

I think it would pay any landowner to let all the cottages upon his property to the labourers themselves direct, exactly as farms are let, giving them security of tenure, so long as rent was forthcoming, with each cottage to add a large garden, or allotment, up to, say, two acres, at an agricultural, and not an accommodation, rent.   Most gardens and allotments are let as a favour at a rent about three times, and in some cases even six times, the agricultural rent of the same soil in the adjoining fields.   Cottagers do not look upon such tenancies—held, too, on suffer-ance—as a favour or kindness, and feel no gratitude nor any attachment to those who permit them to dig and delve at thrice the charge the farmer pays.   Add to these cottages gardens, not necessarily adjoining them, but as near as circumstances allow, up to two acres at a purely agricultural rental.   If, in addition, facilities were to be given for the gradual purchase of the freehold by the labourer on the same terms as are now frequently held out by building societies, it would be still better.   I think it would turn out for the advantage of landowner, tenant, and the country at large to have a settled agricultural population.

The limit of two acres I mention, not that there is any especial virtue in that extent of land, but because I do not think the labourer would profit by having more, since he must then spend his whole time culti-vating his plot.   Experience has proved over and over again that for a man in England to live by spade-husbandry on four or five acres of land is the most miserable existence possible.   He can but just scrape a living, he is always failing, his children are in rags, and debt ultimately consumes him.   He is of no good either to himself or to others or to the country. For in our country agriculture, whether by plough or spade, is confined to three things, to grass, corn, or cattle, and there is no plant like the vine by which a small proprietor may prosper. Wet seasons come, and see—even the broad acres cultivated at such an expense of money produce nothing, and the farmer comes to the verge of ruin. But this verge of ruin to the small proprietor who sees his four acres of crops destroyed means simple extinction. So that the amount of land to be of advantage is that amount which the cottager can cultivate without giving his entire time to it ; so that, in fact, he may also earn wages.

To landowner and farmer the value of a fixed population like this, fixed and independent, and looking only for payment for what was actually done, and not for eleemosynary earnings, would be, I think, very great. There would be a constant supply of first-class labour available all the year round. A supply of labour on an estate is like water-power in America—indispensable. But if you have no resident supply you face two evils—you must pay extra to keep men there when you have no real work for them to do, or you must offer fancy wages in harvest. Now, I think a resident population would do the same work if not at less wages at the time of the work, yet for less money, taking the year through.

I should be in hopes that such a plan would soon breed a race of men of the sturdiest order, the true and natural countrymen ; men standing upright in the face of all, without one particle of servility ; paying their rates, and paying their rents ; absolutely civil and pleasant-mannered, because, being really independent, they would need no impudence of tongue to assert what they did not feel ; men giving a full day's work for a full day's wages (which is now seldom seen) ; men demanding to be paid in full for full work, but refusing favours and petty assistance to be recouped hereafter ; able to give their children a fixed home to come back to ; able even to push them in life if they wish to leave employment on the land ; men with the franchise, voting under the protection of the ballot, and voting first and foremost for the demolition of the infernal poor-law and workhouse system.

The men are there. This is no imaginary class to be created, they are there, and they only require homes to become the finest body in the world, a rampart to the nation, a support not only to agriculture but to every industry that needs the help of labour. For physique they have ever been noted, and if it is not valued at home it is estimated at its true value in the colonies. From Australia, America, all countries desiring sinews and strength, come earnest persuasions to these men to emigrate. They are desired above all others as the very foundation of stability. It is only at home that the agricultural labourer is despised. If ever there were grounds for that contempt in his illiterate condition they have disappeared. I have always maintained that intelligence exists outside education, that men who can neither read nor write often possess good natural parts. The labourer at large possesses such parts, but until quite lately he has had no opportunity of displaying them. Of recent years he or his children have had an opportunity of displaying their natural ability, since education was brought within reach of them all. Their natural power has at once shown itself, and all the young men and young women are now solidly educated. The reproach of being illiterate can no longer be hurled at them. They never were illiterate mentally; they are now no more illiterate in the partial sense of book-knowledge. A young agricultural labourer to-day can speak almost as well as the son of a gentleman. There is, of course, a little of the country accent remaining, and some few technical words are in use. Why should they not be? Do not gentlemen on the Exchange use technical terms? I cannot see myself that 'contango' is any better English, or 'backwardation' more indicative of intelligence, than the terms used in the field. The labourer of to-day reads, and thinks about what he reads. The young, being educated, have brought education to their parents, the old have caught the new tone from the young. It is acknowledged that the farm labourer is the most peaceful of all men, the least given to agitation for agitation's sake. Permit him to live and he is satisfied. He has no class ill-feeling, either against farmer or landowner, and he resists all attempts to introduce ill-feeling. He maintains a steady and manly attitude, calm, and considering, without a trace of hasty revolutionary sentiments.

I say that such a race of men are not to be despised; I say that they are the very foundation of a nation's stability. I say that in common justice they deserve settled homes; and further, that as a matter of sound policy they should be provided with them.

ON THE DOWNS

A TRAILING beam of light sweeps through the combe, broadening out where it touches the ground, and narrowing up to the cloud with which it travels. The hollow groove between the hills is lit up where it falls as with a ray cast from a mirror. It is an acre wide on the sward, and tapers up to the invisible slit in the cloud; a mere speck of light from the sky enlightens the earth, and one thought opens the hearts of all men. On the slope here the furze is flecked with golden spots, and black-headed stonechats perch on ant-hills or stray flints, taking no heed of a quiet wanderer. Afar, blue line upon blue line of down is drawn along in slow curves, and beneath, the distant sea appears a dim plain with five bright streaks, where the sunshine pours through as many openings in the clouds. The wind smells like an apple fresh plucked; suddenly the great beam of light vanishes as the sun comes out, and at once the single beam is merged in the many.

Light and colour, freedom and delicious air, give exquisite pleasure to the senses; but the heart searches deeper, and draws forth food for itself from sunshine, hills and sea. Desiring their beauty so deeply, the desire in a measure satisfies itself. It is a thirst which slakes itself to grow the stronger. It springs afresh from the light, from the blue hill-line yonder, from the gorse-flower at hand; to seize upon something that seems in them, which they symbolize and speak of; to take it away within oneself; to absorb it and feel conscious of it—a something that cannot be defined, but which corresponds with all that is highest, truest, and most ideal within the mind. It says, Hope and aspire, strive for largeness of thought. The wind blows, and declares that the mind has capacity for more than has ever yet been brought to it. The wind is wide, and blows not only here, but along the whole range of hills—the hills are not broad enough for it; nor is the sea—it crosses the ocean and spreads itself whither it will. Though invisible, it is material, and yet it knows no limit. As the wind to the fixed boulder lying deep in the sward, so is the immaterial mind to the wind. There is capacity in it for more than has ever yet been placed before it. No system, no philosophy yet organized in logical sequence satisfies the inmost depth—fills and fully occupies the well of thought. Read the system, and with the last word it is over— the mind passes on and requires more. It is but a crumb tasted and gone: who should remember a crumb? But the wind blows, not one puff and then stillness: it continues; if it does cease there remains the same air to be breathed. So that the physical part of man thus always provided with air for breath- ing is infinitely better cared for than his mind, which gets but little crumbs, as it were, coming from old times. These are soon gone, and there remains nothing. Somewhere surely there must be more. An ancient thinker considered that the atmosphere was full of faint images—spectra, reflections, or emanations retaining shape, though without substance—that they crowded past in myriads by day and night. Perhaps there may be thoughts invisible, but floating round us, if we could only render ourselves sensitive to their impact. Such a remark must not be taken literally—it is only an effort to convey a meaning, just as shadow throws up light. The light is that there are further thoughts yet to be found.

The fulness of Nature and the vacancy of mental existence are strangely contrasted. Nature is full everywhere ; there is no chink, no unfurnished space. The mind has only a few thoughts to recall, and those old, and that have been repeated these centuries past. Unless the inner mind (not that which deals with little matters of daily labour) lets itself rest on every blade of grass and leaf, and listens to the soothing wind, it must be vacant—vacant for lack of something to do, not from limit of capacity. For it is too strong and powerful for the things it has to grasp; they are crushed like wheat in a mill. It has capacity for so much, and it is supplied with so little. All the centuries that have gone have gathered hardly a bushel, as it were, and these dry grains are quickly rolled under strong thought and reduced to dust. The mill must then cease, not

that it has no further power, but because the supply
stops. Bring it another bushel, and it will grind as
long as the grain is poured in. Let fresh images
come in a stream like the apple-scented wind; there
is room for them, the storehouse of the inner mind
expands to receive them, wide as the sea which
receives the breeze. The Downs are now lit with
sunlight—the night will cover them presently—but
the mind will sigh as eagerly for these things as in
the glory of day. Sooner or later there will surely
come an opening in the clouds, and a broad beam of
light will descend. A new thought scarcely arrives
in a thousand years, but the sweet wind is always
here, providing breath for the physical man. Let
hope and faith remain, like the air, always, so that
the soul may live. That such a higher thought may
come is the desire—the prayer—which springs on
viewing the blue hill line, the sea, the flower.

Stoop and touch the earth, and receive its influence;
touch the flower, and feel its life; face the wind, and
have its meaning; let the sunlight fall on the open
hand as if you could hold it. Something may be
grasped from them all, invisible yet strong. It is the
sense of a wider existence—wider and higher. Illustrations drawn from material things (as they needs must
be) are weak to convey such an idea. But much
may be gathered indirectly by examining the powers
of the mind—by the light thrown on it from physical
things. Now, at this moment, the blue dome of the
sky, immense as it is, is but a span to the soul.
The eye-glance travels to the horizon in an instant—

the soul-glance travels over all matter also in a moment.   By no possibility could a world, or a series of worlds, be conceived which the mind could not traverse instantaneously.   Outer space itself, therefore, seems limited and with bounds, because the mind is so penetrating it can imagine nothing to the end of which it cannot get.   Space—ethereal space, as far beyond the stars as it is to them—think of it how you will, ends each side in dimness.   The dimness is its boundary.   The mind so instantly occupies all space that space becomes finite, and with limits.   It is the things that are brought before it that are limited, not the power of the mind.

The sweet wind says, again, that the inner mind has never yet been fully employed ; that more than half its power still lies dormant.   Ideas are the tools of the mind.   Without tools you cannot build a ship. The minds of savages lie almost wholly dormant, not because naturally deficient, but because they lack the ideas—the tools—to work with.   So we have had our ideas so long that we have built all we can with them.   Nothing further can be constructed with these materials.   But whenever new and larger materials are discovered we shall find the mind able to build much more magnificent structures.   Let us, then, if we cannot yet discover them, at least wait and watch as ceaselessly as the hills, listening as the wind blows over.   Three-fourths of the mind still sleeps.   That little atom of it needed to conduct the daily routine of the world is, indeed, often strained to the utmost.   That small part of it, again, occasionally exercised in re-learning ancient thoughts, is scarcely half employed—small as it is. There is so much more capacity in the inner mind—a capacity of which but few even dream. Until favourable times and chances bring fresh materials for it, it is not conscious of itself. Light and freedom, colour, and delicious air—sunshine, blue hill lines, and flowers—give the heart to feel that there is so much more to be enjoyed of which we walk in ignorance.

Touching a flower, it seems as if some of this were absorbed from it; it flows from the flower like its perfume. The delicate odour of the violet cannot be written; it is material yet it cannot be expressed. So there is an immaterial influence flowing from it which escapes language. Touching the greensward, there is a feeling as if the great earth sent a mystic influence through the frame. From the sweet wind, too, it comes. The sunlight falls on the hand; the light remains without on the surface, but its influence enters the very being. This sense of absorbing something from earth, and flower, and sunlight is like hovering on the verge of a great truth. It is the consciousness that a great truth is there. Not that the flower and the wind know it, but that they stir unexplored depths in the mind. They are only material—the sun sinks, darkness covers the hills, and where is their beauty then? The feeling or thought which is excited by them resides in the mind, and the purport and drift of it is a wider existence—yet to be enjoyed on earth. Only to think of and imagine it is in itself a pleasure.

The red-tipped hawthorn buds are full of such a thought; the tender green of the leaf just born speaks it. The leaf does not come forth shapeless. Already, at its emergence, there are fine divisions at the edge, markings, and veins. It is wonderful from the commencement. A thought may be put in a line, yet require a life-time to understand in its completeness. The leaf was folded in the tiny red-tipped bud—now it has come forth how long must one ponder to fully appreciate it?

Those things which are symbolized by the leaf, the flower, the very touch of earth, have not yet been put before the mind in a definite form, and shaped so that they can be weighed. The mind is like a lens. A lens can examine nothing of itself, but no matter what is put before it, it will magnify it so that it can be searched into. So whatever is put before the mind in such form that it may be perceived, the mind will search into and examine. It is not that the mind is limited, and unable to understand; it is that the facts have not yet been placed in front of it. But because as yet these things are like the leaf folded in the bud, that is no reason why we should say they are beyond hope of comprehension.

Such a course inflicts the greatest moral injury on the world. Remaining content upon a mental level is fatal, saying to ourselves, ' There is nothing more, this is our limit; we can go no farther,' is the ruin of the mind, as much sleep is the ruin of the body. Looking back through history, it is evident that thought has forced itself out on the world by its own power and against an immense inertia. Thought has worked its way by dint of its own energy, and not because it was welcomed. So few care or hope for a higher mental level; the old terrace of mind will do; let us rest; be assured no higher terrace exists. Experience, however, from time to time has proved that higher terraces did exist. Without doubt there are others now. Somewhere behind the broad beam of life sweeping so beautifully through the combe, somewhere behind the flower, and in the wind. Yet to come up over the blue hill line, there are deeper, wider thoughts still. Always let us look higher, in spite of the narrowness of daily life. The little is so heavy that it needs a strong effort to escape it. The littleness of daily routine; the care felt and despised, the minutiæ which grow against our will, come in time to be heavier than lead. There should be some comfort in the thought that, however these may strain the mind, it is certain that hardly a fiftieth part of its real capacity is occupied with them. There is an immense power in it un-used. By stretching one muscle too much it be-comes overworked; still, there are a hundred other muscles in the body. In truth, we do not fully understand our own earth, our own life, yet. Never, never let us permit the weight of little things to bear us wholly down. If any object that these are vague aspirations, so is the wind vague, yet it is real. They may direct us as strongly as the wind presses on the sails of a ship.

The blue hill line arouses a perception of a current of thought which lies for the most part unrecognized within—an unconscious thought. By looking at this blue hill line this dormant power within the mind becomes partly visible ; the heart wakes up to it.

The intense feeling caused by the sunshine, by the sky, by the flowers and distant sea is an increased consciousness of our own life. The stream of light—the rush of sweet wind—excites a deeper knowledge of the soul. An unutterable desire at once arises for more of this; let us receive more of the inner soul life which seeks and sighs for purest beauty. But the word beauty is poor to convey the feelings intended. Give us the thoughts which correspond with the feeling called up by the sky, the sea afar, and the flower at hand. Let us really be in ourselves the sunbeam which we use as an illustration. The recognition of its loveliness, and of the delicious air, is really a refined form of prayer—the purer because it is not associated with any object, because of its width and openness. It is not prayer in the sense of a benefit desired, it is a feeling of rising to a nobler existence.

It does not include wishes connected with routine and labour. Nor does it depend on the brilliant sun —this mere clod of earth will cause it, even a little crumble of mould. The commonest form of matter thus regarded excites the highest form of spirit. The feelings may be received from the least morsel of brown earth adhering to the surface of the skin on the hand that has touched the ground. Inhaling this deep feeling, the soul, perforce, must pray—a rude imperfect word to express the aspiration—with every glimpse of sunlight, whether it come in a room amid routine, or in the solitude of the hills; with every flower, and grass-blade, and the vast earth underfoot; with the gleam on the distant sea, with the song of the lark on high, and the thrush lowly in the hawthorn.

From the blue hill lines, from the dark copses on the ridges, the shadows in the combes, from the apple-sweet wind and rising grasses, from the leaf issuing out of the bud to question the sun—there comes from all of these an influence which forces the heart to lift itself in earnest and purest desire.

The soul knows itself, and would live its own life.

THE SUN AND THE BROOK

THE sun first sees the brook in the meadow where some roach swim under a bulging root of ash. Leaning against the tree, and looking down into the water, there is a picture of the sky. Its brightness hides the sandy floor of the stream as a picture conceals the wall where it hangs, but, as if the water cooled the rays, the eye can bear to gaze on the image of the sun. Over its circle thin threads of summer cloud are drawn; it is only the reflection, yet the sun seems closer seen in the brook, more to do with us, like the grass, and the tree, and the flowing stream. In the sky it is so far, it cannot be approached, nor even gazed at, so that by the very virtue and power of its own brilliance it forces us to ignore, and almost forget it. The summer days go on, and no one notices the sun. The sweet water slipping past the green flags, with every now and then a rushing sound of eager haste, receives the sky, and it becomes a part of the earth and of life. No one can see his own face without a glass; no one can sit down and deliberately think of the soul till it appears a visible thing. It eludes—the mind cannot grasp it. But hold a flower in the hand—a rose, this later honeysuckle, or this the first hare-bell—and in its beauty you can recognize your own soul reflected as the sun in the brook. For the soul finds itself in beautiful things.

Between the bulging root and the bank there is a tiny oval pool, on the surface of which the light does not fall. There the eye can see deep down into the stream, which scarcely moves in the hollow it has worn for itself as its weight swings into the concave of the bend. The hollow is illumined by the light which sinks through the stream outside the root ; and beneath, in the green depth, five or six roach face the current. Every now and then a tiny curl appears on the surface inside the root, and must rise up to come there. Unwinding as it goes, its raised edge lowers and becomes lost in the level. Dark moss on the base of the ash darkens the water under. The light green leaves overhead yield gently to the passing air ; there are but few leaves on the tree, and these scarcely make a shadow on the grass beyond that of the trunk. As the branch swings, the gnats are driven farther away to avoid it. Over the verge of the bank, bending down almost to the root in the water, droop the heavily seeded heads of tall grasses which, growing there, have escaped the scythe.

These are the days of the convolvulus, of ripening berry, and dropping nut. In the gateways, ears of wheat hang from the hawthorn boughs, which seized them from the passing load. The broad aftermath is without flowers ; the flowers are gone to the uplands and the untilled wastes. Curving opposite the south, the hollow side of the brook has received the sunlight like a silvered speculum every day that the sun has shone. Since the first violet of the meadow, till now that the berries are ripening, through all the long drama of the summer, the rays have visited the stream. The long, loving touch of the sun has left some of its own mystic attraction in the brook. Resting here, and gazing down into it, thoughts and dreams come flowing as the water flows. Thoughts without words, mobile like the stream, nothing compact that can be grasped and stayed : dreams that slip silently as water slips through the fingers. The grass is not grass alone ; the leaves of the ash above are not leaves only. From tree, and earth, and soft air moving, there comes an invisible touch which arranges the senses to its waves as the ripples of the lake set the sand in parallel lines. The grass sways and fans the reposing mind ; the leaves sway and stroke it, till it can feel beyond itself and with them, using each grass blade, each leaf, to abstract life from earth and ether. These then become new organs, fresh nerves and veins running afar out into the field, along the winding brook, up through the leaves, bringing a larger existence. The arms of the mind open wide to the broad sky.

Some sense of the meaning of the grass, and leaves of the tree, and sweet waters hovers on the confines of thought, and seems ready to be resolved into definite form. There is a meaning in these things, a meaning in all that exists, and it comes near to declare itself. Not yet, not fully, nor in such shape that it may be formulated—if ever it will be—but sufficiently so to leave, as it were, an unwritten impression that will remain when the glamour is gone, and grass is but grass, and a tree a tree.

NATURE AND ETERNITY

THE goldfinches sing so sweetly hidden in the top-most boughs of the apple-trees that heart of man cannot withstand them. These four walls, though never so well decorated with pictures, this flat white ceiling, feels all too small, and dull and tame. Down with books and pen, and let us away with the gold-finches, the princes of the birds. For thirty of their generations they have sung and courted and built their nests in those apple-trees, almost under the very windows—a time in their chronology equal to a thousand years. For they are so very busy, from earliest morn till night—a long summer's day is like a year. Now flirting with a gaily-decked and coy lady-love, chasing her from tree to tree; now splash-ing at the edge of a shallow stream till the golden feathers glisten and the red topknot shines. Then searching in and out the hedgerow for favourite seeds, and singing, singing all the while, verily a ' song without an end.' The wings never still, the bill never idle, the throat never silent, and the tiny heart within the proud breast beating so rapidly that, reckoning time by change and variety, an hour must be a day. A life all joy and freedom, without thought,

and full of love. What a great god the sun must be
to the finches from whose wings his beams are reflected
in glittering gold! The abstract idea of a deity apart,
as they feel their life-blood stirring, their eyelids
opening, with the rising sun ; as they fly to satisfy
their hunger with those little fruits they use ; as they
revel in the warm sunshine, and utter soft notes of
love to their beautiful mates, they cannot but feel
a sense, unnamed, indefinite, of joyous gratitude
towards that great orb which is very nearly akin to
the sensual worship of ancient days. Darkness and
cold are Typhon and Ahriman, light and warmth,
Osiris and Ormuzd, indeed to them ; with song they
welcome the spring and celebrate the awakening of
Adonis. Lovely little idolaters, my heart goes with
them. Deep down in the mysteries of organic life
there are causes for the marvellously extended grasp
which the worship of light once held upon the world,
hardly yet guessed at, and which even now play a
part unsuspected in the motives of men. Even yet,
despite our artificial life, despite railroads, telegraphs,
printing-press, in the face of firm monotheistic convictions, once a year the old, old influence breaks
forth, driving thousands and thousands from cities
and houses out into field and forest, to the seashore
and mountain-top, to gather fresh health and strength
from the Sun, from the Air—Jove—and old Ocean.
So the goldfinches rejoice in the sunshine, and who
can sit within doors when they sing?

Foolish fashion has banished the orchard from the
mansion—the orchard which Homer tells us kings

once valued as part of their demesne—and has substituted curious evergreens to which the birds do not
take readily. But this orchard is almost under the
windows, and in summer the finches wake the sleeper
with their song, and in autumn the eye looks down
upon the yellow and rosy fruit. Up the scaling bark
of the trunks the brown tree-climbers run, peering
into every cranny, and few are the insects which
escape those keen eyes. Sitting on a bench under
a pear-tree, I saw a spider drop from a leaf fully
nine feet above the ground, and disappear in the
grass, leaving a slender rope of web, attached at the
upper end to a leaf, and at the lower to a fallen pear.
In a few minutes a small white caterpillar, barely an
inch long, began to climb this rope. It grasped the
thread in the mouth and drew up its body about
a sixteenth of an inch at a time, then held tight with
the two fore-feet, and, lifting its head, seized the
rope a sixteenth higher; repeating this operation
incessantly, the rest of the body swinging in the air.
Never pausing, without haste and without rest, this
creature patiently worked its way upwards, as a man
might up a rope. Let anyone seize a beam overhead
and attempt to lift the chest up to a level with it, the
expenditure of strength is very great; even with long
practice, to 'swarm' up a pole or rope to any distance
is the hardest labour the human muscles are capable
of. This despised 'creeping thing,' without the
slightest apparent effort, without once pausing to
take breath, reached the leaf overhead in rather under
half an hour, having climbed a rope fully 108 times

its own length. To equal this a man must climb 648 feet, or more than half as high again as St. Paul's. The insect on reaching the top at once commenced feeding, and easily bit through the hard pear-leaf: how delicately then it must have grasped the slender spider's web, which a touch would destroy! The thoughts which this feat call forth do not end here, for there was no necessity to go up the thread; the insect could to all appearance have travelled up the trunk of the tree with ease, and it is not to be supposed that its mouth and feet were specially adapted to climb a web, a thing which I have never seen done since, and which was to all appearance merely the result of the *accident* of the insect coming along just after the spider had left the thread. Another few minutes, and the first puff of wind would have carried the thread away—as a puff actually did soon afterwards. I claim a wonderful amount of *original* intelligence—as opposed to the ill-used term instinct—of patience and perseverance for this creature. It is so easy to imagine that because man is big, brain power cannot exist in tiny organizations; but even in man the seat of thought is so minute that it escapes discovery, and his very life may be said to lie in the point of contact of two bones of the neck. Put the mind of man within the body of the caterpillar— what more could it have done? Accustomed to bite and eat its way through hard leaves, why did not the insect snip off and destroy its rope? These are matters to think over dreamily while the finches sing overhead in the apple-tree.

They are not the only regular inhabitants, still less the only visitors. As there are wide plains even in thickly populated England where man has built no populous city, so in bird-life there are fields and woods almost deserted by the songsters, who at the same time congregate thickly in a few favourite resorts, where experience gathered in slow time has shown them they need fear nothing from human beings. Such a place, such a city of the birds and beasts, is this old orchard. The bold and handsome bullfinch builds in the low hawthorn hedge which bounds it upon one side. In the walls of the arbour formed of thick ivy and flowering creepers, the robin and thrush hide their nests. On the topmost branches of the tall pear-trees the swallows rest and twitter. The noble blackbird, with full black eye, pecks at the decaying apples upon the sward, and takes no heed of a footstep. Sometimes the loving pair of squirrels who dwell in the fir-copse at the end of the meadow find their way down the hedges—staying at each tree as an inn by the road—into the orchard, and play their fantastic tricks upon the apple-boughs. The flycatchers perch on a branch clear from the tree, and dart at the passing flies. Merriest of all, the tomtits chatter and scold, hanging under the twigs, head downwards, and then away to their nest in the crumbling stone wall which encloses one side of the orchard. They have worked their way by a cranny deep into the thick wall. On the other side runs the king's highway, and ever and anon the teams go by, making music with their bells. One day a

whole nation of martins savagely attacked this wall.
Pressure of population probably had compelled them
to emigrate from the sand quarry, and the chinks in
the wall pleased their eyes.   Five-and-thirty brown
little birds went to work like miners at twelve or
fourteen holes, tapping at the mortar with their bills,
scratching out small fragments of stone, twittering
and talking all the time, and there undoubtedly they
would have founded a colony had not the jingling
teams and now and then a barking dog disturbed
them.   Resting on the bench and leaning back against
an apple-tree, it is easy to watch the eager starlings
on the chimney-top, and see them tear out the straw
of the thatch to form their holes.   They are all
orators born.   They live in a democracy, and fluency
of speech leads the populace.   Perched on the edge
of the chimney, his bronze-tinted wings flapping
against his side to give greater emphasis—as a
preacher moves his hands—the starling pours forth
a flood of eloquence, now rising to screaming-pitch,
now modulating his tones to soft persuasion, now
descending to deep, low, complaining, regretful sounds
—a speech without words—addressed to a dozen
birds gravely listening on the ash-tree yonder.   He
is begging them to come with him to a meadow
where food is abundant.   In the ivy close under the
window there, within reach of the hand, a water-
wagtail built its nest.   To this nest one lovely afternoon came a great bird like a hawk, to the fearful
alarm and intense excitement of all the bird population.   It was a cuckoo, and after three or four visits,

despite a curious eye at the window, there was a strange egg in that nest. Inside that window, huddled fearfully in the darkest corner of the room, there was once a tiny heap of blue and yellow feathers. A tomtit straying through the casement had been chased by the cat till it dropped exhausted, and the cat was fortunately frightened by a footstep. The bird was all but dead—the feathers awry and ruffled, the eyelids closed, the body limp and helpless—only a faint fluttering of the tiny heart. When placed tenderly on the ledge of the casement, where the warm sunshine fell and the breeze came softly, it dropped listlessly on one side. But in a little while the life-giving rays quickened the blood, the eyelids opened, and presently it could stand perched upon the finger. Then, lest with returning consciousness fear should again arise, the clinging claws were transferred from the finger to a twig of wall-pear. A few minutes more, and with a chirp the bird was gone into the flood of sunlight. What intense joy there must have been in that little creature's heart as it drank the sweet air and felt the loving warmth of its great god Ra, the Sun!

Throwing open the little wicket-gate, by a step the greensward of the meadow is reached. Though the grass has been mown and the ground is dry, it is better to carry a thick rug, and cast it down in the shadow under the tall horse-chestnut-tree. It is only while in a dreamy, slumbrous, half-mesmerized state that nature's ancient papyrus roll can be read—only when the mind is at rest, separated from care and labour ; when the body is at ease, luxuriating in warmth and delicious languor ; when the soul is in accord and sympathy with the sunlight, with the leaf, with the slender blades of grass, and can feel with the tiniest insect which climbs up them as up a mighty tree. As the genius of the great musicians, without an articulated word or printed letter, can carry with it all the emotions, so now, lying prone upon the earth in the shadow, with quiescent will, listening, thoughts and feelings rise respondent to the sunbeams, to the leaf, the very blade of grass. Resting the head upon the hand, gazing down upon the ground, the strange and marvellous inner sight of the mind penetrates the solid earth, grasps in part the mystery of its vast extension upon either side, bearing its majestic mountains, its deep forests, its grand oceans, and almost feels the life which in ten thousand thousand forms revels upon its surface. Returning upon itself, the mind joys in the know-ledge that it too is a part of this wonder—akin to the ten thousand thousand creatures, akin to the very earth itself. How grand and holy is this life ! how sacred the temple which contains it !

Out from the hedge, not five yards distant, pours a rush of deep luscious notes, succeeded by the sweetest trills heard by man. It is the nightingale, which tradition assigns to the night only, but which in fact sings as loudly, and to my ear more joyously, in the full sunlight, especially in the morning, and always close to the nest. The sun has moved onward upon his journey, and this spot is no longer completely

shaded, but the foliage of a great oak breaks the force
of his rays, and the eye can even bear to gaze at his
disc for a few moments. Living for this brief hour
at least in unalloyed sympathy with nature, apart from
all disturbing influences, the sight of that splendid
disc carries the soul with it till it feels as eternal as
the sun. Let the memory call up a picture of the
desert sands of Egypt—upon the kings with the
double crown, upon Rameses, upon Sesostris, upon
Assurbanipal the burning beams of this very sun
descended, filling their veins with tumultuous life,
three thousand years ago. Lifted up in absorbing
thought, the mind feels that these three thousand
years are in truth no longer past than the last beat
of the pulse. It throbbed—the throb is gone ; their
pulse throbbed, and it seems but a moment since, for
to thought, as to the sun, there is no time. This
little petty life of seventy years, with its little petty
aims and hopes, its despicable fears and contemptible
sorrows, is no more the life with which the mind is
occupied. This golden disc has risen and set, as the
graven marks of man alone record, full eight thousand
years. The hieroglyphs of the rocks speak of a fiery
sun shining inconceivable ages before that. Yet even
this almost immortal sun had a beginning—perhaps
emerging as a ball of incandescent gas from chaos :
how long ago was that ? And onwards, still onwards
goes the disc, doubtless for ages and ages to come.
It is time that our measures should be extended ;
these paltry divisions of hours and days and years—
aye, of centuries—should be superseded by terms

conveying some faint idea at least of the vastness of space. For in truth, when thinking thus, there is no *time* at all. The mind loses the sense of time and reposes in eternity. This hour, this instant is eternity; it extends backwards, it extends forwards, and we are in it. It is a grand and an ennobling feeling to know that at this moment illimitable time extends on either hand. No conception of a supernatural character formed in the brain has ever or will ever surpass the mystery of this endless existence as exemplified—as made manifest by the physical sun—a visible sign of immortality. This—this hour is part of the immortal life. Reclining upon this rug under the chestnut-tree, while the graceful shadows dance, a passing bee hums and the nightingale sings, while the oak foliage sprinkles the sunshine over us, we are really and in truth in the midst of eternity. Only by walking hand in hand with nature, only by a reverent and loving study of the mysteries for ever around us, is it possible to disabuse the mind of the narrow view, the contracted belief that time is now and eternity to-morrow. Eternity is to-day. The goldfinches and the tiny caterpillars, the brilliant sun, if looked at lovingly and thoughtfully, will lift the soul out of the smaller life of human care that is of selfish aims, bounded by seventy years, into the greater, the limitless life which has been going on over universal space from endless ages past, which is going on now, and which will for ever and for ever, in one form or another, continue to proceed.

Dreamily listening to the nightingale's song, let

us look down upon the earth as the sun looks down upon it. In this meadow how many millions of blades of grass are there, each performing wonderful operations which the cleverest chemist can but poorly indicate, taking up from the earth its sap, from the air its gases, in a word living, living as much as ourselves, though in a lower form? On the oak-tree yonder, how many leaves are doing the same? Just now we felt the vastness of the earth—its extended majesty, bearing mountain, forest, and sea. Not a blade of grass but has its insect, not a leaf; the very air as it softly woos the cheek bears with it living germs, and upon all those mountains, within those forests, and in every drop of those oceans, life in some shape moves and stirs. Nay, the very solid earth itself, the very chalk and clay and stone and rock has been built up by once living organisms. But at this instant, looking down upon the earth as the sun does, how can words depict the glowing wonder, the marvellous beauty of all the plant, the insect, the animal life, which presses upon the mental eye? It is impossible. But with these that are more immediately around us—with the goldfinch, the caterpillar, the nightingale, the blades of grass, the leaves—with these we may feel, into their life we may in part enter, and find our own existence thereby enlarged. Would that it were possible for the heart and mind to enter into *all* the life that glows and teems upon the earth—to feel with it, hope with it, sorrow with it—and thereby to become a grander, nobler being. Such a being, with such a

sympathy and larger existence, must hold in scorn
the feeble, cowardly, selfish desire for an immortality of pleasure only, whose one great hope is to
escape pain! No. Let me joy with all living
creatures; let me suffer with them all—the reward
of feeling a deeper, grander life would be amply
sufficient.

What wonderful patience the creatures called
'lower' exhibit! Watch this small red ant travelling
among the grass-blades. To it they are as high as
the oak-trees to us, and they are entangled and
matted together as a forest overthrown by a tornado.
The insect slowly overcomes all the difficulties of its
route—now climbing over the creeping roots of the
buttercups, now struggling under a fallen leaf, now
getting up a bennet, up and down, making one inch
forward for three vertically, but never pausing,
always onwards at racing speed. A shadow sweeps
rapidly over the grass—it is that of a rook which
has flown between us and the sun. Looking upwards into the deep azure of the sky, intently
gazing into space and forgetting for a while the
life around and beneath, there comes into the mind
an intense desire to rise, to penetrate the height, to
become part and parcel of that wondrous infinity
which extends overhead as it extends along the
surface. The soul full of thought grows concentrated in itself, marvels only at its own destiny,
labours to behold the secret of its own existence,
and, above all, utters without articulate words a
prayer forced from it by the bright sun, by the blue

sky, by bird and plant:—Let me have wider feelings, more extended sympathies, let me feel with all living things, rejoice and praise with them. Let me have deeper knowledge, a nearer insight, a more reverent conception. Let me see the mystery of life—the secret of the sap as it rises in the tree—the secret of the blood as it courses through the vein. Reveal the broad earth and the ends of it—make the majestic ocean open to the eye down to its inmost recesses. Expand the mind till it grasps the idea of the unseen forces which hold the globe suspended and draw the vast suns and stars through space. Let it see the life, the organisms which dwell in those great worlds, and feel with them their hopes and joys and sorrows. Ever upwards, onwards, wider, deeper, broader, till capable of all—all. Never did vivid imagination stretch out the powers of deity with such a fulness, with such intellectual grasp, vigour, omniscience as the human mind could reach to, if only its organs, its means, were equal to its thought. Give us, then, greater strength of body, greater length of days; give us more vital energy, let our limbs be mighty as those of the giants of old. Supplement such organs with nobler mechanical engines—with extended means of locomotion; add novel and more minute methods of analysis and discovery. Let us become as demi-gods. And why not? Whoso gave the gift of the mind gave also an infinite space, an infinite matter for it to work upon, an infinite time in which to work. Let no one presume to define the boundaries of that divine gift—that mind—for all the experience of eight thousand years proves beyond a question that the limits of its powers will never be reached, though the human race dwell upon the globe for eternity. Up, then, and labour : and let that labour be sound and holy. Not for immediate and petty reward, not that the appetite or the vanity may be gratified, but that the sum of human perfection may be advanced ; labouring as consecrated priests, for true science is religion. All is possible. A grand future awaits the world. When man has only partially worked out his own conceptions — when only a portion of what the mind foresees and plans is realized—then already earth will be as a paradise.

Full of love and sympathy for this feeble ant climbing over grass and leaf, for yonder nightingale pouring forth its song, feeling a community with the finches, with bird, with plant, with animal, and reverently studying all these and more—how is it possible for the heart while thus wrapped up to conceive the desire of crime? For ever anxious and labouring for perfection, shall the soul, convinced of the divinity of its work, halt and turn aside to fall into imperfection? Lying thus upon the rug under the shadow of the oak and horse-chestnut-tree, full of the joy of life—full of the joy which all organisms feel in living alone—lifting the eye far, far above the sphere even of the sun, shall we ever conceive the idea of murder, of violence, of aught that degrades ourselves? It is impossible while in this frame. So thus reclining, and thus occupied, we require no judge, no prison, no law, no punishment—and, further, no army, no monarch. At this moment, did neither of these institutions exist our conduct would be the same. Our whole existence at this moment is permeated with a reverent love, an aspiration—a desire of a more perfect life ; if the very name of religion was extinct, our hopes, our wish would be the same. It is but a simple transition to conclude that with more extended knowledge, with wider sympathies, with greater powers—powers more equal to the vague longings of their minds, the human race would be as we are at this moment in the shadow of the chestnut-tree. No need of priest and lawyer ; no need of armies or kings. It is probable that with the progress of knowledge it will be possible to satisfy the necessary wants of existence much more easily than now, and thus to remove one great cause of discord. And all these thoughts because the passing shadow of a rook caused the eye to gaze upwards into the deep azure of the sky. There is no limit, no number to the thoughts which the study of nature may call forth, any more than there is a limit to the number of the rays of the sun.

This blade of grass grows as high as it can, the nightingale there sings as sweetly as it can, the goldfinches feed to their full desire and lay down no arbitrary rules of life ; the great sun above pours out its heat and light in a flood unrestrained. What is the meaning of this hieroglyph, which is repeated in a thousand thousand other ways and shapes, which meets us at every turn ? It is evident that all living creatures, from the zoophyte upwards, plant, reptile, bird, animal, and in his natural state—in his physical frame—man also, strive with all their powers to obtain as perfect an existence as possible. It is the one great law of their being, followed from birth to death. All the efforts of the plant are put forth to obtain more light, more air, more moisture—in a word, more food—upon which to grow, expand, and become more beautiful and perfect. The aim may be unconscious, but the result is evident. It is equally so with the animal ; its lowest appetites subserve the one grand object of its advance. Whether it be eating, drinking, sleeping, procreating, all tends to one end, a fuller development of the individual, a higher condition of the species ; still further, to the production of new races capable of additional progress. Part and parcel as we are of the great community of living beings, indissolubly connected with them from the lowest to the highest by a thousand ties, it is impossible for us to escape from the operation of this law ; or if, by the exertion of the will, and the resources of the intellect, it is partially suspended, then the individual may perhaps pass away unharmed, but the race must suffer. It is, rather, the province of that inestimable gift, the mind, to aid nature, to smooth away the difficulties, to assist both the physical and mental man to increase his powers and widen his influence. Such efforts have been made from time to time, but unfortunately upon purely empirical principles, by arbitrary inter-ference, without a long previous study of the delicate

organization it was proposed to amend.   If there is
one thing our latter-day students have demonstrated
beyond all reach of cavil, it is that both the physical
and the mental man are, as it were, a mass of inherited
structures—are built up of partially absorbed rudimentary organs and primitive conceptions, much as
the trunks of certain trees are formed by the absorp-
tion of the leaves.   He is made up of the Past.
This is a happy and an inspiriting discovery, insomuch as it holds out a resplendent promise that
there may yet come a man of the future made out of
our present which will then be the past.   It is a
discovery which calls upon us for new and larger
moral and physical exertion, which throws upon us
wider and nobler duties, for upon us depends the
future.   At one blow this new light casts aside those
melancholy convictions which, judging from the evil
blood which seemed to stain each new generation
alike, had elevated into a faith the depressing idea
that man could not advance.   It explains the causes
of that stain, the reason of those imperfections, not
necessary parts of the ideal man, but inherited from
a lower order of life, and to be gradually expunged.

But this marvellous mystery of inheritance has
brought with it a series of mental instincts, so to say ;
a whole circle of ideas of moral conceptions, in a sense
belonging to the Past—ideas which were high and
noble in the rudimentary being, which were beyond
the capacity of the pure animal, but which are now
in great part merely obstructions to advancement.
Let these perish.   We must seek for enlightenment

and for progress, not in the dim failing traditions of a period but just removed from the time of the rudimentary or primeval man—we must no longer allow the hoary age of such traditions to blind the eye and cause the knee to bend—we must no longer stultify the mind by compelling it to receive as infallible what in the very nature of things must have been fallible to the highest degree. The very plants are wiser far. They seek the light of to-day, the heat of the sun which shines at this hour ; they make no attempt to guide their life by the feeble reflection of rays which were extinguished ages ago. This slender blade of grass, beside the edge of our rug under the chestnut-tree, shoots upwards in the fresh air of to-day ; its roots draw nourishment from the moisture of the dew which heaven deposited this morning. If it does make use of the past—of the soil, the earth that has accumulated in centuries—it is to advance its present growth. Root out at once and for ever these primeval, narrow, and contracted ideas ; fix the mind upon the sun of the present, and prepare for the sun that must rise to-morrow. It is our duty to develop both mind and body and soul to the utmost : as it is the duty of this blade of grass and this oak-tree to grow and expand as far as their powers will admit. But the blade of grass and the oak have this great disadvantage to work against— they can only labour in the lines laid down for them, and unconsciously ; while man can think, foresee, and plan. The greatest obstacle to progress is the lack now beginning to be felt all over the world, but more especially in the countries most highly civilized, of a true ideal to work up to. It is necessary that some far-seeing master-mind, some giant intellect, should arise, and sketch out in bold, unmistakable outlines the grand and noble future which the human race should labour for. There have been weak attempts—there are contemptible makeshifts now on their trial, especially in the new world—but the whole of these, without exception, are simply diluted reproductions of systems long since worn out. These can only last a little while ; if anything, they are worse than the prejudices and traditions which form the body of wider-spread creeds. The world cries out for an intellect which shall draw its inspiration from the unvarying and infallible laws regulating the universe ; which shall found its faith upon the teaching of grass, of leaf, of bird, of beast, of hoary rock, great ocean, star and sun ; which shall afford full room for the development of muscle, sense, and above all of the wondrous brain ; and which without fettering the individual shall secure the ultimate apotheosis of the race. No such system can spring at once, complete, perfect in detail, from any one mind. But assuredly when once a firm basis has been laid down, when an outline has been drawn, the converging efforts of a thousand thousand thinkers will be brought to bear upon it, and it will be elaborated into something approaching a reliable guide. The faiths of the past, of the ancient world, now extinct or feebly lingering on, were each inspired by one mind only. The faith of the future, in strong contrast, will spring from the researches of a thousand thousand thinkers, whose minds, once brought into a focus, will speedily burn up all that is useless and worn out with a fierce heat, and evoke a new and brilliant light. This converging thought is one of the greatest blessings of our day, made possible by the vastly extended means of communication, and almost seems specially destined for this very purpose. Thought increases with the ages. At this moment there are probably as many busy brains studying, reflecting, collecting scattered truths, as there were thinkers—effectual thinkers—in all the recorded eighty centuries gone by. Daily and hourly the noble army swells its numbers, and the sound of its mighty march grows louder ; the inscribed roll of its victories fills the heart with exultation.

There is a slight rustle among the bushes and the fern upon the mound. It is a rabbit who has peeped. forth into the sunshine. His eye opens wide with wonder at the sight of us; his nostrils work nervously as he watches us narrowly. But in a little while the silence and stillness reassure him ; he nibbles in a desultory way at the stray grasses on the mound, and finally ventures out into the meadow almost within reach of the hand. It is so easy to make the acquaintance—to make friends with the children of Nature. From the tiniest insect upwards they are so ready to dwell in sympathy with us—only be tender, quiet, considerate, in a word, *gentlemanly*, towards them and they will freely wander around. And they have all such marvellous tales to tell—

intricate problems to solve for us. This common wild rabbit has an ancestry of almost unsearchable antiquity. Within that little body there are organs and structures which, rightly studied, will throw a light upon the mysteries hidden in our own frames. It is a peculiarity of this search that nothing is despicable ; nothing can be passed over—nót so much as a fallen leaf, or a grain of sand. Literally everything bears stamped upon it characters in the hieratic, the sacred handwriting, not one word of which shall fall to the ground.

Sitting indoors, with every modern luxury around, rich carpets, artistic furniture, pictures, statuary, food and drink brought from the uttermost ends of the earth, with the telegraph, the printing-press, the railway at immediate command, it is easy to say, ' What have *I* to do with all this ? I am neither an animal nor a plant, and the sun is nothing to me. This is *my* life which I have created ; I am apart from the other inhabitants of the earth.' But go to the window. See—there is but a thin, transparent sheet of brittle glass between the artificial man and the air, the light, the trees, and grass. So between him and the other innumerable organisms which live and breathe there is but a thin feeble crust of prejudice and social custom. Between him and those irresistible laws which keep the sun upon its course there is absolutely no bar whatever. Without air he cannot live. Nature cannot be escaped. Then face the facts, and having done so, there will speedily arise a calm pleasure beckoning onwards.

The shadows of the oak and chestnut-tree no longer shelter our rug; the beams of the noonday sun fall vertically on us; we will leave the spot for a while. The nightingale and the goldfinches, the thrushes and blackbirds, are silent for a time in the sultry heat. But they only wait for the evening to burst forth in one exquisite chorus, praising this wondrous life and the beauties of the earth.

THE DAWN

THERE came to my bedside this morning a visitant that has been present at the bedside of everyone who has lived for ten thousand years. In the darkness I was conscious of a faint light not visible if I looked deliberately to find it, but seen sideways, and where I was not gazing. It slipped from direct glance as a shadow may slip from a hand-grasp, but it was there floating in the atmosphere of the room. I could not say that it shone on the wall or lit the distant corner. Light is seen by reflection, but this light was visible of itself like a living thing, a visitant from the unknown. The dawn was in the chamber, and by degrees this intangible and slender existence would enlarge and deepen into day. Ever since I used to rise early to bathe, or shoot, or see the sunrise, the habit has remained of waking at the same hour, so that I see the dawn morning after morning, though I may sleep again immediately. Sometimes the change of the seasons makes it broad sunlight, sometimes it is still dark ; then again the faint grey light is there, and I know that the distant hills are becoming defined along the sky. But though so familiar, that spectral light in the silence has never lost its meaning, the violets are sweet year by year though never so many summers pass away; indeed, its meaning grows wider and more difficult as the time goes on. For think, this spectre of the light—light's double-ganger—has stood by the couch of every human being for thousands and thousands of years. Sleeping or waking, happily dreaming, or wrenched with pain, whether they have noticed it or not, the finger of this light has pointed towards them. When they were building the pyramids, five thousand years ago, straight the arrow of light shot from the sun, lit their dusky forms, and glowed on the endless sand. Endless as that desert sand may be, innumerable in multitude its grains, there was and is a ray of light for each. A ray for every invisible atom that dances in the air—for the million million changing facets of the million ocean waves. Immense as these numbers may be, they are not incomprehensible. The priestess at Delphi in her moment of inspiration declared that she knew the number of the sands. Such number falls into insignificance before the mere thought of light, its speed, its quantity, its existence over space, and yet the idea of light is easy to the mind. The mind is the priestess of the Delphic temple of our bodies, and sees and understands things for which language is imperfect, and notation deficient. There is a secret alphabet in it to every letter of which we unconsciously assign a value, just as the mathematician may represent a thousand by the letter A. In my own mind the idea of light is associated with the colour yellow, not the yellow

of the painters, or of flowers, but a quick flash.
This quick bright flash of palest yellow in the
thousandth of an instant reminds me, or rather conveys in itself, the whole idea of light—the accumulated idea of study and thought. I suppose it to be
a memory of looking at the sun—a quick glance at
the sun leaves something such an impression on the
retina. With that physical impression all the calculations that I have read, and all the ideas that have
occurred to me, are bound up. It is the sign—the
letter—the expression of light. To the builders of
the pyramids came the arrow from the sun, tinting
their dusky forms, and glowing in the sand. To me
it comes white and spectral in the silence, a finger
pointed, a voice saying, 'Even now you know
nothing.' Five thousand years since they were fully
persuaded that they understood the universe, the
course of the stars, and the secrets of life and death.
What did they know of the beam of light that shone
on the sonorous lap of their statue Memnon? The
telescope, the microscope, and the prism have parted
light and divided it, till it seems as if further discovery were impossible. This beam of light brings
an account of the sun, clear as if written in actual
letters, for example stating that certain minerals are
as certainly there as they are here. But when in the
silence I see the pale visitant at my bedside, and the
mind rushes in one spring back to the builders of the
pyramids who were equally sure with us, the thought
will come to me that even now there may be messages
in that beam undeciphered. With a turn of the

heliograph, a mere turn of the wrist, a message is
easily flashed twenty miles to the observer. You
cannot tell what knowledge may not be pouring
down in every ray; messages that are constant and
perpetual, the same from age to age. These are
physical messages. There is beyond this just a
possibility that beings in distant earths possessed of
greater knowledge than ourselves may be able to
transmit their thoughts along, or by the ray, as we
do along wires. In the days to come, when a
deeper insight shall have been gained into the
motions and properties of those unseen agents we
call forces, such as magnetism, electricity, gravitation, perhaps a method will be devised to use them
for communication. If so, communication with
distant earths is quite within reasonable hypothesis.
At this hour it is not more impossible than the
transmission of a message to the antipodes in a few
minutes would have been to those who lived a
century since. The inhabitants of distant earths
may have endeavoured to communicate with us in
this way for ought we know time after time. Such
a message is possibly contained sometimes in the
pale beam which comes to my bedside. That beam
always impresses me with a profound, an intense
and distressful sense of ignorance, of being outside
the intelligence of the universe, as if there were
a vast civilization in view and yet not entered.
Mere villagers and rustics creeping about a sullen
earth, we know nothing of the grandeur and intellectual brilliance of that civilization. This beam

fills me with unutterable dissatisfaction. Discontent, restless longing, anger at the denseness of the perception, the stupidity with which we go round and round in the old groove till accident shows us a fresh field. Consider, all that has been wrested from light has been gained by mere bits of glass. Mere bits of glass in curious shapes—poor feeble glass, quickly broken, made of flint, of the flint that mends the road. To this almost our highest conceptions are due. Could we employ the ocean as a lens we might tear truth from the sky. Could the greater intelligences that dwell on the planets and stars communicate with us, they might enable us to conquer the disease and misery which bear down the masses of the world. Perhaps they do not die. The pale visitor hints that the stars are not the outside and rim of the universe, any more than the edge of horizon is the circumference of our globe. Beyond the star-stratum, what? Mere boundless space. Mind says certainly not. What then? At present we cannot conceive a universe without a central solar orb for it to gather about and swing around. But that is only because hitherto our positive, physical knowledge has gone no farther. It can as yet only travel as far as this, as analogous beams of light. Light comes from the uttermost bounds of our star system—to that rim we can extend a positive thought. Beyond, and around it, whether it is solid, or fluid, or ether, or whether, as is most probable, there exist things absolutely different to any that have come under eyesight yet is not known.

May there not be light we cannot see? Gravitation is an unseen light; so too magnetism; electricity or its effect is sometimes visible, sometimes not. Besides these there may be more delicate forces not instrumentally demonstrable. A force, or a wave, or a motion—an unseen light—may at this moment be flowing in upon us from that unknown space without and beyond the stellar system. It may contain messages from thence as this pale visitant does from the sun. It may outstrip light in speed as light outstrips an arrow. The more delicate, the more ethereal, then the fuller and more varied the knowledge it holds. There may be other things beside matter and motion, or force. All natural things known to us as yet may be referred to those two conditions: One, Force; Two, Matter. A third, a fourth, a fifth—no one can say how many conditions—may exist in the ultra-stellar space, beyond the most distant stars. Such a condition may even be about us now unsuspected. Something which is neither force nor matter is difficult to conceive; the mind cannot give it tangible shape even as a thought. Yet I think it more than doubtful if the entire universe, visible and invisible, is composed of these two. To me it seems almost demonstrable by rational induction that the entire universe must consist of more than two conditions. The grey dawn every morning warns me not to be certain that all is known. Analysis by the prism alone has quite doubled the knowledge that was previously available. In the light itself there may still exist as much more to be learnt, and then there may be other forces and other conditions to be first found out and next to tell their story. As at present known the whole system is so easy and simple, one body revolving round another, and so on ; it is as easy to understand as the motion of a stone that has been thrown. This simplicity makes me misdoubt. Is it all ? Space—immeasurable space—offers such possibilities that the mind is forced to the conclusion that it is not, that there must be more. I cannot think that the universe can be so very very easy as this.

RICHARD JEFFERIES

THE GAMEKEEPER AT HOME and THE AMATEUR POACHER

With an introduction by Richard Fitter

With the first appearance of these two books in 1878 and 1879, Richard Jefferies was recognized as a nature writer of the first rank. *The Gamekeeper at Home* recaptures long hours of his early youth, and springs spontaneously from acute nostalgia for his native meadows and downs, woods and streams, aided by a razor-sharp memory for countryside sights and smells. *The Amateur Poacher* deals with the more illicit characters and pastimes of rural life: badger-baiting, ferreting, poaching the churchyard pheasants. It is perhaps the finest example of Jefferies' acute sensitivity to the moods of nature and his remarkable talent for articulating the essence of the countryside.

RICHARD JEFFERIES

AFTER LONDON: WILD ENGLAND

With an introduction by John Fowles

After London (1885) is an extraordinary novel in which Jefferies makes a voyage, through fantasy, away from the corruptions and determinism of his age. London has suffocated in noxious filth, and its people relapse into barbarism; Felix escapes across the lake which has formed over the south of England. Although the centre of social and economic evil has collapsed, the fragmented rural poverty which ensues is no better.

John Fowles, in his introduction to this edition, links *After London* with Butler's *Erewhon* and Morris's *News from Nowhere*, and concludes that Jefferies' novel is 'profounder in its implications'.

A VICTORIAN POACHER:
JAMES HAWKER'S JOURNAL

Edited by Garth Christian
Illustrated by Lynton Lamb

James Hawker was born in 1836, a tailor's son in the village
of Oadby, Leicestershire. Times were hard and Hawker lived
according to his own moral code, poaching with great dex-
terity in order to feed his family. Rather than face unemploy-
ment he worked at many labouring trades, but never gave up
the habit of poaching. He could often be seen, wearing a long
coat with secret pockets where hares and pheasants could be
hidden, walking off to the forbidden estates, limping slightly
because of the sawn-off rifle which he carried down his
trouser leg. He continued to outwit admiring gamekeepers
until the day he died, aged 84. His memoirs, first published in
1961, portray the life of a remarkable man: shrewd, vigorous,
humorous, learned in country lore, a first-rate field naturalist,
and eloquent in his exposition of the poacher's craft.

L. P. JACKS

MAD SHEPHERDS

Snarley Bob is the main character in this series of stories set
in the Cotswold village of Deadborough at the turn of the
century. Gruff and often rude to people he considers foolish,
at other times gentle, and always wise, he can understand the
song of the nightingale and the movements of the stars. This
empathy with nature is his philosophy of life, known to others
as 'snarleychology'. Among the other figures who appear are
Shoemaker Hankin, an ardent atheist who has read the works
of J. S. Mill, and the parson's wife Mrs Abel, who used to be
an actress and is considered 'not proper' by her well-to-do
neighbours. The author, one-time Dean of Manchester
College, Oxford, has a dry sense of humour which makes
Mad Shepherds charming and unsentimental; it was first
published in 1910.

M. V. HUGHES

A LONDON CHILD
OF THE 1870s

Molly Hughes's account of growing up in London in the 1870s ranks with Flora Thompson's best-selling *Lark Rise to Candleford* and *Still Glides the Stream* as a classic description of life in Victorian England. But whereas Flora Thompson describes the rural, Molly Hughes describes the urban scene. *A London Child* was published in 1934, and the reaction of *Country Life* remains valid today: 'The book has the charm of simplicity and frankness with faithfulness to fact and impression, and is delightfully human . . .'

M. V. HUGHES

A LONDON GIRL
OF THE 1880s

In this sequel to *A London Child of the 1870s*, equally charming and delightful, Molly Hughes continues her account of growing up in Victorian London. All the hardships and triumphs of school life, the pleasure of outings to museums and theatres, and the comforts of an affectionate family are remembered and recorded in vivid detail.

M. V. HUGHES

A LONDON HOME
IN THE 1890s

The final book in Molly Hughes's autobiographical trilogy covers a decade crammed with adventure: a new career in a teacher-training college, travels to Europe and America, and marriage to Arthur Hughes in the year of Queen Victoria's Diamond Jubilee. The birth and tragic death of her daughter are movingly related, as is – more light-heartedly – the election campaign in which her husband stood against Lloyd George.

This trilogy is available in a boxed set entitled A Victorian Family.

A LONDON FAMILY
BETWEEN THE WARS

M. V. HUGHES

The Hughes family – a widower with three sons – were not well off financially, but were rich in affection. This is a gentle, often humorous account of a family growing up in the rural environs of London in the 1920s and 1930s. It recaptures the charms of a now vanished world, in which *The Times* arrives by bicycle, household necessities are supplied by a hawker with a pony cart, and making a telephone call is an adventure.

FLORA THOMPSON

STILL GLIDES THE STREAM

Like her well-loved trilogy *Lark Rise to Candleford*, this book depicts the vanished life of the countryside which Flora Thompson knew as a child in the 1880s. Cast in a fictional form, it is an enchanting portrait of an Oxfordshire village and its inhabitants around the time of Queen Victoria's Golden Jubilee.

'... reading it is a perfect pleasure' *Benny Green*

J. M. SYNGE

THE ARAN ISLANDS

In this book, illustrated by his own photographs, the famous Irish playwright recounts his travels and encounters on the Aran Islands. He describes the magic wells, poteen drinkers, and fishing expeditions in currachs, and records the stories told him by the solemn Pat Dirane of islanders who fell victim to the druids and the fairies.

PEIG SAYERS

AN OLD WOMAN'S REFLECTIONS

'The Queen of Gaelic story-tellers' spent the greater part of her long life on the Great Blasket Island. Here she reflects on the days of her youth spent on her beloved island.

THOMAS BEWICK:
A MEMOIR

Edited by Iain Bain

Thomas Bewick (1753–1828) remains unrivalled as an artist-engraver. Though he was principally a metal engraver and copper-plate printer, his fame rests on his superb wood engravings of birds and animals. His delightful *Memoir*, long regarded as a minor classic, provides a remarkable picture of a north-country childhood in Georgian England and an account of Bewick's apprenticeship, trade, and publications. This edition is much enhanced by the exquisite engravings it reproduces and by the excellent introduction, note on Bewick's engraving techniques, and other explanatory material supplied by the editor, himself a Bewick collector and accomplished printer from Bewick's blocks.

WILLIAM WORDSWORTH

GUIDE TO THE LAKES

Complete with illustrations, notes, and a map, this is the best-selling guide to the part of England that inspired one of its greatest poets.

'... the archetypal book for the Lake District connoisseur ... a classic of committed prose about a passionately loved landscape' *Melvyn Bragg*